PHYSICAL ANTHROPOLOGY 92/93

Editor

Elvio Angeloni
Pasadena City College

Elvio Angeloni received his B.A. from UCLA in 1963, his M.A. in anthropology from UCLA in 1965, and his M.A. in communication arts from Loyola Marymount University in 1976. He has produced several films, including "Little Warrior," winner of the Cinemedia VI Best Bicentennial Theme, and "Broken Bottles," shown on PBS. He most recently served as an academic advisor on the instructional television series, "Faces of Culture."

Annual Editions
A Library of Information from the Public Press

Cover illustration by Mike Eagle

The Dushkin Publishing Group, Inc.
Sluice Dock, Guilford, Connecticut 06437

VOLUMES AVAILABLE

series

Annual Editions is a series of over 55 volumes designed to provide the reader with convenient, low-cost access to a wide range of current, carefully selected articles from some of the most important magazines, newspapers, and journals published today. Annual Editions are updated on an annual basis through a continuous monitoring of over 300 periodical sources. All Annual Editions have a number of features designed to make them particularly useful, including topic guides, annotated tables of contents, unit overviews, and indexes. For the teacher using Annual Editions in the classroom, an Instructor's Resource Guide with test questions is available for each volume.

Africa
Aging
American Government
American History, Pre-Civil War
American History, Post-Civil War
Anthropology
Biological Anthropology
Biology
Business and Management
Business Ethics
Canadian Politics
China
Comparative Politics
Computers in Education
Computers in Business
Computers in Society
Criminal Justice
Drugs, Society, and Behavior
Early Childhood Education
Economics
Educating Exceptional Children
Education
Educational Psychology
Environment
Geography
Global Issues
Health
Human Development
Human Resources
Human Sexuality
International Business

Japan
Latin America
Life Management
Macroeconomics
Management
Marketing
Marriage and Family
Microeconomics
Middle East and the Islamic World
Money and Banking
Nutrition
Personal Growth and Behavior
Psychology
Public Administration
Race and Ethnic Relations
Social Problems
Sociology
Soviet Union and Eastern Europe
State and Local Government
Third World
Urban Society
Violence and Terrorism
Western Civilization,
   Pre-Reformation
Western Civilization,
   Post-Reformation
Western Europe
World History, Pre-Modern
World History, Modern
World Politics

Library of Congress Cataloging in Publication Data
Main entry under title: Annual editions: Physical anthropology. 1992/93.
   1. Physical anthropology—Periodicals. I. Angeloni, Elvio, *comp.* II. Title: Physical anthropology.
ISBN 1–56134–054–5   573′.05

First Edition

Manufactured by The Banta Company, Harrisonburg, Virginia 22801

Editors/Advisory Board

To the Reader

In publishing ANNUAL EDITIONS we recognize the enormous role played by the magazines, newspapers, and journals of the *public press* in providing current, first-rate educational information in a broad spectrum of interest areas. Within the articles, the best scientists, practitioners, researchers, and commentators draw issues into new perspective as accepted theories and viewpoints are called into account by new events, recent discoveries change old facts, and fresh debate breaks out over important controversies.

Many of the articles resulting from this enormous editorial effort are appropriate for students, researchers, and professionals seeking accurate, current material to help bridge the gap between principles and theories and the real world. These articles, however, become more useful for study when those of lasting value are carefully *collected, organized, indexed,* and *reproduced* in a *low-cost format*, which provides easy and permanent access when the material is needed. That is the role played by *Annual Editions*. Under the direction of each volume's *Editor*, who is an expert in the subject area, and with the guidance of an *Advisory Board*, we seek each year to provide in each ANNUAL EDITION a current, well-balanced, carefully selected collection of the best of the public press for your study and enjoyment. We think you'll find this volume useful, and we hope you'll take a moment to let us know what you think.

This first edition of *Annual Editions: Physical Anthropology 92/93* contains a variety of articles relating to human evolution. The articles were selected for their timeliness, relevance to issues not easily treated in the standard physical anthropology textbook, and clarity of presentation.

Whereas textbooks tend to reflect the consensus within the field, *Annual Editions: Physical Anthropology 92/93* will provide a forum for the controversial. We do this in order to convey to the student the sense that the study of human development is in itself an evolving entity in which each discovery encourages further research, and each added piece of the puzzle raises new questions about the total picture.

Our final criterion for selecting articles has to do with their readability. All too often, the excitement of a new discovery or a fresh idea is deadened by the weight of a ponderous presentation. We seek to avoid this by incorporating essays written with enthusiasm and with the desire to communicate some very special ideas to the general public.

Included in this volume are a number of features designed to be useful for students, researchers, and professionals in the field of anthropology. While the articles are arranged along the lines of broadly unifying subject area, the *topic guide* can be used to establish specific reading assignments tailored to the needs of a particular course of study. Other useful features include the *table of contents abstracts*, which summarize each article and present key concepts in bold italics, and a comprehensive *index*. In addition, each unit is preceded by an overview that provides a background for informed reading of the articles, emphasizes critical issues, and presents *challenge questions*.

In contrast to the usual textbook, which by its nature cannot be easily revised, this book will be continually updated in order to reflect the dynamic, changing character of its subject. Those involved in producing *Annual Editions: Physical Anthropology 92/93* wish to make the next one as useful and effective as possible. Your criticism and advice are welcomed. Please fill out the article rating form on the last page of the book and let us know your opinions. Any anthology can be improved, and this will continue to be.

Elvio Angeloni

Elvio Angeloni
Editor

Contents

Unit 1

Natural Selection

Seven articles examine the link between genetics and the process of natural selection.

Unit 2

Primates

Six articles examine some of the social relationships in the primate world and how they mirror human society.

The concepts in bold italics are developed in the article. For further expansion please refer to the Topic Guide and the Index.

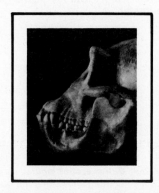

Unit 3

The Fossil Evidence

Six selections discuss theories of human origin and the importance of recently discovered fossil evidence.

The concepts in bold italics are developed in the article. For further expansion please refer to the Topic Guide and the Index.

Unit 4

Late Hominid Evolution

Seven selections examine the enigma of early human evolution and some of the newest fossil discoveries that add further clues to humanity's development.

The concepts in bold italics are developed in the article. For further expansion please refer to the Topic Guide and the Index.

The concepts in bold italics are developed in the article. For further expansion please refer to the Topic Guide and the Index.

Topic Guide

This topic guide suggests how the selections in this book relate to topics of traditional concern to students and professionals involved with the study of physical anthropology. It is useful for locating articles that relate to each other for reading and research. The guide is arranged alphabetically according to topic. Articles may, of course, treat topics that do not appear in the topic guide. In turn, entries in the topic guide do not necessarily constitute a comprehensive listing of all the contents of each selection.

TOPIC AREA	TREATED IN:	TOPIC AREA	TREATED IN:
Aggression	8. Everything *Else* You Always Wanted to Know About Sex 9. Machiavellian Monkeys 10. These Are Real Swinging Primates 11. What Are Friends For? 22. Hard Times Among the Neanderthals 26. Is It Our Culture, Not Our Genes, That Makes Us Killers?	Dominance Hierarchy	10. These Are Real Swinging Primates 11. What Are Friends For? 12. Suburban Chimp
		Fire	21. Bamboo and Human Evolution
		Fluorine Testing	16. Dawson's Dawn Man: The Hoax of Piltdown
Anatomy	22. Hard Times Among the Neanderthals	Genes	2. Pox Upon Our Genes 3. Ticking of a Time Bomb 4. Curse and Blessing of the Ghetto 26. Is It Our Culture, Not Our Genes, That Makes Us Killers?
Archeology	20. What Was the Acheulean Hand Ax? 21. Bamboo and Human Evolution 26. Is It Our Culture, Not Our Genes, That Makes Us Killers?		
Australopithecines	14. Bone Wars 16. Dawson's Dawn Man: The Hoax of Piltdown 17. New Fossil Is Forcing Family Tree Revisions 18. Sizing Up Human Intelligence	Genetic Drift	1. Growth of Evolutionary Science 4. Curse and Blessing of the Ghetto
		Genetic Testing	3. Ticking of a Time Bomb 4. Curse and Blessing of the Ghetto
Biostratigraphy	21. Bamboo and Human Evolution	Homo Erectus	14. Bone Wars 15. Scars of Human Evolution 16. Dawson's Dawn Man: The Hoax of Piltdown 18. Sizing Up Human Intelligence 21. Bamboo and Human Evolution 23. Search for Adam and Eve
Bipedalism	13. Lucy's Uncommon Forebear 15. Scars of Human Evolution 19. Scavenger Hunt		
Blood Groups	7. Racial Odyssey	Homo Habilis	14. Bone Wars 17. New Fossil Is Forcing Family Tree Revision 18. Sizing Up Human Intelligence
Brain Size	18. Sizing Up Human Intelligence		
Cannibalism	26. Is It Our Culture, Not Our Genes, That Makes Us Killers?	Homo Sapiens	14. Bone Wars 17. New Fossil Is Forcing Family Tree Revision 18. Sizing Up Human Intelligence 23. Search for Adam and Eve 24. Novel Notion of Neanderthal
Catastrophism	1. Growth of Evolutionary Science		
Chain of Being	1. Growth of Evolutionary Science		
Creationism	1. Growth of Evolutionary Science	Hunting and Gathering	19. Scavenger Hunt 20. What Was the Acheulean Hand Ax? 21. Bamboo and Human Evolution 22. Hard Times Among the Neanderthals 25. Life as a Hunter-Gatherer
Cro-Magnons	16. Dawson's Dawn Man: The Hoax of Piltdown 24. Novel Notion of Neanderthal		
DNA (Deoxyribonucleic Acid)	4. Curse and Blessing of the Ghetto 13. Lucy's Uncommon Forebear 23. Search for Adam and Eve 24. Novel Notion of Neanderthal	Hunting Hypothesis	11. What Are Friends For? 19. Scavenger Hunt
		Locomotion	10. These Are Real Swinging Primates
Disease	2. Pox Upon Our Genes 4. Curse and Blessing of the Ghetto 5. Emerging Viruses 6. Germ Wars 7. Racial Odyssey	Mutation	1. Growth of Evolutionary Science 23. Search for Adam and Eve

TOPIC AREA	TREATED IN:	TOPIC AREA	TREATED IN:
Natural Selection	1. Growth of Evolutionary Science 2. Pox Upon Our Genes 3. Ticking of a Time Bomb 4. Curse and Blessing of the Ghetto 5. Emerging Viruses 7. Racial Odyssey	**Sexuality**	8. Everything *Else* You Always Wanted to Know About Sex 10. These Are Real Swinging Primates 13. Lucy's Uncommon Forebear
Neanderthals	16. Dawson's Dawn Man: The Hoax of Piltdown 22. Hard Times Among the Neanderthals 23. Search for Adam and Eve 24. Novel Notion of Neanderthal	**Social Relationships**	8. Everything *Else* You Always Wanted to Know About Sex 10. These Are Real Swinging Primates 11. What Are Friends For? 12. Suburban Chimp 25. Life as a Hunter-Gatherer
		Species	1. Growth of Evolutionary Science
Paleoanthropology	14. Bone Wars 17. New Fossil Is Forcing Family Tree Revisions 23. Search for Adam and Eve	**Taxonomy**	1. Growth of Evolutionary Science 7. Racial Odyssey 13. Lucy's Uncommon Forebear 14. Bone Wars 23. Search for Adam and Eve 24. Novel Notion of Neanderthal
Piltdown Hoax	16. Dawson's Dawn Man: The Hoax of Piltdown		
Primates	8. Everything *Else* You Always Wanted to Know About Sex 10. These Are Real Swinging Primates 11. What Are Friends For? 12. Suburban Chimp 13. Lucy's Uncommon Forebear 18. Sizing Up Human Intelligence	**Technology**	20. What Was the Acheulean Hand Ax? 21. Bamboo and Human Evolution 25. Life as a Hunter-Gatherer
		Territoriality	26. Is It Our Culture, Not Our Genes, That Makes Us Killers?
Race	7. Racial Odyssey 23. Search for Adam and Eve	**Theology**	1. Growth of Evolutionary Science
Reproductive Strategy	10. These Are Real Swinging Primates 11. What Are Friends For?	**Thermo-luminescence**	24. Novel Notion of Neanderthal
Scavenging	19. Scavenger Hunt	**Uniformitarianism**	1. Growth of Evolutionary Science
Scientific Method	1. Growth of Evolutionary Science	**Viruses**	2. Pox Upon Our Genes 5. Emerging Viruses 6. Germ Wars
Sex Roles	8. Everything *Else* You Always Wanted to Know About Sex 10. These Are Real Swinging Primates 25. Life as a Hunter-Gatherer		

Natural Selection

As the twentieth century draws to a close and we reflect upon where science has taken us over the past 100 years, it should come as no surprise that the field of genetics has swept us along a path of profound insight into the human condition, as well as heightened controversy as to how to handle this potentially dangerous knowledge of ourselves.

Certainly, Gregor Mendel in the late nineteenth century could not have anticipated that his study of pea plants would ultimately lead to the better understanding of over 3,000 genetically caused diseases, such as sickle-cell anemia, Huntington's Chorea, and Tay-Sachs disease. Nor could he have foreseen the present-day controversies over such matters as surrogate motherhood, cloning, and genetic engineering.

The significance of Mendel's work, of course, was his discovery that hereditary traits are conferred by particular units that we now call "genes," a then-revolutionary notion that has been followed by a better understanding of how and why such units change. It is the knowledge of the process of "mutation," or the alteration of the chemical structure of the gene, which is now providing us with the potential to control the genetic fate of individuals.

The other side of the evolutionary coin, as discussed in "The Growth of Evolutionary Science," is *natural selection*, a concept provided by Charles Darwin and Alfred Wallace. This refers to the "weeding out" of unfavorable mutations and the perpetuation of favorable ones, thus accounting for the peculiarly human characteristics described by Boyce Rensberger in "Racial Odyssey." It seems that as we gain a better understanding of both of these processes, mutation and natural selection, we draw nearer to that time when we may even control the evolutionary direction of our species. Knowledge itself, of course, is neutral—its potential for good or ill being determined by those who happen to be in the position to use it. Consider the possibility of eliminating some of the harmful hereditary traits discussed in "A Pox Upon Our Genes" and in "Curse and Blessing of the Ghetto," both by Jared Diamond. While it is true that many deleterious genes do get weeded out of the population by means of natural selection, there are other harmful ones, Diamond points out, that may actually have a good side to them and will therefore be perpetuated. It may be, for example, that some men are dying from a genetically caused over-abundance of iron in their blood systems in a trade-off that allows some women to absorb sufficient amounts of the element to guarantee their own survival. The question of whether or not we should eliminate such a gene would seem to depend upon which sex we decide should reap the benefit. Even when a gene is obviously harmful, as illustrated by the case of Huntington's Chorea in "The Ticking of a Time Bomb" by Denise Grady, the fore-knowledge of the manner of one's own death may be so devastating that many people simply elect not to know.

The issue of just what is a beneficial application of scientific knowledge is a matter for debate. Who will have the final word as to how these technological break-throughs will be employed in the future? Even with the best of intentions, how can we be certain of the long-range consequences of our actions in such a complicated field? Note, for example, the sweeping effects of ecological change upon the viruses of the world, which in turn seem to be paving the way for new waves of human epidemics. Generally speaking, there is an element of purpose and design in our machinations. This is no better illustrated than in "Germ Wars" by Melissa Hendricks, who shows us that while biological warfare is not by any means new, it has become a very important and dangerous aspect of the arms race as a whole. Yet, even with this clearly in mind, the whole process seems to be escalating out of human control. As John Langone reports in "Emerging Viruses," it seems that the whole world has become an experimental laboratory in which we know not what we do until we have already done it.

As we read the articles in this section and contemplate the significance of genetic diseases for human evolution, we can hope that a better understanding of congenital diseases will lead to a reduction of human suffering. At the same time, we must remain aware that, rather than reduce the misery that exists in the world, someone, at some time, may actually use the same knowledge to increase it.

Looking Ahead: Challenge Questions

In nature, how is it that design can occur without a designer, orderliness without purpose?

Why is it difficult to study natural selection in humans?

Why are epidemic diseases more common today than in our hunting and gathering past?

How and why might the ABO blood group be related to epidemic diseases?

Should people be told they are going to die of a disease from which they are presently suffering and for which there is no cure?

How is it possible to test for deleterious genes?

Charles Darwin

Why is Tay-Sachs disease so common among Eastern European Jews?

How do ecological changes cause new viruses to emerge?

Can and should biological weapons be developed for purely defensive purposes?

Can the human species be subdivided into racial categories?

The Growth of Evolutionary Science

Douglas J. Futuyma

Today, the theory of evolution is an accepted fact for everyone but a fundamentalist minority, whose objections are based not on reasoning but on doctrinaire adherence to religious principles.

—James D. Watson, 1965*

In 1615, Galileo was summoned before the Inquisition in Rome. The guardians of the faith had found that his "proposition that the sun is the center [of the solar system] and does not revolve about the earth is foolish, absurd, false in theology, and heretical, because expressly contrary to Holy Scripture." In the next century, John Wesley declared that "before the sin of Adam there were no agitations within the bowels of the earth, no violent convulsions, no concussions of the earth, no earthquakes, but all was unmoved as the pillars of heaven." Until the seventeenth century, fossils were interpreted as "stones of a peculiar sort, hidden by the Author of Nature for his own pleasure." Later they were seen as remnants of the Biblical deluge. In the middle of the eighteenth century, the great French naturalist Buffon speculated on the possibility of cosmic and organic evolution and was forced by the clergy to recant: "I abandon everything in my book respecting the formation of the earth, and generally all of which may be contrary to the narrative of Moses." For had not St. Augustine written, "Nothing is to be accepted save on the authority of Scripture, since greater is that authority than all the powers of the human mind"?

When Darwin published *The Origin of Species,* it was predictably met by a chorus of theological protest. Darwin's theory, said Bishop Wilberforce, "contradicts the revealed relations of creation to its Creator." "If the Darwinian theory is true," wrote another clergyman, "Genesis is a lie, the whole framework of the book of life falls to pieces, and the revelation of God to man, as we Christians know it, is a delusion and a snare." When *The Descent of Man* appeared, Pope Pius IX was moved to write that Darwinism is "a system which is so repugnant at once to history, to the tradition of all peoples, to exact science, to observed facts, and even to Reason herself, [that it] would seem to need no refutation, did not alienation from God and the leaning toward materialism, due to depravity, eagerly seek a support in all this tissue of fables."[1] Twentieth-century creationism continues this battle of medieval theology against science.

One of the most pervasive concepts in medieval and post-medieval thought was the "great chain of being," or *scala naturae.*[2] Minerals, plants, and animals, according to his concept, formed a gradation, from the lowliest and most material to the most complex and spiritual, ending in man, who links the animal series to the world of intelligence and spirit. This "scale of nature" was the manifestation of God's infinite benevolence. In his goodness, he had conferred existence on all beings of which he could conceive, and so created a complete chain of being, in which there were no gaps. All his creatures must have been created at once, and none could ever cease to exist, for then the perfection of his divine plan would have been violated. Alexander Pope expressed the concept best:

Vast chain of being! which from God
  began,
Natures aethereal, human, angel, man,
Beast, bird, fish, insect, what no eye
  can see,
No glass can reach; from Infinite to
  thee,
From thee to nothing.—On superior
  pow'rs
Were we to press, inferior might on
  ours;
Or in the full creation leave a void,
Where, one step broken, the great
  scale's destroy'd;
From Nature's chain whatever link you
  strike,
Tenth, or ten thousandth, breaks the
  chain alike.

Coexisting with this notion that all of which God could conceive existed so as to complete his creation was the idea that all things existed for man. As the philosopher Francis Bacon put it, "Man, if we look to final causes, may be regarded as the centre of the world . . . for the whole world works

*James D. Watson, a molecular biologist, shared the Nobel Prize for his work in discovering the structure of DNA.

together in the service of man . . . all things seem to be going about man's business and not their own."

"Final causes" was another fundamental concept of medieval and post-medieval thought. Aristotle had distinguished final causes from efficient causes, and the Western world saw no reason to doubt the reality of both. The "efficient cause" of an event is the mechanism responsible for its occurrence: the cause of a ball's movement on a pool table, for example, is the impact of the cue or another ball. The "final cause," however, is the goal, or purpose for its occurrence: the pool ball moves because I wish it to go into the corner pocket. In post-medieval thought there was a final cause—a purpose—for everything; but purpose implies intention, or foreknowledge, by an intellect. Thus the existence of the world, and of all the creatures in it, had a purpose; and that purpose was God's design. This was self-evident, since it was possible to look about the world and see the palpable evidence of God's design everywhere. The heavenly bodies moved in harmonious orbits, evincing the intelligence and harmony of the divine mind; the adaptations of animals and plants to their habitats likewise reflected the divine intelligence, which had fitted all creatures perfectly for their roles in the harmonious economy of nature.

Before the rise of science, then, the causes of events were sought not in natural mechanisms but in the purposes they were meant to serve, and order in nature was evidence of divine intelligence. Since St. Ambrose had declared that "Moses opened his mouth and poured forth what God had said to him," the Bible was seen as the literal word of God, and according to St. Thomas Aquinas, "Nothing was made by God, after the six days of creation, absolutely new." Taking Genesis literally, Archbishop Ussher was able to calculate that the earth was created in 4004 B.C. The earth and the heavens were immutable, changeless. As John Ray put it in 1701 in *The Wisdom of God Manifested in the Works of the Creation,* all living and nonliving things were "created by God at first,

and by Him conserved to this Day in the same State and Condition in which they were first made."[3]

The evolutionary challenge to this view began in astronomy. Tycho Brahe found that the heavens were not immutable when a new star appeared in the constellation Cassiopeia in 1572. Copernicus displaced the earth from the center of the universe, and Galileo found that the perfect heavenly bodies weren't so perfect: the sun had spots that changed from time to time, and the moon had craters that strongly implied alterations of its surface. Galileo, and after him Buffon, Kant, and many others, concluded that change was natural to all things.

A flood of mechanistic thinking ensued. Descartes, Kant, and Buffon concluded that the causes of natural phenomena should be sought in natural laws. By 1755, Kant was arguing that the laws of matter in motion discovered by Newton and other physicists were sufficient to explain natural order. Gravitation, for example, could aggregate chaotically dispersed matter into stars and planets. These would join with one another until the only ones left were those that cycled in orbits far enough from each other to resist gravitational collapse. Thus order might arise from natural processes rather than from the direct intervention of a supernatural mind. The "argument from design"—the claim that natural order is evidence of a designer—had been directly challenged. So had the universal belief in final causes. If the arrangement of the planets could arise merely by the laws of Newtonian physics, if the planets could be born, as Buffon suggested, by a collision between a comet and the sun, then they did not exist for any purpose. They merely came into being through impersonal physical forces.

From the mutability of the heavens, it was a short step to the mutability of the earth, for which the evidence was far more direct. Earthquakes and volcanoes showed how unstable terra firma really is. Sedimentary rocks showed that materials eroded from mountains could be compacted over the ages. Fossils of marine shells on mountain-

tops proved that the land must once have been under the sea. As early as 1718, the Abbé Moro and the French academician Bernard de Fontenelle had concluded that the Biblical deluge could not explain the fossilized oyster beds and tropical plants that were found in France. And what of the great, unbroken chain of being if the rocks were full of extinct species?

To explain the facts of geology, some authors—the "catastrophists"—supposed that the earth had gone through a series of great floods and other catastrophes that successively extinguished different groups of animals. Only this, they felt, could account for the discovery that higher and lower geological strata had different fossils. Buffon, however, held that to explain nature we should look to the natural causes we see operating around us: the gradual action of erosion and the slow buildup of land during volcanic eruptions. Buffon thus proposed what came to be the foundation of geology, and indeed of all science, the principle of uniformitarianism, which holds that the same causes that operate now have always operated. By 1795, the Scottish geologist James Hutton had suggested that "in examining things present we have data from which to reason with regard to what has been." His conclusion was that since "rest exists not anywhere," and the forces that change the face of the earth move with ponderous slowness, the mountains and canyons of the world must have come into existence over countless aeons.

If the entire nonliving world was in constant turmoil, could it not be that living things themselves changed? Buffon came close to saying so. He realized that the earth had seen the extinction of countless species, and supposed that those that perished had been the weaker ones. He recognized that domestication and the forces of the environment could modify the variability of many species. And he even mused, in 1766, that species might have developed from common ancestors:

If it were admitted that the ass is of the family of the horse, and different from the horse only because it has varied from the original form, one could equally well say that the ape is of the family of man, that he is a degenerate man, that man and ape have a common origin; that, in fact, all the families among plants as well as animals have come from a single stock, and that all animals are descended from a single animal, from which have sprung in the course of time, as a result of process or of degeneration, all the other races of animals. For if it were once shown that we are justified in establishing these families; if it were granted among animals and plants there has been (I do not say several species) but even a single one, which has been produced in the course of direct descent from another species . . . then there would no longer be any limit to the power of nature, and we should not be wrong in supposing that, with sufficient time, she has been able from a single being to derive all the other organized beings.[4]

This, however, was too heretical a thought; and in any case, Buffon thought the weight of evidence was against common descent. No new species had been observed to arise within recorded history, Buffon wrote; the sterility of hybrids between species appeared an impossible barrier to such a conclusion; and if species had emerged gradually, there should have been innumerable intermediate variations between the horse and ass, or any other species. So Buffon concluded: "But this [idea of a common ancestor] is by no means a proper representation of nature. We are assured by the authority of revelation that all animals have participated equally in the grace of direct Creation and that the first pair of every species issued fully formed from the hands of the Creator."

Buffon's friend and protégé, Jean Baptiste de Monet, the Chevalier de Lamarck, was the first scientist to take the big step. It is not clear what led Lamarck to his uncompromising belief in evolution; perhaps it was his studies of fossil molluscs, which he came to believe were the ancestors of similar species living today. Whatever the explanation, from 1800 on he developed the notion that fossils were not evidence of extinct species but of ones that had gradually been transformed into living species. To be sure, he wrote, "an enormous time and wide variation in successive conditions must doubtless have been required to enable

nature to bring the organization of animals to that degree of complexity and development in which we see it at its perfection"; but "time has no limits and can be drawn upon to any extent."

Lamarck believed that various lineages of animals and plants arose by a continual process of spontaneous generation from inanimate matter, and were transformed from very simple to more complex forms by an innate natural tendency toward complexity caused by "powers conferred by the supreme author of all things." Various specialized adaptations of species are consequences of the fact that animals must always change in response to the needs imposed on them by a continually changing environment. When the needs of a species change, so does its behavior. The animal then uses certain organs more frequently than before, and these organs, in turn, become more highly developed by such use, or else "by virtue of the operations of their own inner senses." The classic example of Lamarckism is the giraffe: by straining upward for foliage, it was thought, the animal had acquired a longer neck, which was then inherited by its offspring.

In the nineteenth century it was widely believed that "acquired" characteristics—alterations brought about by use or disuse, or by the direct influence of the environment—could be inherited. Thus it was perfectly reasonable for Lamarck to base his theory of evolutionary change partly on this idea. Indeed, Darwin also allowed for this possibility, and the inheritance of acquired characteristics was not finally prove impossible until the 1890s.

Lamarck's ideas had a wide influence; but in the end did not convince many scientists of the reality of evolution. In France, Georges Cuvier, the foremost paleontologist and anatomist of his time, was an influential opponent of evolution. He rejected Lamarck's notion of the spontaneous generation of life, found it inconceivable that changes in behavior could produce the exquisite adaptations that almost every species shows, and emphasized that in both the fossil record and among living

animals there were numerous "gaps" rather than intermediate forms between species. In England, the philosophy of "natural theology" held sway in science, and the best-known naturalists continued to believe firmly that the features of animals and plants were evidence of God's design. These devout Christians included the foremost geologist of the day, Charles Lyell, whose *Principles of Geology* established uniformitarianism once and for all as a guiding principle. But Lyell was such a thorough uniformitarian that he believed in a steady-state world, a world that was always in balance between forces such as erosion and mountain building, and so was forever the same. There was no room for evolution, with its concept of steady change, in Lyell's world view, though he nonetheless had an enormous impact on evolutionary thought, through his influence on Charles Darwin.

Darwin (1809–1882) himself, unquestionably one of the greatest scientists of all time, came only slowly to an evolutionary position. The son of a successful physician, he showed little interest in the life of the mind in his early years. After unsuccessfully studying medicine at Edinburgh, he was sent to Cambridge to prepare for the ministry, but he had only a half-hearted interest in his studies and spent most of his time hunting, collecting beetles, and becoming an accomplished amateur naturalist. Though he received his B.A. in 1831, his future was quite uncertain until, in December of that year, he was enlisted as a naturalist aboard *H.M.S. Beagle,* with his father's very reluctant agreement. For five years (from December 27, 1831, to October 2, 1836) the *Beagle* carried him about the world, chiefly along the coast of South America, which it was the *Beagle's* mission to survey. For five years Darwin collected geological and biological specimens, made geological observations, absorbed Lyell's *Principles of Geology,* took voluminous notes, and speculated about everything from geology to anthropology. He sent such massive collections of specimens back to England that by the time he returned he had already gained a substantial reputation as a naturalist.

Shortly after his return, Darwin married and settled into an estate at Down where he remained, hardly traveling even to London, for the rest of his life. Despite continual ill health, he pursued an extraordinary range of biological studies: classifying barnacles, breeding pigeons, experimenting with plant growth, and much more. He wrote no fewer than sixteen books and many papers, read voraciously, corresponded extensively with everyone, from pigeon breeders to the most eminent scientists, whose ideas or information might bear on his theories, and kept detailed notes on an amazing variety of subjects. Few people have written authoritatively on so many different topics: his books include not only *The Voyage of the Beagle, The Origin of Species,* and *The Descent of Man,* but also *The Structure and Distribution of Coral Reefs* (containing a novel theory of the formation of coral atolls which is still regarded as correct), *A Monograph on the Sub-class Cirripedia* (the definitive study of barnacle classification), *The Various Contrivances by Which Orchids are Fertilised by Insects, The Variation of Animals and Plants Under Domestication* (an exhaustive summary of information on variation, so crucial to his evolutionary theory), *The Effects of Cross and Self Fertilisation in the Vegetable Kingdom* (an analysis of sexual reproduction and the sterility of hybrids between species), *The Expression of the Emotions in Man and Animals* (on the evolution of human behavior from animal behavior), and *The Formation of Vegetable Mould Through the Action of Worms.* There is every reason to believe that almost all these books bear, in one way or another, on the principles and ideas that were inherent in Darwin's theory of evolution. The worm book, for example, is devoted to showing how great the impact of a seemingly trivial process like worm burrowing may be on ecology and geology if it persists for a long time. The idea of such cumulative slight effects is, of course, inherent in Darwin's view of evolution: successive

slight modifications of a species, if continued long enough, can transform it radically.

When Darwin embarked on his voyage, he was a devout Christian who did not doubt the literal truth of the Bible, and did not believe in evolution any more than did Lyell and the other English scientists he had met or whose books he had read. By the time he returned to England in 1836 he had made numerous observations that would later convince him of evolution. It seems likely, however, that the idea itself did not occur to him until the spring of 1837, when the ornithologist John Gould, who was working on some of Darwin's collections, pointed out to him that each of the Galápagos Islands, off the coast of Ecuador, had a different kind of mockingbird. It was quite unclear whether they were different varieties of the same species, or different species. From this, Darwin quickly realized that species are not the discrete, clear-cut entities everyone seemed to imagine. The possibility of transformation entered his mind, and it applied to more than the mockingbirds: "When comparing . . . the birds from the separate islands of the Galápagos archipelago, both with one another and with those from the American mainland, I was much struck how entirely vague and arbitrary is the distinction between species and varieties."

In July 1837 he began his first notebook on the "Transmutation of Species." He later said that the Galápagos species and the similarity between South American fossils and living species were at the origin of all his views.

During the voyage of the *Beagle* I had been deeply impressed by discovering in the Pampean formation great fossil animals covered with armour like that on the existing armadillos; secondly, by the manner in which closely allied animals replace one another in proceeding southward over the continent; and thirdly, by the South American character of most of the productions of the Galápagos archipelago, and more especially by the manner in which they differ slightly on each island of the group; none of these islands appearing to be very ancient in a geological sense. It was evident that such facts as these, as well as many others, could be explained on the supposition that species gradually

become modified; and the subject has haunted me.

The first great step in Darwin's thought was the realization that evolution had occurred. The second was his brilliant insight into the possible cause of evolutionary change. Lamarck's theory of "felt needs" had not been convincing. A better one was required. It came on September 18, 1838, when after grappling with the problem for fifteen months, "I happened to read for amusement Malthus on Population, and being well prepared to appreciate the struggle for existence which everywhere goes on from long-continued observation of the habits of animals and plants, it at once struck me that under these circumstances favorable variations would tend to be preserved, and unfavorable ones to be destroyed. The result of this would be the formation of new species. Here, then, I had at last got a theory by which to work."

Malthus, an economist, had developed the pessimistic thesis that the exponential growth of human populations must inevitably lead to famine, unless it were checked by war, disease, or "moral restraint." This emphasis on exponential population growth was apparently the catalyst for Darwin, who then realized that since most natural populations of animals and plants remain fairly stable in numbers, many more individuals are born than survive. Because individuals vary in their characteristics, the struggle to survive must favor some variant individuals over others. These survivors would then pass on their characteristics to future generations. Repetition of this process generation after generation would gradually transform the species.

Darwin clearly knew that he could not afford to publish a rash speculation on so important a subject without developing the best possible case. The world of science was not hospitable to speculation, and besides, Darwin was dealing with a highly volatile issue. Not only was he affirming that evolution had occurred, he was proposing a purely material explanation for it, one that demolished the argument from design in a single thrust. Instead of publishing his theory, he patiently amassed

Figure 1. *Some species of Galápagos finches. Several of the most different species are represented here; intermediate species also exist. Clockwise from lower left are a male ground-finch (the plumage of the female resembles that of the tree-finches); the vegetarian tree-finch; the insectivorous tree-finch; the warbler-finch; and the woodpecker-finch, which uses a cactus spine to extricate insects from crevices. The slight differences among these species, and among species in other groups of Galápagos animals such as giant tortoises, were one of the observations that led Darwin to formulate his hypothesis of evolution. (From D. Lack, Darwin's Finches [Oxford: Oxford University Press, 1944].)*

establish the priority of his ideas, and on July 1, 1858, they presented to the Linnean Society of London both Wallace's paper and extracts from Darwin's 1844 essay. Darwin abandoned his big book on natural selection and condensed the argument into a 490-page "abstract" that was published on November 24, 1859, under the title *The Origin of Species by Means of Natural Selection; or, the Preservation of Favored Races in the Struggle for Life.* Because it was an abstract, he had to leave out many of the detailed observations and references to the literature that he had amassed, but these were later provided in his other books, many of which are voluminous expansions on the contents of *The Origin of Species.*

The first five chapters of the *Origin* lay out the theory that Darwin had conceived. He shows that both domesticated and wild species are variable, that much of that variation is hereditary, and that breeders, by conscious selection of desirable varieties, can develop breeds of pigeons, dogs, and other forms that are more different from each other than species or even families of wild animals and plants are from each other. The differences between related species then are no more than an exaggerated form of the kinds of variations one can find in a single species; indeed, it is often extremely difficult to tell if natural populations are distinct species or merely well-marked varieties.

Darwin then shows that in nature there is competition, predation, and a struggle for life.

a mountain of evidence, and finally, in 1844, collected his thoughts in an essay on natural selection. But he still didn't publish. Not until 1856, almost twenty years after he became an evolutionist, did he begin what he planned to be a massive work on the subject, tentatively titled *Natural Selection.*

Then, in June 1858, the unthinkable happened. Alfred Russel Wallace (1823–1913), a young naturalist who had traveled in the Amazon Basin and in the Malay Archipelago, had also become interested in evolution. Like Darwin,

he was struck by the fact that "the most closely allied species are found in the same locality or in closely adjoining localities and . . . therefore the natural sequence of the species by affinity is also geographical." In the throes of a malarial fever in Malaya, Wallace conceived of the same idea of natural selection as Darwin had, and sent Darwin a manuscript "On the Tendency of Varieties to Depart Indefinitely from the Original Type." Darwin's friends Charles Lyell and Joseph Hooker, a botanist, rushed in to help Darwin

Owing to this struggle, variations, however slight and from whatever cause proceeding, if they be in any degree profitable to the individuals of a species, in their infinitely complex relations to other organic beings and to their physical conditions of life, will tend to the preservation of such individuals, and will generally be inherited by the offspring. The offspring, also, will thus have a better chance of surviving, for, of the many individuals of any species which are periodically born, but a small number can survive. I have called this principle, by which each slight variation, if useful, is preserved, by the term natural selection, in order to mark its relation to man's power of selection.

Darwin goes on to give examples of how even slight variations promote survival, and argues that when populations are exposed to different conditions, different variations will be favored, so that the descendants of a species become diversified in structure, and each ancestral species can give rise to several new ones. Although "it is probable that each form remains for long periods unaltered," successive evolutionary modifications will ultimately alter the different species so greatly that they will be classified as different genera, families, or orders.

Competition between species will impel them to become more different, for "the more diversified the descendants from any one species become in structure, constitution and habits, by so much will they be better enabled to seize on many and widely diversified places in the polity of nature, and so be enabled to increase in numbers." Thus different adaptations arise, and "the ultimate result is that each creature tends to become more and more improved in relation to its conditions. This improvement inevitably leads to the greater advancement of the organization of the greater number of living beings throughout the world." But lowly organisms continue to persist, for "natural selection, or the survival of the fittest, does not necessarily include progressive development—it only takes advantage of such variations as arise and are beneficial to each creature under its complex relations of life." Probably no organism has reached a peak of perfection, and many lowly forms of life continue to exist, for "in some cases variations or individual differences of a favorable nature may never have arisen for natural selection to act on or accumulate. In no case, probably, has time sufficed for the utmost possible amount of development. In some few cases there has been what we must call retrogression of organization. But the main cause lies in the fact that under very simple conditions of life a high organization would be of no service. . . ."

In the rest of *The Origin of Species,* Darwin considers all the objections that might be raised against his theory;

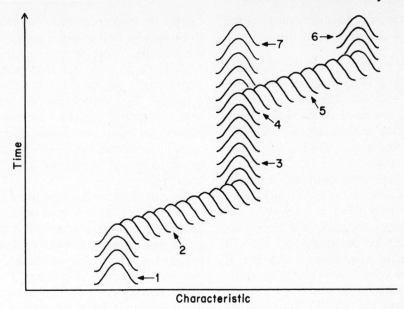

Figure 2. *Processes of evolutionary change. A characteristic that is variable (1) often shows a bell-shaped distribution—individuals vary on either side of the average. Evolutionary change (2) consists of a shift in successive generations, after which the characteristic may reach a new equilibrium (3). When the species splits into two different species (4), one of the species may undergo further evolutionary change (5) and reach a new equilibrium (6). The other may remain unchanged (7) or not. Each population usually remains variable throughout this process, but the average is shifted, ordinarily by natural selection.*

discusses the evolution of a great array of phenomena—hybrid sterility, the slave-making instinct of ants, the similarity of vertebrate embryos; and presents an enormous body of evidence for evolution. He draws his evidence from comparative anatomy, embryology, behavior, geographic variation, the geographic distribution of species, the study of rudimentary organs, atavistic variations ("throwbacks"), and the geological record to show how all of biology provides testimony that species have descended with modification from common ancestors.

Darwin's triumph was in synthesizing ideas and information in ways that no one had quite imagined before. From Lyell and the geologists he learned uniformitarianism: the cause of past events must be found in natural forces that operate today; and these, in the vastness of time, can accomplish great change. From Malthus and the nineteenth-century economists he learned of competition and the struggle for existence. From his work on barnacles, his travels, and his knowledge of domesticated varieties he learned that

species do not have immutable essences but are variable in all their properties and blend into one another gradually. From his familiarity with the works of Whewell, Herschel, and other philosophers of science he developed a powerful method of pursuing science, the "hypothetico-deductive" method, which consists of formulating a hypothesis or speculation, deducing the logical predictions that must follow from the hypothesis, and then testing the hypothesis by seeing whether or not the predictions are verified. This was by no means the prevalent philosophy of science in Darwin's time.[5]

Darwin brought biology out of the Middle Ages. For divine design and unknowable supernatural forces he substituted natural material causes that could be studied by the methods of science. Instead of catastrophes unknown to physical science he invoked forces that could be studied in anyone's laboratory or garden. He replaced a young, static world by one in which there had been constant change for countless aeons. He established that life had a history, and this proved the essential view that differentiated evolutionary thought from all that had gone before.

For the British naturalist John Ray, writing in 1701, organisms had no history—they were the same at that moment, and lived in the same places, doing the same things, as when they were first created. For Darwin, organisms spoke of historical change. If there has indeed been such a history, then fossils in the oldest rocks must differ from those in younger rocks: trilobites, dinosaurs, and mammoths will not be mixed together but will appear in some temporal sequence. If species come from common ancestors, they will have the same characteristics, modified for different functions: the same bones used by bats for flying will be used by horses for running. If species come from ancestors that lived in different environments, they will carry the evidence of their history with them in the form of similar patterns of embryonic development and in vestigial, rudimentary organs that no longer serve any function. If species have a history, their geographical distribution will reflect it: oceanic islands won't have elephants because they wouldn't have been able to get there.

Once the earth and its living inhabitants are seen as the products of historical change, the theological philosophy embodied in the great chain of being ceases to make sense; the plenitude, or fullness, of the world becomes not an eternal manifestation of God's bountiful creativity but an illusion. For most of earth's history, most of the present species have not existed; and many of those that did exist do so no longer. But the scientific challenge to medieval philosophy goes even deeper. If evolution has occurred, and if it has proceeded from the natural causes that Darwin envisioned, then the adaptations of organisms to their environment, the intricate construction of the bird's wing and the orchid's flower, are evidence not of divine design but of the struggle for existence. Moreover, and this may be the deepest implication of all, Darwin brought to biology, as his predecessors had brought to astronomy and geology, the sufficiency of efficient

causes. No longer was there any reason to look for final causes or goals. To the questions "What purpose does this species serve? Why did God make tapeworms?" the answer is "To no purpose." Tapeworms were not put here to serve a purpose, nor were planets, nor plants, nor people. They came into existence not by design but by the action of impersonal natural laws.

By providing materialistic, mechanistic explanations, instead of miraculous ones, for the characteristics of plants and animals, Darwin brought biology out of the realm of theology and into the realm of science. For miraculous spiritual forces fall outside the province of science; all of science is the study of material causation.

Of course, *The Origin of Species* didn't convince everyone immediately. Evolution and its material cause, natural selection, evoked strong protests from ecclesiastical circles, and even from scientists.[6] The eminent geologist Adam Sedgwick, for example, wrote in 1860 that species must come into existence by creation,

a power I cannot imitate or comprehend; but in which I can believe, by a legitimate conclusion of sound reason drawn from the laws and harmonies of Nature. For I can see in all around me a design and purpose, and a mutual adaptation of parts which I *can* comprehend, and which prove that there is exterior to, and above, the mere phenomena of Nature a great prescient and designing cause. . . . The pretended physical philosophy of modern days strips man of all his moral attributes, or holds them of no account in the estimate of his origin and place in the created world. A cold atheistical materialism is the tendency of the so-called material philosophy of the present day.

Among the more scientific objections were those posed by the French paleontologist François Pictet, and they were echoed by many others. Since Darwin supposes that species change gradually over the course of thousands of generations, then, asked Pictet, "Why don't we find these gradations in the fossil record . . . and why, instead of collecting thousands of identical individuals, do we not find more intermediary forms? . . . How is

it that the most ancient fossil beds are rich in a variety of diverse forms of life, instead of the few early types Darwin's theory leads us to expect? How is it that no species has been seen to evolve during human history, and that the 4000 years which separates us from the mummies of Egypt have been insufficient to modify the crocodile and the ibis?" Pictet protested that, although slight variations might in time alter a species slightly, "all known facts demonstrate . . . that the prolonged influence of modifying causes has an action which is constantly restrained within sufficiently confined limits."

The anatomist Richard Owen likewise denied "that . . . variability is progressive and unlimited, so as, in the course of generations, to change the species, the genus, the order, or the class." The paleontologist Louis Agassiz insisted that organisms fall into discrete groups, based on uniquely different created plans, between which no intermediates could exist. He chose the birds as a group that showed the sharpest of boundaries. Only a few years later, in 1868, the fossil *Archaeopteryx,* an exquisite intermediate between birds and reptiles, demolished Agassiz's argument, and he had no more to say on the unique character of the birds.

Within twelve years of *The Origin of Species,* the evidence for evolution had been so thoroughly accepted that the philosopher and mathematician Chauncey Wright could point out that among the students of science, "orthodoxy has been won over to the doctrine of evolution." However, Wright continued, "While the general doctrine of evolution has thus been successfully redeemed from theological condemnation, this is not yet true of the subordinate hypothesis of Natural Selection."

Natural selection turned out to be an extraordinarily difficult concept for people to grasp. St. George Mivart, a Catholic scholar and scientist, was not unusual in equating natural selection with chance. "The theory of Natural Selection may (though it need not) be taken in such a way as to lead man to regard the present organic world as formed, so to speak, *accidentally*, beautiful and wonderful as is the confessedly haphazard result." Many like him simply refused to understand that natural selection is the antithesis of chance and consequently could not see how selection might cause adaptation or any kind of progressive evolutionary change. Even in the 1940s there were those, especially among paleontologists, who felt that the progressive evolution of groups like the horses, as revealed by the fossil record, must have had some unknown cause other than natural selection. Paradoxically, then, Darwin had convinced the scientific world of evolution where his predecessors had failed; but he had not convinced all biologists of his truly original theory, the theory of natural selection.

Natural selection fell into particular disrepute in the early part of the twentieth century because of the rise of genetics—which, as it happened, eventually became the foundation of the modern theory of evolution. Darwin's supposition that variation was unlimited, and so in time could give rise to strikingly different organisms, was not entirely convincing because he had no good idea of where variation came from. In 1865, the Austrian monk Gregor Mendel discovered, from his crosses of pea plants, that discretely different characteristics such as wrinkled versus smooth seeds were inherited from generation to generation without being altered, as if they were caused by particles that passed from parent to offspring. Mendel's work was ignored for thirty-five years, until, in 1900, three biologists discovered his paper and realized that it held the key to the mystery of heredity. One of the three, Hugo de Vries, set about to explore the problem as Mendel had, and in the course of his studies of evening primroses observed strikingly different variations arise, *de novo*. The new forms were so different that de Vries believed they represented new species, which had arisen in a single step by alteration or, as he called it, mutation, of the hereditary material.

In the next few decades, geneticists working with a great variety of organisms observed many other drastic changes arise by mutation: fruit flies (*Drosophila*), for example, with white instead of red eyes or curled instead of straight wings. These laboratory geneticists, especially Thomas Hunt Morgan, an outstanding geneticist at Columbia University, asserted that evolution must proceed by major mutational steps, and that mutation, not natural selection, was the cause of evolution. In their eyes, Darwin's theory was dead on two counts: evolution was not gradual, and it was not caused by natural selection. Meanwhile, naturalists, taxonomists, and breeders of domesticated plants and animals continued to believe in Darwinism, because they saw that populations and species differed quantitatively and gradually rather than in big jumps, that most variation was continuous (like height in humans) rather than discrete, and that domesticated species could be altered by artificial selection from continuous variation.

The bitter conflict between the Mendelian geneticists and the Darwinians was resolved in the 1930s in a "New Synthesis" that brought the opposing views into a "neo-Darwinian" theory of evolution.[7] Slight variations in height, wing length, and other characteristics proved, under careful genetic analysis, to be inherited as particles, in the same way as the discrete variations studied by the Mendelians. Thus a large animal simply has inherited more particles, or genes, for large size than a smaller member of the species has. The Mendelians were simply studying particularly well marked variations, while the naturalists were studying more subtle ones. Variations could be very slight, or fairly pronounced, or very substantial, but all were inherited in the same manner. All these variations, it was shown, arose by a process of mutation of the genes.

Three mathematical theoreticians, Ronald Fisher and J. B. S. Haldane in England and Sewall Wright in the United States, proved that a newly mutated gene would not automatically form a new species. Nor would it automatically replace the preexisting form of the gene, and so transform the species. Replacement of one gene by a mutant form of the gene, they said, could happen in two ways. The mutation could enable its possessors to survive or reproduce more effectively than the old form; if so, it would increase by natural selection, just as Darwin had said. The new characteristic that evolved in this way would ordinarily be considered an improved adaptation.

Sewall Wright pointed out, however, that not all genetic changes in species need be adaptive. A new mutation might be no better or worse than the preexisting gene—it might simply be "neutral." In small populations such a mutation could replace the previous gene purely by chance—a process he called random genetic drift. The idea, put crudely, is this. Suppose there is a small population of land snails in a cow pasture, and that 5 percent of them are brown and the rest are yellow. Purely by chance, a greater percentage of yellow snails than of brown ones get crushed by cows' hooves in one generation. The snails breed, and there will now be a slightly greater percentage of yellow snails in the next generation than there had been. But in the next generation, the yellow ones may suffer more trampling, purely by chance. The proportion of yellow offspring will then be lower again. These random events cause fluctuations in the percentage of the two types. Wright proved mathematically that eventually, if no other factors intervene, these fluctuations will bring the population either to 100 percent yellow or 100 percent brown, purely by chance. The population will have evolved, then, but not by natural selection; and there is no improvement of adaptation.

During the period of the New Synthesis, though, genetic drift was emphasized less than natural selection, for which abundant evidence was discovered. Sergei Chetverikov in Russia, and later Theodosius Dobzhansky working in the United States, showed that wild populations of fruit flies contained an immense amount of genetic variation, including the same kinds of mutations that the geneticists had found arising in their laboratories. Dobzhansky and other workers went on to show that these variations affected survival and reproduction: that natural selection was a reality. They showed, moreover, that the genetic differences among related species were indeed compounded of the same kinds of slight genetic variations that they found within species. Thus the taxonomists and the geneticists converged onto a neo-Darwinian theory of evolution: evolution is due not to mutation *or* natural selection, but to both. Random mutations provide abundant genetic variation; natural selection, the antithesis of randomness, sorts out the useful from the deleterious, and transforms the species.

In the following two decades, the paleontologist George Gaylord Simpson showed that this theory was completely adequate to explain the fossil record, and the ornithologists Bernhard Rensch and Ernst Mayr, the botanist G. Ledyard Stebbins, and many other taxonomists showed that the similarities and differences among living species could be fully explained by neo-Darwinism. They also clarified the meaning of "species." Organisms belong to different species if they do not interbreed when the opportunity presents itself, thus remaining genetically distinct. An ancestral species splits into two descendant species when different populations of the ancestor, living in different geographic regions, become so genetically different from each other that they will not or cannot interbreed when they have the chance to do so. As a result, evolution can happen without the formation of new species: a single species can be genetically transformed without splitting into several descendants. Conversely, new species can be formed without much genetic change. If one population becomes different from the rest of its species in, for example, its mating behavior, it will not interbreed with the other populations. Thus it has become a new species, even though it may be identical to its "sister species" in every respect except its behavior.

Such a new species is free to follow a new path of genetic change, since it does not become homogenized with its sister species by interbreeding. With time, therefore, it can diverge and develop different adaptations.

The conflict between the geneticists and the Darwinians that was resolved in the New Synthesis was the last major conflict in evolutionary science. Since that time, an enormous amount of research has confirmed most of the major conclusions of neo-Darwinism. We now know that populations contain very extensive genetic variation that continually arises by mutation of pre-existing genes. We also know what genes are and how they become mutated. Many instances of the reality of natural selection in wild populations have been documented, and there is extensive evidence that many species form by the divergence of different populations of an ancestral species.

The major questions in evolutionary biology now tend to be of the form, "All right, factors x and y both operate in evolution, but how important is x compared to y?" For example, studies of biochemical genetic variation have raised the possibility that nonadaptive, random change (genetic drift) may be the major reason for many biochemical differences among species. How important, then, is genetic drift compared to natural selection? Another major question has to do with rates of evolution: Do species usually diverge very slowly, as Darwin thought, or does evolution consist mostly of rapid spurts, interspersed with long periods of constancy? Still another question is raised by mutations, which range all the way from gross changes of the kind Morgan studied to very slight alterations. Does evolution consist entirely of the substitution of mutations that have very slight effects, or are major mutations sometimes important too? Partisans on each side of all these questions argue vigorously for their interpretation of the evidence, but they don't doubt that the major factors of evolution are known. They simply emphasize one factor or another. Minor battles of pre-

cisely this kind go on continually in every field of science; without them there would be very little advancement in our knowledge.

Within a decade or two of *The Origin of Species,* the belief that living organisms had evolved over the ages was firmly entrenched in biology. As of 1982, the historical existence of evolution is viewed as fact by almost all biologists. To explain how the fact of evolution has been brought about, a theory of evolutionary mechanisms—mutation, natural selection, genetic drift, and isolation—has been developed.[8] But exactly what is the evidence for the fact of evolution?

NOTES

1. Andrew Dickson White, *A History of the Warfare of Science with Theology in Christendom* vol. I (London: Macmillan, 1896; reprint ed., New York: Dover, 1960).

2. A. O. Lovejoy, *The Great Chain of Being* (Cambridge, Mass.: Harvard University Press, 1936).

3. Much of this history is provided by J. C. Greene, *The Death of Adam: Evolution and its Impact on Western Thought* (Ames: Iowa State University Press, 1959).

4. A detailed history of this and other developments in evolutionary biology is given by Ernst Mayr, *The Growth of Biological Thought: Diversity, Evolution, Inheritance* (Cambridge, Mass.: Harvard University Press, 1982).

5. See D. L. Hull, *Darwin and His Critics* (Cambridge, Mass.: Harvard University Press, 1973).

6. *Ibid.*

7. E. Mayr and W. B. Provine, *The Evolutionary Synthesis* (Cambridge, Mass.: Harvard University Press, 1980).

8. Our modern understanding of the mechanisms of evolution is described in many books. Elementary textbooks include G. L. Stebbins, *Processes of Organic Evolution,* (Englewood Cliffs, N.J.: Prentice-Hall, 1971), and J. Maynard Smith, *The Theory of Evolution* (New York: Penguin Books, 1975). More advanced textbooks include Th. Dobzhansky, F. J. Ayala, G. L. Stebbins, and J. W. Valentine, *Evolution* (San Francisco: Freeman, 1977), and D. J. Futuyma, *Evolutionary Biology* (Sunderland, Mass.: Sinauer, 1979). Unreferenced facts and theories described in the text are familiar enough to most evolutionary biologists that they will be found in most or all of the references cited above.

A Pox Upon Our Genes

*Smallpox vanished twelve years ago, but its genetic legacy
may still linger within us*

Jared Diamond

*Jared Diamond teaches physiology at
UCLA and studies the evolution of New
Guinea birds.*

Human evolution holds a special fascination for us. Granted, it's much
easier to study natural selection in
creatures like bacteria and fruit flies,
which we manipulate experimentally
without compunction. Granted, the
general principles thereby uncovered
may also apply to humans. But let's
face it: bacteria and general principles
aren't what we're most curious about.
What we really want to know are the
particulars of how we came to be who
we are.

Unfortunately, attempts to study natural selection in humans face daunting
obstacles. You can't take any woman
you choose and mate her to any man
you choose in order to observe the
resultant progeny. You can't irradiate,
heat shock, or dissect humans. You
can't inoculate them with lethal diseases, although that experiment would
be especially interesting because diseases were a major selective force on
us until the advent of modern medicine.

This piece is about an ingenious
attempt to study natural selection in
humans without resorting to morally
unacceptable manipulations. Twenty-
five years ago, nature visited a tragic
experiment on rural areas of India in
the form of a virulent outbreak of
smallpox. Nature used abominably excellent experimental design, matching
children who died against brothers or
sisters who survived. Analysis of the
results by two scientists yielded insights into the scars that smallpox, one
of the great modern killers of humans,
has left on our genes.

The study that resulted was unique
in the annals of medicine. It will never
be repeated because smallpox itself has
been eliminated. Thus, it will be remembered as our last, and best, chance
to understand what may have been an
important determinant of our blood
groups.

Despite the virtual halt in human
skeletal evolution since the end of the
Ice Age, the genes for our soft tissues
(including blood cells) continue to undergo changes in response to natural
selection. However, the important selective agents are no longer large, visible enemies, like lions, but tiny,
invisible ones: microbes. With the beginnings of agriculture about 10,000
years ago, infectious diseases probably
began to claim an increasing toll of
human life, eventually becoming the
leading cause of our mortality. As human numbers soared, we became susceptible to diseases that tend to die out
in small populations but that can maintain themselves in large ones, which
offer continuing supplies of not-yet-
infected victims. Agriculture also made
us sedentary, and we began to live in
the midst of our own effluents and
hence to infect one another more easily
with pathogens in our feces, urine, and
exhaled air. As we domesticated animals and came to live amidst them, we
caught still other diseases.

It's true of some infectious diseases,
as of some other causes of death, that
certain people are genetically more
susceptible than others. Since more
resistant individuals are more likely to
survive and to leave more offspring,
selection operating over the last 10,000
years must have caused a genetic revolution in our soft tissues. In a previous
[article] ("Blood, Genes, and Malaria," *Natural History,* February
1989), I discussed genetic resistance to
malaria, the leading infectious disease
of the Old World tropics. But a disease
much more familiar to Americans and
Europeans is smallpox. Until the recent eradication of smallpox, American citizens traveling abroad required
two pieces of paper in order to reenter
the United States: a valid passport and
proof of recent smallpox vaccination.

Smallpox is caused by one of a
group of microbes called pox viruses.
While the virus (and hence the disease)
is confined to humans, it is closely
related to viruses that cause similar
diseases in various domestic animals,
including cows (cowpox), sheep, goats,
horses, and pigs. The smallpox virus
probably developed by mutations from
one of these animal viruses after we
began living in close association with
animals.

Imagine smallpox suddenly being
introduced into a small and isolated
population without any previous expo-

sure to smallpox or related viruses. If all the people have plenty of contact with one another, then smallpox will quickly spread, infecting everybody. Many people will die, but those who survive will develop antibodies to smallpox and will thereby become resistant. As a result, smallpox will have killed or immunized the whole population and will die out, because the virus doesn't infect animals.

Although the disease thus can't persist for long in a small, isolated population, it can last indefinitely as it spreads through a large population in contact with other large populations. Going from one area to another, it can return to an area after a new crop of previously unexposed babies has become available for infection. This need for large numbers of hosts, plus the close similarity of the smallpox virus to domestic animal viruses, is the reason for believing that smallpox probably appeared only after the rise of agriculture.

Just where and when did smallpox first infect us? It must have evolved somewhere in the Old World, since the New World was free of smallpox until it arrived with Spanish conquistadors about 1507. Our oldest certain evidence consists of three Egyptian mummies, dating from the period 1570–1085 B.C., with well-preserved skins that show the characteristic rash caused by smallpox. One of the mummies was Pharaoh Ramses V, whose titles of Mighty Bull, Repulser of Millions, Golden God of the Sun, and Lord of the Two Lands were powerless to protect him against this virus. Smallpox is also known to have existed in India and China before the time of Christ. But it remains unclear how much earlier than 1570 B.C., and exactly where within the Old World, the fatal mutation that transformed some animal virus into smallpox first occurred.

Many devastating smallpox epidemics are known to have killed one-quarter to one-half of the affected populations. Thus, smallpox has often changed the course of human history. It may have caused the famous plague that decimated Athens in 430 B.C. and helped seal her doom in her war against Sparta. Epidemics beginning

about A.D. 165 may have contributed to the decline of the Roman Empire. Titled victims besides Ramses V include Marcus Aurelius of Rome, Peter II of Russia, and Louis XV of France.

But the most far-reaching effects of smallpox were in the New World, where Spanish explorers carrying the disease encountered Indian populations large enough to sustain smallpox but with no previous exposure and no antibodies. Hence the disease played a decisive role in the astonishing conquests of the Aztec and Inca empires, each with millions of inhabitants, by groups of just a few hundred Spaniards. In Mexico, after Cortés had lost two-thirds of his tiny force and retreated to the coast from the Aztec capital of Tenochtitlán (modern Mexico City), a smallpox epidemic killed half of the Aztecs, including Montezuma's successor, Cuitláhuac. In Peru an epidemic that spread southward from Central America, before Pizarro and other Spaniards reached the area, killed the Inca emperor Huayna Capac, killed his designated heir, Ninan Cuyoche, and plunged the empire into civil war between the rival would-be emperors Huáscar and Atahualpa. Cortés and Pizarro triumphed not only because smallpox had killed so many Indian soldiers, including their commanders, but also because a disease that killed Indians, and spared the already resistant Spaniards, demoralized those Indians who survived the epidemic.

As is true of other diseases, individuals must vary in their genetic resistance to smallpox, and the more resistant individuals are more likely to survive epidemics. In populations exposed to the virus for many generations, the frequencies of genes associated with resistance must have risen. Today, only twelve years since smallpox claimed its last victim, those resistant genes should still be common. What might those genes be? For reasons that I shall mention, the genes responsible for our so-called ABO blood types are likely candidates. I must now digress for a simplified crash course in hematology.

Blood is typed according to various protein-and-sugar compounds occupying the surfaces of our red blood cells (hence the name "blood group substances"). While most such substances are found only on our red cells, the ABO substances, which are the best known, are also present on other cells of our body. Each of us has either substance A alone, B alone, both A and B, or neither, and is correspondingly classified as having blood type A, B, AB, or O, respectively. (Strictly speaking, we have two copies of each gene, one inherited from our father and one from our mother, and each copy may be either the A, B, or O form, or allele. Thus, a type-A person has either two As or else one A and one O allele, while a type-O person must have two O alleles.)

In addition, each of us in infancy develops antibodies to the substances he or she lacks. People of type O develop antibodies to both the A and B substances; those of type A develop antibodies only to the B substance, and vice versa; and those of type AB develop neither antibody.

We pay attention to our blood types mainly when they cause us trouble. For example, if a patient of type B receives a transfusion of type-A blood, the transfused cells with the A substance are destroyed by the patient's anti-A antibody, with possibly lethal consequences to the patient. This problem appeared only with the rise of modern medicine and blood transfusions, but a similar problem can arise naturally when a woman is pregnant with a fetus bearing a blood group substance against which she has antibodies. For instance, if a type-O mother carries a fetus that inherited group A from the father, the mother's anti-A antibodies may cause the fetus to abort or may leave it damaged at birth. That doesn't mean, though, that all you type-O women should reject a type-A or type-B suitor, or that you should fret through your pregnancy if you marry that suitor. Only a small fraction of pregnancies in ABO-incompatible marriages actually result in medical complications.

Why, since almost all known effects of blood group substances are thus harmful, do we have differing blood types at all? The reason remains unclear. Perhaps they function as chemical passwords to help us distinguish our own cells from invading microbes or cancer cells that we ought to destroy.

In almost all human populations the O allele is more frequent than the A and B alleles combined. The occasional loss of type-A or type-B fetuses because of incompatibility with their mothers would therefore tend to eliminate the A and B alleles if there were no other important selective factors acting on ABO genes. In fact, as predicted by this reasoning, the O allele tends to be especially common in isolated human populations on islands or mountains out of the mainstream of migration and, therefore, out of the path of infection. But A and B are common in mainstream populations of the Old World, with A being especially frequent in Europe, B in Asia. What compensating advantage peculiar to group A in Europe accounts for its higher frequency there, and similarly for group B in Asia?

One possibility is that certain of the ABO blood groups might confer resistance against fatal diseases common (or formerly common) on certain continents but not on others. Beginning in 1953, convincing associations between ABO blood type and susceptibility to cancer began to be discovered. For example, the risk of stomach cancer is 20 percent higher for Europeans of type A than those of type O. But cancers are not major causes of death in children and young adults and therefore should not be the major determinants of blood type.

A much more plausible explanation for ABO gene frequencies is that they were influenced by the infectious diseases that were major killers of humans. A potential mechanism for such an influence is that the surfaces of some microbes prove to bear substances similar to the ABO blood groups. This suggests a clever evolutionary trick by the microbes to deceive their hosts. For instance, if a microbe's surface is coated with the microbe's own peculiar substances, the host is likely to recognize the microbe

as foreign, develop antibodies against it, and destroy it. But a microbe coated with the A substance would slip past the defenses of a type-A person, since we do not normally develop antibodies against our own proteins.

In the 1960s two kinds of evidence were advanced for a susceptibility of type-A people to smallpox. The first was a still-unresolved claim that a virus closely related to the smallpox virus does have substances like group A on its surface. The second consisted of two statistical studies that compared how frequencies of blood group A and of smallpox varied among different areas of India and Africa. Areas with high frequencies of smallpox proved to have low frequencies of group A, suggesting that smallpox had killed off people with group A.

As recently as the 1960s, in rural areas of India, lack of resources for vaccination, limited access to modern medical care, and lack of understanding of hygiene and disease transmission combined to make smallpox epidemics virtually annual occurrences. Children sick with smallpox shared the same room, and often the same bed, with their brothers and sisters, thereby insuring widespread exposure to the disease. As many as half of the smallpox patients died.

In 1965 and 1966 two scientists, Dr. F. Vogel and Dr. M. R. Chakravartti, realizing that a comparative study of survivors and victims might yield clues about genetic resistance to the disease, attempted to locate all cases of smallpox during severe epidemics in some villages and small towns. They found a total of 415 unvaccinated smallpox patients. For all but eight of these patients, they were also able to find a healthy brother or sister to consider as a "control subject"—that is, someone as similar as possible genetically to the patient and living in the same house, but differing in not having contracted smallpox despite close exposure. Drops of blood drawn from the fingertips sufficed to identify the ABO blood types of the patients and their siblings. Although 52 percent of the patients— 217 out of 415—died in this severe

epidemic, risk of death varied greatly with ABO blood type.

Among the 415 patients, 261 carried blood group A (that is, their blood type was A or AB), while 154 lacked A (their blood type was B or O). Among the 407 healthy subjects, only 80 carried group A, while 327 lacked it— which strongly suggests that the As were susceptible and the non-As resistant. The ratio of A to non-A among the patients (261:154), divided by the ratio of A to non-A among the controls (80:327), was 7—meaning that a person with group A had a seven times greater risk of contracting smallpox than someone without group A.

The 415 patients were then classified according to the severity or the mildness of their symptoms. Among the 283 severe cases, most (201) had blood group A, and only 82 lacked it. Among the mild cases, only 60 had group A, while 72 lacked it. Hence, once they had contracted smallpox, patients with group A were three times more likely to develop a severe case.

When the 415 patients were classified as to whether they died or survived, most (155) of the 217 who died had group A, and only 62 lacked it. The proportions were more nearly equal among those who survived: 106 had group A, and 92 lacked it. Hence, once a person had contracted smallpox, patients with group A had a doubled risk of dying.

Since people with group A are much more likely to contract smallpox, to develop a severe case of it, and to die of it, why hasn't the gene for group A been virtually eliminated in India, Europe, and other areas where smallpox has been a major killer for a long time, leaving all the survivors with group O or B?

Perhaps the answer is that other, equally widespread infectious diseases spared people with group A and penalized those with other blood groups. There is suggestive evidence that the Black Death (bubonic plague), which killed about one-third of medieval Europe's population, preferentially attacked the bearers of group O, as does cholera, whose death toll in India rivaled that of smallpox. These two dis-

15

eases may have favored A at the expense of O in India and Europe. Conversely, those with blood type O may be relatively resistant to syphilis, which may have originated in the New World and thus contributed to the very high frequencies (approaching 100 percent) of group O among Central and South American Indians. Thus, ABO blood group frequencies may represent a compromise among the selective effects of numerous diseases. If so, why do geneticists consider the evidence little more than speculative?

In the case of smallpox, although the study by Vogel and Chakravartti yielded a clear picture, three other studies in India and one in Brazil failed to detect differences in ABO frequencies between smallpox patients and controls. Vogel and Chakravartti noted many reasons why the considered their 1965–66 study much more convincing. Most of their patients were unvaccinated children without medical care, exposed to an especially virulent epidemic, while many patients in the other studies were apparently vaccinated adults receiving medical care in large urban hospitals and possibly exposed to a less virulent epidemic. As a result, mortality in the other studies was only 0–16 percent, compared to 52 percent in the 1965–66 study. Vogel and Chakravartti studied all patients that

they could locate in a small area and compared the patients with siblings living in the same house. The other studies used the biased sample of patients presenting themselves as an urban hospital and compared their blood groups with those of "control subjects" from other areas. However, blood group frequencies vary greatly with caste, religion, ethnic affiliation, and locality within India. Thus, Vogel and Chakravartti appear to me correct in claiming that their study involved a much less biased set of "experimental" subjects, a set of control subjects much better matched to the experimental subjects, and a much greater selective effect of the smallpox epidemic, which in this case was severe.

If the study had involved mice, these claims, counterclaims, and discrepancies would have been resolved by further studies. Larger blood samples would have been drawn to permit measurement of other possible genetic resistance factors besides ABO blood groups. But—thank God—the opportunity to continue studies of smallpox in humans has vanished. As a result of a major effort that began in 1966 to eliminate smallpox throughout the world, no natural cases have been recorded since Ali Maow Maalin developed the telltale rash in Merka Town, Somalia, on October 26, 1977. Hence,

the study by Vogel and Chakravartti will remain unique. Similarly, our prospects for learning more about the genetic influences of bubonic plague and syphilis are slim, since plague has virtually vanished except in remote areas, while syphilis can now be treated as soon as it is detected.

Does this mean that these killers of the past are now of purely academic interest? Not al all. First, the slow-healing scars that they left on our genes, possibly in the form of altered ABO frequencies, will linger in us for many generations. But—perhaps more important—what they did to us in the past serves as a model for what AIDS is doing to us today.

It's well known that individuals exposed to AIDS vary in their risk of becoming infected, and that infected individuals vary in the rate at which their disease progresses. These facts suggest the possibility of genetic differences in susceptibility to AIDS, as is true of many other diseases. In some areas of the world the eventual AIDS-related mortality rate may come to rival that of the great past epidemics of smallpox and plague. If so, AIDS too may be in the process of causing big shifts in human gene frequencies, although we can't yet specify which genes are involved. Natural selection is not a theoretical postulate, but a grimly continuing reality.

The Ticking of a Time Bomb in the Genes

Denise Grady

The first time she called, she said she was a friend of someone I had interviewed, and she used his name to avoid revealing her own. The second time, she said, "Hello, this is . . . um," and she hesitated a moment or two. "I'm a friend of, er . . ." Later, I suggested that she make up a name for herself, to avoid my inadvertently choosing her real one, and to make it easier for her to leave messages. She chose Catherine, and then she laughed and said, "I guess you noticed I got stuck back there, trying to think of his name and remember who I was supposed to be."

I realized then that I had noticed—and had thought, almost unconsciously, *Has she got it?* Here was a high-level executive who was so busy that she was working nights and weekends, and yet had been generous enough to call me, a stranger, to accept my guarantee of anonymity, and to answer my questions about a brain-destroying disease that she might have inherited from her mother. She had made that one verbal fumble on the telephone—far fewer than I had—and I automatically started wondering whether she was losing her mind. No wonder she didn't want her name in print, didn't want anyone at work to know.

That's how it is with Huntington's disease. People who, like Catherine, are "at risk"—meaning that because a parent had the disease, they have a fifty-fifty chance of getting it—can't stumble, lose their temper, misplace their keys, or get tongue-tied without wondering, or causing somebody else to wonder, whether their brain cells are starting to burn out.

If it's possible to label one aspect of this terrible disease the worst, it's probably that the abnormal—and as yet unidentified—gene that's to blame usually gives no sign of its presence until its victims are in their thirties or forties. Those who are unaware of their family histories are shocked to find themselves becoming disabled during their most productive years. Those who know it's in the family must wait decades to see if the disease will strike them. Some decide never to have children, because if a parent has the gene, each child has a fifty-fifty chance of inheriting it—and everybody who has the gene gets the disease. By the time you're in the clear—past the age when the disease would have come on—it's usually too late to have children. So some gamble when they're young and raise families anyway.

The early symptoms are often ambiguous: irritability, clumsiness, depression, forgetfulness, difficulty getting along with others. Only when the constant and uncontrollable movements known as chorea set in, when the victim begins to stagger, fall, slur his speech, grimace, compulsively clench and unclench his fists, and fling his arms and legs around does the diagnosis become inescapable. Gradually, victims lose the ability to talk, swallow, or remember recent events. Their scores on simple mental tests become progressively lower, and some develop serious psychiatric disorders. They take a long time to die—fifteen or twenty years—and many retain a mute, agonized awareness of what's happening to them.

Even though Huntington's disease was described in the medical literature more than a hundred years ago, scientists still don't know how this gene, present from birth, wreaks such havoc decades later. Indeed, practically every aspect of the disease remains unexplained. Somehow, it destroys brain cells, primarily in regions called the caudate nuclei. The symptoms usually come on between the ages of 35 and 45, but some people escape until their fifties and even sixties. A few have a more rapidly progressing form that comes on during adolescence or even childhood. Most juvenile patients inherit the disease from their fathers; even in the adult form, symptoms develop three years earlier on the average when the gene is passed on by the father rather than the mother. No one knows why. (Unlike the genes that cause hemophilia and color blindness, the Huntington's gene doesn't reside on the chromosomes that determine sex.) Nor is there any explanation for the weight loss that often occurs early in the disease, and persists even when victims apparently eat more than enough calories to make up for the energy drained away by chorea.

The best hope—probably the only hope—for answering any of these questions lies in identifying the gene that causes Huntington's, analyzing the protein that it may direct cells to produce, and figuring out what the protein does. Several research groups are working on these issues; some answers are likely within a few years.

In the meantime, research has yielded the one piece of information whose value, at least to patients, is the most debatable. As a result of groundbreaking work in 1983 by Harvard molecular geneticist James Gusella and his colleagues, it's now possible to test some people at risk, and tell them with 96 percent certainty whether they carry the Huntington's gene (*see box*). But if they do have it, no one can help them. There's no cure, and, except for drugs that may relieve depression and control the chorea for a time, no treatment.

About 25,000 Americans have Huntington's disease, and 125,000 more are at risk. Most of the people who've heard of it know it as the disease that killed folk singer Woody Gutherie. But it's more than a topic of morbid curiosity. Most important, it's a late-onset, degenerative disease of the nervous system, like Alzheimer's, which also appears to be hereditary in at least some cases. If the studies that have made it possible to predict Huntington's disease fulfill their promise of also identifying its cause, they may reveal something important about this other incurable brain disease, which afflicts 2.5 million Americans.

It's noteworthy that Huntington's disease is caused by a dominant gene. Genes come in pairs; we inherit one member of each pair from our father and the other from our mother. A gene is said to be dominant when it takes just one, from one parent, to have an effect. Although dominant genes are to blame for about half of the 4,000 or so genetic diseases that afflict man, they're poorly understood. Through genetic research, Huntington's may become one of the few dominant disorders to be well characterized, and thus offer clues about the workings of other dominant genes.

The social dilemmas created by the Huntington's test are at least as important as its scientific ramifications, and they foreshadow the difficulties that are likely to arise as similar techniques are applied to other diseases. Molecular biologists have begun finding mutant genes much faster than doctors can devise treatments for the illnesses those genes cause. In the past two years alone, scientists have turned up genes or genetic markers (bit of DNA linked to the gene) implicated in cystic fibrosis, phenylketonuria (PKU), Alzheimer's disease, Duchenne muscular dystrophy, manic depression, Gaucher's disease, and a rare eye cancer called retinoblastoma (*Discover*, March 1987). They have also made progress toward identifying the genetic underpinnings of several other types of cancer, as well as heart disease.

*People say they want to find out if they have the gene. But they really want to find out they **don't** have it. The trouble is that 50 percent of them do*

Things would be far simpler if doctors could offer a cure for a disease before telling you you're going to get it. Unfortunately, they can't find a cure until they find the marker and the gene, and once they find those, it becomes possible to make life and death predictions.

As more and more errant bits of DNA are revealed, more and more people will have to decide whether they want to know if they will one day fall victim to a dreadful and incurable disease. The question we must answer is, Really, do we want to find out how and when we're going to die?

Last fall the Johns Hopkins Hospital in Baltimore and the Massachusetts General Hospital in Boston began offering the Huntington's test to adults at risk. The College of Physicians and Surgeons at Columbia University in New York will start doing so soon.

Surveys taken before the test became available indicated that between 60 and 80 percent of those at risk would want it. Now that it's being offered, many seem to have backed down. At Hopkins, which notified 350 people at risk, only about 70 have signed up so far. Of 1,500 at risk in New England, many of whom heard about the test through local chapters of the Huntington's Disease Society of America, only 32 have gone in for preliminary counseling.

At Hopkins, people who have inquired about the test often want it to help them decide whether to have children. "They're in their thirties," says neuropsychologist Jason Brandt, "and they hear that biological clock ticking." Some of those at risk are so desperate for the information that they've offered to move to Maryland just to be within the 150-mile limit set for test subjects. Others, who already have families, want the test because they're worried about their children (each child of a parent at 50 percent risk has 25 percent chance of inheriting the gene).

Childbearing has been less of a concern in the Boston group, according to Richard Myers, a medical geneticist and psychologist. "Most of them say every life decision is influenced by the threat of having HD. Should we buy this house or sink more money into disability insurance? Should I change jobs? This one is more stimulating, but that one has better benefits. It's not any one thing, but the day-in, day-out uncertainty."

"When people say they want this test to find out if they have the gene so they can make decisions," says Graciela Penchaszadeh, a genetic counselor at Columbia, "they really want to find out that they *don't* have it. The trouble is that fifty percent of them do. And there's no way to prepare them."

Not everybody who wants the test gets it. Some of those at risk don't have enough living relatives to enable geneticists to trace the marker; others turn out not to need it because neurological examinations reveal that they already have the disease. And some who qualify change their minds after the initial counseling. So far only 18 people have been (or are being) tested in Boston and six in Baltimore. At both centers, some of the tests have turned out to be uninformative, because it was impossible to tell which marker traveled with the gene. As for tests that have yielded results, both hospitals are fiercely protective of their patients' privacy and refuse to say anything about the findings except that some have been negative and some positive. In the hands of employers or insurance companies, the information could be put to devastating use.

There's also fear, reasonable enough, that people who learn they have the gene will become depressed and unable to function at work or at home. The greatest worry is that they'll kill themselves. Huntington's victims already have a high suicide rate: about 25 percent are thought to try it, and six percent succeed. Hopkins therapists will do psychological follow-ups for three years after the test; Massachusetts General requires those being tested to go to the hospital for counseling and to find psychotherapists in their own communities. What concerns Myers isn't only the immediate effect of the test results but also the repercussions in ten or twenty years, when symptoms begin to appear. "It will be hard to tell if the information we're giving them now will have an effect on the suicide rate later," he says. "I don't know that I'll be here then if they need help, or that they'll be willing or able to seek help on their own."

"There are two schools of thought about suicide," says Brandt. "One says it can be rational—and if that's true anywhere, it's true here and with terminal cancer. But I subscribe to the school that says one must choose life over death, and that to say death is the only way to end the suffering is a restricted, constrained world view. Depression is a major symptom of HD and a major cause of suicide; it's treatable. We won't offer to test someone who is suicidal."

But what if a patient admits that he might want to kill himself later, when the symptoms come on? "We haven't had a case like that," Brandt says. "I

hope it doesn't happen. If a person said, 'Huntington's disease is the most horrible thing I can think of, and in the terminal stages death is better,' a trap door wouldn't open automatically under that person to drop him out of the study.

Scientists still don't know how the Huntington's gene, which is present from birth, wreaks such havoc when its victims are forty or so

---

"You know, it's very painful for us, too, to give bad news. One of my secret fantasies is to tell everybody, regardless of the results, that they don't have the gene:" 'Nah, you don't have it. Nah, you don't have it.' "

Given the nature of Huntington's disease, says Nancy Wexler, a psychologist at Columbia and president of the Hereditary Disease Foundation, "suicide is not unreasonable. It's not so awful that we can't discuss it or consider it." It's impossible to talk to anybody who knows anything about this disease without hearing Wexler's name. She is vibrant, articulate, incisive, and one of the top researchers in the field. At 41, she's also at the peak of risk; her mother died of Huntington's in 1978. "People at risk sometimes feel a tremendous sense of lack of control," she says. "Considering suicide as one of various options can be a way of knowing you have control. Sometimes, knowing that you *can* do it takes off some of the heat to do it. But I'd feel terrible if somebody jumped out the window this year, and a cure was found next year. You always have time to jump. The disease is very slow, and research is moving much faster."

When Wexler first pondered taking the test, she says, "my feeling was that the advantages of knowing, even if the answer was yes, outweighed the disadvantages." Now she's not so sure, because she feels that those people who think the test will end uncertainty may be kidding themselves. "They'll have

just as much uncertainty, only a different kind: the waiting game will become 'When?' instead of 'What if?' " she says. "You still won't know, why am I depressed, why did I drop this, why did I yell at my husband? The test has good potential, but it can also be monstrously destructive."

The darker possibilities become clear when she imagined what it would be like to find out that she or her older sister, or both, had the gene, and when she thought of what that knowledge would do to them and to their father. Milton Wexler, a psychoanalyst, has said, "I do believe my children have been spared." He has also said, emphatically, that he doesn't want them tested.

Will Nancy Wexler take the test? Has she? That, she says, is none of anybody's business.

Catherine, the woman who telephoned me, has taken it. She said she would tell me the results, but not until we finished talking. First, she wanted to try to make me understand what it means to be at risk. "I was in graduate school when I learned that my mother might have Huntington's disease," she said. "All I knew was that it was incurable and hereditary. So hearing that my mother might have it was sort of like having a bomb go off in my life. I was married, but the marriage was not in particularly good shape, and it didn't last much beyond that.

"At first it seemed that being at risk affected every aspect of my life all the time. I would say that lasted for some years. I felt as if I was going to develop this terrible disease tomorrow, and I wouldn't be able to cope with it. What helped most—more than any doctor or professional counselor—was meeting other people at risk or with HD. I know that I may develop it, even in the near future"—she's in her early forties—"and I think I would be able to cope with it. But even so, I can think only about the fairly early stages."

Her mother is alive, in a nursing home, 17 years after her symptoms started. They came on late, when she was fifty, and worsened slowly. Hers is a relatively mild case. "Mentally, she's in very good condition," Catherine

HOW TO PREDICT HUNTINGTON'S DISEASE—AT LEAST SOME OF THE TIME

If scientists could just read off the more than 200 million chemical bases that make up chromosome four, where the mysterious gene for Huntington's disease resides, the gene probably would've been identified by now, and the test for it would be 100 per cent accurate. Unfortunately, genes don't reveal themselves so readily. Although techniques exist for decoding short stretches of DNA, the stuff of which chromosomes are made, human chromosomes are too long, and the techniques for unraveling them too laborious, to allow whole chromosomes to be analyzed at once. So biologists take short cuts that enable them to scan a chromosome for markers, segments of DNA associated with a particular gene.

Markers aren't part of the gene, but they're near by on the same chromosome and can be used as flags to track the gene through successive generations of a family. The markers for Huntington's disease, for example, are just normal, harmless pieces of DNA. They come in at least sixty forms, and everybody, well or ill, has one form or another.

Scientists find the markers by "chopping up" chromosomes into fragments of varying lengths, using enzymes that cut DNA when they encounter a specific sequence of its chemical bases. The resulting pattern of fragments varies from person to person, and the presence or absence of particular fragments serves as the marker. This is how molecular geneticist James Gusella and his colleagues at Harvard and Indiana University found the Huntington's marker. In 1983, after analyzing DNA samples from members of two large families, they discovered that within each family there were certain fragment patterns that were almost always inherited with the disease. Since the disease can be linked to any pattern (the pattern that identifies a bad gene in one family may identify the good gene in another), geneticists must trace the marker all over again every time they test a new family.

Once it's established that a certain form of the marker travels with the Huntington's gene in a particular family, any person who has that form has a 96 per cent chance of carrying the gene. The four per cent error represents the chance that the gene and the marker became separated before the person was conceived, by the normal process of rearrangement of chromosomes that takes place when the sperm and egg develop. If they did, the person at risk can have the marker but not the gene, or vice versa. Marker tests like this are now used to detect Huntington's disease, cystic fibrosis, and several other inherited diseases.

In some cases there aren't enough living family members to pin down a marker. Or the test is uninformative because healthy and afflicted relatives carry the same marker, making it impossible to tell good chromosomes from bad.

Nevertheless, the markers still serve as guides to the location of the gene, and once the gene is found, the test becomes absolutely accurate. But that only intensifies the ethical dilemma, since it removes the last vestige of doubt about whether a person will get the disease.

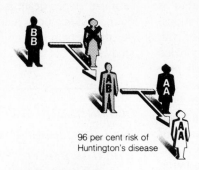

96 per cent risk of Huntington's disease

A TEST THAT DOESN'T REVEAL ANYTHING

Though the grandparents are dead, the markers of their afflicted (grey) and healthy (black) children show that the bad gene is linked to marker A. But it's impossible to tell whether the A of the granddaughter (white) came from her afflicted mother or her dead father (whose markers are unknown), so the test is uninformative.

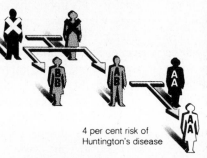

4 per cent risk of Huntington's disease

A NON-DISCLOSING PRENATAL TEST

There is a 50 per cent chance that a woman (white) inherited Huntington's from her afflicted father (grey), both of whose copies of chromosome four had marker B. Since her unborn child inherited the same B, it shares her 50 per cent risk. Should she later develop symptoms of the disease, the child's risk would jump to 96 per cent.

A TEST THAT SHOWS THE BAD GENE IS THERE

A woman (white), whose two copies of chromosome four both have marker A, wants to know if she inherited Huntington's from her afflicted father (grey). Since the healthy grandfather (black) had only B, the bad gene must be linked to the A that the father got from the grandmother (deceased) and passed to the woman.

50 per cent risk of Huntington's disease

A TEST THAT GIVES THE ANSWER YOU WANT

Again, both grandparents are dead and their markers are unknown. But studies of their two afflicted children (grey) show that the Huntington's gene in this family must be linked to B. Since the granddaughter (white) didn't inherit B, there's only a slim (4 per cent) chance that she got the bad gene.

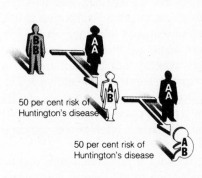

50 per cent risk of Huntington's disease

50 per cent risk of Huntington's disease

ILLUSTRATIONS BY JOE LERTOLA

said. "She has some problems with memory, particularly short-term. But she's quite alert and aware of what's going on. She still likes to talk to her friends and relatives on the phone. It's difficult to understand her, but it's not impossible. She can get around. She sometimes uses a wheelchair, and she spends a lot of time lying down. Her chorea is still increasing. It's hard to say whether she's suffering. She says this isn't the worst disease that one could have. And she very seldom complains. But the relentlessness of the disease must be incredibly difficult. I look at her and think, she's taking it so remarkably well. I hope I could deal with it as well as she does."

Catherine hasn't remarried, although being at risk would not stop her if she met someone. "It would stop me from having kids, though," she says. "Giving them a twenty-five percent chance of having a disease that has been called one of the worst diseases of mankind seems too high a risk.

"Being at risk has also made me more cautious and conservative in other ways. It became important to finish school and get a good job and do well professionally. I think I always tended to be an overachiever. But once I learned I was at risk, if I could do something outstanding, that was sort of proof that I didn't have HD."

But it wasn't proof enough. "As long as I've known I was at risk—since I was twenty-three—I've wanted to take a predictive test. I want it less for making plans now than I would have then. I'd just like to know my condition as accurately as possible. But I've also come to realize that if the answer came back, 'You don't have the gene,' it would result in a very substantial change in my image of myself: being at risk for HD is almost as fundamental to my identity as being a woman."

The test has led to situations that would have been difficult to anticipate. One set of parents, offered the chance to adopt an infant at risk, would take it only if the baby could be tested and proved free of Huntington's. "It bothered me that they would ask that," says Michael Conneally, a professor of medical genetics and neurology at In-

diana University, who was called in to advise the couple. "There's a consensus that no minors should ever be tested, because the child's right to decide, once he comes of age, whether he or anybody else should know always overrides the parents' right to the information." Conneally recommended that the baby be given to another couple.

Given the symptoms, "suicide is not unreasonable. It's not so awful that we can't discuss it or consider it."

Sometimes a parent asks that a child be tested because the other parent is at risk or already has the disease. "They're torn up inside," says Conneally. "They look at their children and think, 'My God, which one has it? I've got to find out.'" The answer is still no.

Prenatal testing—looking at markers in fetal cells during pregnancy—is an especially sensitive subject. Both Hopkins and Massachusetts General have done some tests of this sort, but they won't say how the cases worked out. In addition to the usual debate over abortion, the issue here is whether it's reasonable to end a pregnancy when the fetus may well have forty good years ahead. To that Wexler responds, "The way you die is very disagreeable—a twenty-year decline. You don't wish that on somebody you love. People deciding whether to have children are often watching a parent die, and most say, no way am I going to let that happen to anybody else in my family."

The fact that the test detects a marker rather than the gene itself makes for weird possibilities. If a parent-to-be doesn't want to be tested—or can't be, for lack of relatives—it may still be possible to learn something about the fetus's risk without revealing anything about the parent's. A test called a nondisclosing prenatal (*see diagram*) can tell whether a fetus has a

50 percent risk, as its parent does, or only a four percent risk. Those who want to be as sure as possible of having a child without the gene can abort any fetus with a fifty-fifty risk. Some healthy babies will be lost, but that situation isn't unique to Huntington's: until recently the only way that women carrying the gene for Duchenne muscular dystrophy (a disease that almost never occurs in females) could be virtually assured of having healthy children was to abort all boys, even though half might not have the gene.

If a couple decides not to abort a fetus with a fifty-fifty risk, and if the parent at risk turns out to have Huntington's, the child's risk leaps to 96 percent. The parents know it, and the test has done something it was supposed to avoid: revealed the fate of a minor.

A study published in February in the *New England Journal of Medicine* suggested that there might be another way—it's still experimental—to detect the gene in people who appear healthy. For the past seven years, doctors at the University of California at Los Angeles have been using PET scans to measure brain activity in adults, either at risk or with the disease. Not surprisingly, those who already have symptoms have abnormally low activity in the caudate nuclei. But some of those at risk—18 of 58—had abnormal scans too, which suggests that things start to go awry in the brain even before the damage produces symptoms or becomes visible on X-rays. The numbers match the researchers' prediction, based on ages and family histories, of the proportion of the at-risk group that would have the gene—provocative evidence that the scans are picking out those who will get Huntington's. Moreover, four patients with abnormal scans have since developed symptoms, while none of those who tested normal have become ill.

The UCLA study would be convincing if another paper, published a few weeks later in the *Archives of Neurology*, hadn't contradicted it. Doctors at the University of Michigan did PET scans on 29 people at risk, and found that not one had any sign of abnormality. In addition, the Michigan group tested several people in the early stages of Huntington's—including one with a positive marker test—and found their scans normal, too.

Surveys taken before the test was available indicated that 60 to 80 percent of those at risk would want it. Now many seem to have backed down

---

The two groups of researchers are now trying to reconcile the differences. Anne Young, a neurologist who's the director of the Michigan study, offers three possible explanations: the researchers may be reading the scans differently; the Michigan patients, younger on average than those at UCLA, may be too far from the onset of symptoms for brain damage to show up; or, because of differences in diagnostic criteria, UCLA's "asymptomatic" group may include some people with subtle symptoms. Young says she doubts that PET will prove a reliable way to pick out gene carriers, except possibly those in whom the disease is just about to manifest itself.

The leaders of the UCLA team think it's too early to tell. Gusella is doing marker studies on some of their patients to see if the scans did indeed pick out people with the gene. If they did, it will be a matter of waiting to see how long it takes for symptoms to show up. The UCLA team has begun studying younger people, some in their early twenties, to see when brain function first turns abnormal and to find out whether PET can be used to predict the age at which symptoms will start. "We get calls all the time from people who want this test," says UCLA neurologist John Hoffman, "but we can't do it." Not even patients in the study are told the results. It's hard to imagine which would be worse: telling people they'll get Huntington's when they won't, or giving a clean bill of health to people who later fall ill. "Unless we're absolutely sure, the information shouldn't be given out," says Hoffman.

Wexler is less interested in PET as a high-tech fortuneteller than in what the test may reveal about the disease. "We have a major question: When does this gene kick in?" she says. "Some people think the brain of a Huntington's victim is different from the start, and, if you look hard enough at it, you'll find something funny."

The UCLA study supports the idea that brain abnormalities begin well before the onset of symptoms, but the Michigan research suggests the opposite. "Rather than a long curve reflecting a lifetime of deterioration," says Wexler, "you might see a flat line of normal braincell activity and then a sudden downturn"—as if a dormant gene were abruptly activated. Regardless of which proves true, the scans will provide crucial information about the course of the disease, and will be a good way of testing treatments—if any come along.

In an effort to gain further understanding of the disease, Wexler has traveled regularly to Venezuela since 1979 to lead a study of the world's largest family of Huntington's victims, scattered in villages along the shores of Lake Maracaibo. The family tree is made up of 7,000 people so far, including more than 300 (living and dead) with the disease and 1,000 still living and known to be at 50 percent risk. (It was blood samples from this group that enabled Gusella to confirm the location of the marker.) During her trips Wexler records the condition—and all too often the decline—of people who, like her, are at risk. It may seem strange, unbearable even, for Wexler to devote herself to studying the thing that may kill her. But she says, "When I felt there was nothing I or anybody else could do except sit back and wait to see if it happened, that made me very depressed. The possibility of doing something is actually elating."

And she and her colleagues have made an important and surprising discovery. According to classical Mendelian genetics, two copies of a dominant gene ought to have no more of an effect than one. Yet real genes don't obey this rule strictly. A double dose of a dominant gene almost always packs more wallop than a single dose, so researchers have long suspected that two copies of the Huntington's gene could be fatal in the womb or during early childhood. Indeed, in two rare cases in which both father and mother had Huntington's disease, an infant died of unknown causes with a few days of birth—which led to speculation that a double dose of the gene was the cause.

But in the March 12 issue of *Nature*, Wexler and her colleagues challenge that idea. They found a Venezuelan family in which both parents have the disease, ten of their fourteen children carry the Huntington's marker, and four of the ten almost certainly have two copies of the gene. These four are no worse off than their brothers and sisters with one copy. The Huntington's gene seems to prove a rare—perhaps even unique—example of complete dominance.

For the first time since I learned about HD, it seems there's a significant chance there'll be a treatment within my lifetime

---

Wexler thinks this says something about the way the gene works. Genetic defects often take something away—an important enzyme, for instance. One bad gene reduces the enzyme level and may or may not cause illness, but two copies kill by removing the enzyme entirely. This can't be the case with Huntington's, because one gene seems as bad as two. Wexler offers two theories. The gene might cause an enzyme level to dip below some critical threshold; two genes could then do no further damage. Or the gene might add something: a normal protein that proves toxic in excess, or that belongs to a different time in development or a different part of the body.

In any event, she says, because the Venezuelans with the double doses of the gene have no normal copy of the gene to confound the search, their chromosomes should prove exceedingly useful—and perhaps even permit biologists to identify the protein responsible for the disease.

Like many people at risk, Catherine follows such investigations closely in the scientific literature. "For the first time since I learned about HD, it seems to me that there's a significant chance that there'll be an effective treatment within my lifetime," she says. "I hope it happens in time to help my mother and other people I know who have HD.

"And now you'd probably like to know the results of my test. Well, it was completely uninformative." Her family was too small (the second diagram on page 20 shows Catherine's family; she's the woman in white). "I was left with the same probability I had started out with. I felt relieved that it wasn't bad news, and disappointed that it wasn't good news. One of my friends had bought a bottle of champagne, and said, 'Let's drink it anyway.' I felt glad that I had tried to find out. I realized at the end that it would be very difficult to tell my mother and my other relatives if I had the gene, but I never doubted that I wanted to know myself. If they find the gene, I'll definitely be tested."

It seemed to me that drinking the champagne had been the right thing to do, and I found myself wishing that Catherine would leave things alone. If you can't be sure you haven't got the gene, can there be a wiser diagnosis than the one she told me? She seems to have brought grace and discipline to bear against the strain of not knowing. Uncertainty, at least, leaves room for hope.

Curse and Blessing of the Ghetto

Tay-Sachs disease is a choosy killer, one that for centuries targeted Eastern European Jews above all others. By decoding its lethal logic, we can learn a lot about how genetic diseases evolve—and how they can be conquered.

Jared Diamond

Contributing editor Jared Diamond is a professor of physiology at the UCLA School of Medicine.

Marie and I hated her at first sight, even though she was trying hard to be helpful. As our obstetrician's genetics counselor, she was just doing her job, explaining to us the unpleasant results that might come out of the genetic tests we were about to have performed. As a scientist, though, I already knew all I wanted to know about Tay-Sachs disease, and I didn't need to be reminded that the baby sentenced to death by it could be my own.

Fortunately, the tests would reveal that my wife and I were not carriers of the Tay-Sachs gene, and our preparenthood fears on that matter at least could be put to rest. But at the time I didn't yet know that. As I glared angrily at that poor genetics counselor, so strong was my anxiety that now, four years later, I can still clearly remember what was going through my mind: If I were an evil deity, I thought, trying to devise exquisite tortures for babies and their parents, I would be proud to have designed Tay-Sachs disease.

Tay-Sachs is completely incurable, unpreventable, and preprogrammed in the genes. A Tay-Sachs infant usually appears normal for the first few months after birth, just long enough for the parents to grow to love him. An exaggerated "startle reaction" to sounds

is the first ominous sign. At about six months the baby starts to lose control of his head and can't roll over or sit without support. Later he begins to drool, breaks out into unmotivated bouts of laughter, and suffers convulsions. Then his head grows abnormally large, and he becomes blind. Perhaps what's most frightening for the parents is that their baby loses all contact with his environment and becomes virtually a vegetable. By the child's third birthday, if he's still alive, his skin will turn yellow and his hands pudgy. Most likely he will die before he's four years old.

My wife and I were tested for the Tay-Sachs gene because at the time we rated as high-risk candidates, for two reasons. First, Marie was carrying twins, so we had double the usual chance to bear a Tay-Sachs baby. Second, both she and I are of Eastern European Jewish ancestry, the population with by far the world's highest Tay-Sachs frequency.

In peoples around the world Tay-Sachs appears once in every 400,000 births. But it appears a hundred times more frequently—about once in 3,600 births—among descendants of Eastern European Jews, people known as Ashkenazim. For descendants of most other groups of Jews—Oriental Jews, chiefly from the Middle East, or Sephardic Jews, from Spain and other Mediterranean countries—the frequency of Tay-Sachs disease is no higher than in non-Jews. Faced with such a clear

correlation, one cannot help but wonder: What is it about this one group of people that produces such an extraordinarily high risk of this disease?

Finding the answer to this question concerns all of us, regardless of our ancestry. Every human population is especially susceptible to certain diseases, not only because of its life-style but also because of its genetic inheritance. For example, genes put European whites at high risk for cystic fibrosis, African blacks for sickle-cell disease, Pacific Islanders for diabetes—and Eastern European Jews for ten different diseases, including Tay-Sachs. It's not that Jews are notably susceptible to genetic diseases in general; but a combination of historical factors has led to Jews' being intensively studied, and so their susceptibilities are far better known than those of, say, Pacific Islanders.

Tay-Sachs exemplifies how we can deal with such diseases; it has been the object of the most successful screening program to date. Moreover, Tay-Sachs is helping us understand how ethnic diseases evolve. Within the past couple of years discoveries by molecular biologists have provided tantalizing clues to precisely how a deadly gene can persist and spread over the centuries. Tay-Sachs may be primarily a disease of Eastern European Jews, but through this affliction of one group of people, we gain a window on how our genes simultaneously curse and bless us all.

The disease's hyphenated name comes from the two physicians—British ophthalmologist W. Tay and New York neurologist B. Sachs—who independently first recognized the disease, in 1881 and 1887, respectively. By 1896 Sachs had seen enough cases to realize that the disease was most common among Jewish children.

Not until 1962, however, were researchers able to trace the cause of the affliction to a single biochemical abnormality: the excessive accumulation in nerve cells of a fatty substance called G_{M2} ganglioside. Normally G_{M2} ganglioside is present at only modest levels in cell membranes, because it is constantly being broken down as well as synthesized. The breakdown depends on the enzyme hexosaminidase A, which is found in the tiny structures within our cells known as lysosomes. In the unfortunate Tay-Sachs victims this enzyme is lacking, and without it the ganglioside piles up and produces all the symptoms of the disease.

We have two copies of the gene that programs our supply of hexosaminidase A, one inherited from our father, the other from our mother; each of our parents, in turn, has two copies derived from their own parents. As long as we have one good copy of the gene, we can produce enough hexosaminidase A to prevent a buildup of G_{M2} ganglioside and we won't get Tay-Sachs. This genetic disease is of the sort termed recessive rather than dominant—meaning that to get it, a child must inherit a defective gene not just from one parent but from both of them. Clearly, each parent must have had one good copy of the gene along with the defective copy—if either had had two defective genes, he or she would have died of the disease long before reaching the age of reproduction. In genetic terms the diseased child is homozygous for the defective gene and both parents are heterozygous for it.

None of this yet gives any hint as to why the Tay-Sachs gene should be most common among Eastern European Jews. To come to grips with that question, we must take a short detour into history.

From their biblical home of ancient Israel, Jews spread peacefully to other Mediterranean lands, Yemen, and India. They were also dispersed violently through conquest by Assyrians, Babylonians, and Romans. Under the Carolingian kings of the eighth and ninth centuries Jews were invited to settle in France and Germany as traders and financiers. In subsequent centuries, however, persecutions triggered by the Crusades gradually drove Jews out of Western Europe; the process culminated in their total expulsion from Spain in 1492. Those Spanish Jews—called Sephardim—fled to other lands around the Mediterranean. Jews of France and Germany—the Ashkenazim—fled east to Poland and from there to Lithuania and western Russia, where they settled mostly in towns, as businessmen engaged in whatever pursuit they were allowed.

It seems unlikely that genetic accidents would have pumped up the frequency of the same gene not once but twice in the same population.

There the Jews stayed for centuries, through periods of both tolerance and oppression. But toward the end of the nineteenth century and the beginning of the twentieth, waves of murderous anti-Semitic attacks drove millions of Jews out of Eastern Europe, with most of them heading for the United States. My mother's parents, for example, fled to New York from the Lithuanian pogroms of the 1880s, while my father's parents fled from the Ukrainian pogroms of 1903–6. The more modern history of Jewish migration is probably well known to you all: most Jews who remained in Eastern Europe were exterminated during World War II, while most the survivors immigrated to the United States and Israel. Of the 13 million Jews alive today, more than three-quarters are Ashkenazim, the descendants of the Eastern European

Jews and the people most at risk for Tay-Sachs.

Have these Jews maintained their genetic distinctness through the thousands of years of wandering? Some scholars claim that there has been so much intermarriage and conversion that Ashkenazic Jews are now just Eastern Europeans who adopted Jewish culture. However, modern genetic studies refute that speculation.

First of all, there are those ten genetic diseases that the Ashkenazim have somehow acquired, by which they differ both from other Jews and from Eastern European non-Jews. In addition, many Ashkenazic genes turn out to be ones typical of Palestinian Arabs and other peoples of the Eastern Mediterranean areas where Jews originated. (In fact, by genetic standards the current Arab-Israeli conflict is an internecine civil war.) Other Ashkenazic genes have indeed diverged from Mediterranean ones (including genes of Sephardic and Oriental Jews) and have evolved to converge on genes of Eastern European non-Jews subject to the same local forces of natural selection. But the degree to which Ashkenazim prove to differ genetically from Eastern European non-Jews implies an intermarriage rate of only about 15 percent.

Can history help explain why the Tay-Sachs gene in particular is so much more common in Ashkenazim than in their non-Jewish neighbors or in other Jews? At the risk of spoiling a mystery, I'll tell you now that the answer is yes, but to appreciate it, you'll have to understand the four possible explanations for the persistence of the Tay-Sachs gene.

First, new copies of the gene might be arising by mutation as fast as existing copies disappear with the death of Tay-Sachs children. That's the most likely explanation for the gene's persistence in most of the world, where the disease frequency is only one in 400,000 births—that frequency reflects a typical human mutation rate. But for this explanation to apply to the Ashkenazim would require a mutation rate of at least one per 3,600 births—far above the frequency observed for any human gene. Furthermore, there would be no precedent for one particular gene mutating so much more often in one human population than in others.

As a second possibility, the Ashkenazim might have acquired the Tay-Sachs gene from some other people who already had the gene at high frequency. Arthur Koestler's controversial book *The Thirteenth Tribe,* for example, popularized the view that the Ashkenazim are really not a Semitic people but are instead descended from the Khazar, a Turkic tribe whose rulers converted to Judaism in the eighth century. Could the Khazar have brought the Tay-Sachs gene to Eastern Europe? This speculation makes good romantic reading, but there is no good evidence to support it. Moreover, it fails to explain why deaths of Tay-Sachs children didn't eliminate the gene by natural selection in the past 1,200 years, nor how the Khazar acquired high frequencies of the gene in the first place.

The third hypothesis was the one preferred by a good many geneticists until recently. It invokes two genetic processes, termed the founder effect and genetic drift, that may operate in small populations. To understand these concepts, imagine that 100 couples settle in a new land and found a population that then increases. Imagine further that one parent among those original 100 couples happens to have some rare gene, one, say, that normally occurs at a frequency of one in a million. The gene's frequency in the new population will now be one in 200 as a result of the accidental presence of that rare founder.

Or suppose again that 100 couples found a population, but that one of the 100 men happens to have lots of kids by his wife or that he is exceptionally popular with other women, while the other 99 men are childless or have few kids or are simply less popular. That one man may thereby father 10 percent rather than a more representative one percent of the next generation's babies, and their genes will disproportionately reflect that man's genes. In other words, gene frequencies will have drifted between the first and second generation.

Through these two types of genetic accidents a rare gene may occur with an unusually high frequency in a small expanding population. Eventually, if the gene is harmful, natural selection will bring its frequency back to normal by killing off gene bearers. But if the resultant disease is recessive—if heterozygous individuals don't get the disease and only the rare, homozygous individuals die of it—the gene's high frequency may persist for many generations.

These accidents do in fact account for the astonishingly high Tay-Sachs gene frequency found in one group of Pennsylvania Dutch: out of the 333 people in this group, 98 proved to carry the Tay-Sachs gene. Those 333 are all descended from one couple who settled in the United States in the eighteenth century and had 13 children. Clearly, one of that founding couple must have carried the gene. A similar accident may explain why Tay-Sachs is also relatively common among French Canadians, who number 5 million today but are descended from fewer than 6,000 French immigrants who arrived in the New World between 1638 and 1759. In the two or three centuries since both these founding events, the high Tay-Sachs gene frequency among Pennsylvania Dutch and French Canadians has not yet had enough time to decline to normal levels.

The same mechanisms were once proposed to explain the high rate of Tay-Sachs disease among the Ashkenazim. Perhaps, the reasoning went, the gene just happened to be overrepresented in the founding Jewish population that settled in Germany or Eastern Europe. Perhaps the gene just happened to drift up in frequency in the Jewish populations scattered among the isolated towns of Eastern Europe.

But geneticists have long questioned whether the Ashkenazim population's history was really suitable for these genetic accidents to have been significant. Remember, the founder effect and genetic drift become significant only in small populations, and the founding populations of Ashkenazim may have been quite large. Moreover, Ashkenazic communities were consid-

erably widespread; drift would have sent gene frequencies up in some towns but down in others. And, finally, natural selection has by now had a thousand years to restore gene frequencies to normal.

Granted, those doubts are based on historical data, which are not always as precise or reliable as one might want. But within the past several years the case against those accidental explanations for Tay-Sachs disease in the Ashkenazim has been bolstered by discoveries by molecular biologists.

Like all proteins, the enzyme absent in Tay-Sachs children is coded for by a piece of our DNA. Along that particular stretch of DNA there are thousands of different sites where a mutation could occur that would result in no enzyme and hence in the same set of symptoms. If molecular biologists had discovered that all cases of Tay-Sachs in Ashkenazim involved damage to DNA at the same site, that would have been strong evidence that in Ashkenazim the disease stems from a single mutation that has been multiplied by the founder effect or genetic drift—in other words, the high incidence of Tay-Sachs among Eastern European Jews is accidental.

In reality, though, several different mutations along this stretch of DNA have been identified in Ashkenazim, and two of them occur much more frequently than in non-Ashkenazim populations. It seems unlikely that genetic accidents would have pumped up the frequency of the same gene not once but twice in the same population.

And that's not the sole unlikely coincidence arguing against accidental explanations. Recall that Tay-Sachs is caused by the excessive accumulation of one fatty substance, G_{M2} ganglioside, from a defect in one enzyme, hexosaminidase A. But Tay-Sachs is one of ten genetic diseases characteristic of Ashkenazim. Among those other nine, two—Gaucher's disease and Niemann-Pick disease—result from the accumulation of two other fatty substances similar to G_{M2} ganglioside, as a result of defects in two other enzymes similar to hexosaminidase A. Yet our bodies contain thousands of different enzymes. It would have been an incredible roll of the genetic dice if, by nothing more than chance, Ashkenazim had independently acquired mutations in three closely related enzymes—and had acquired mutations in one of those enzymes twice.

All these facts bring us to the fourth possible explanation of why the Tay-Sachs gene is so prevalent among Ashkenazim: namely, that something about them favored accumulation of G_{M2} ganglioside and related fats.

For comparison, suppose that a friend doubles her money on one stock while you are getting wiped out with your investments. Taken alone, that could just mean she was lucky on that one occasion. But suppose that she doubles her money on each of two different stocks and at the same time rings up big profits in real estate while also making a killing in bonds. That implies more than lady luck; it suggests that something about your friend—like shrewd judgment—favors financial success.

What could be the blessings of fat accumulation in Eastern European Jews? At first this question sounds weird. After all, that fat accumulation

was noticed only because of the curses it bestows: Tay-Sachs, Gaucher's, or Niemann-Pick disease. But many of our common genetic diseases may persist because they bring both blessings and curses (see "The Cruel Logic of Our Genes," *Discover,* November 1989). They kill or impair individuals who inherit two copies of the faulty gene, but they help those who receive only one defective gene by protecting them against other diseases. The best understood example is the sickle-cell gene of African blacks, which often kills homozygotes but protects heterozygotes against malaria. Natural selection sustains such genes because more heterozygotes than normal individuals survive to pass on their genes, and those extra gene copies offset the copies lost through the deaths of homozygotes.

So let us refine our question and ask, What blessing could the Tay-Sachs gene bring to those individuals who are heterozygous for it? A clue first emerged back in 1972, with the publication of the results of a questionnaire that had asked U.S. Ashkenzaic parents of Tay-Sachs children what their own Eastern European-born parents had

We're not a melting pot, and we won't be for a long time. Each ethnic group has some characteristic genes of its own, a legacy of its distinct history.

died of. Keep in mind that since these unfortunate children had to be homozygotes, with two copies of the Tay-Sachs gene, all their parents had to be heterozygotes, with one copy, and half of the parents' parents also had to be heterozygotes.

As it turned out, most of those Tay-Sachs grandparents had died of the usual causes: heart disease, stroke, cancer, and diabetes. But strikingly, only one of the 306 grandparents had died of tuberculosis, even though TB was generally one of the big killers in these grandparents' time. Indeed, among the general population of large Eastern European cities in the early twentieth century, TB caused up to 20 percent of all deaths.

This big discrepancy suggested that

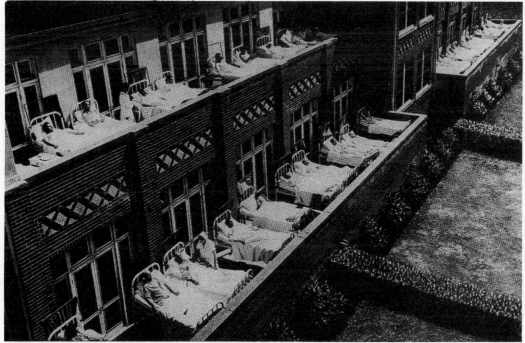

Records at a Jewish TB sanatorium in Denver indicated that among patients born in Europe between 1860 and 1910, Jews from Austria and Hungary were overrepresented. (Photo credit: AMC Cancer Research Center, Denver)

Tay-Sachs heterozygotes might somehow have been protected against TB. Interestingly, it was already well known that Ashkenazim in general had some such protection: even when Jews and non-Jews were compared within the same European city, class, and occupational group (for example, Warsaw garment workers), Jews had only half the TB death rate on non-Jews, despite their being equally susceptible to infection. Perhaps, one could reason, the Tay-Sachs gene furnished part of that well-established Jewish resistance.

A second clue to a heterozygote advantage conveyed by the Tay-Sachs gene emerged in 1983, with a fresh look at the data concerning the distributions of TB and the Tay-Sachs gene within Europe. The statistics showed that the Tay-Sachs gene was nearly three times more frequent among Jews originating from Austria, Hungary, and Czechoslovakia—areas where an amazing 9 to 10 percent of the population were heterozygotes—than among Jews from Poland, Russia, and Germany. At the same time records from an old Jewish TB sanatorium in Denver in 1904 showed that among patients born in Europe between 1860 and 1910, Jews from Austria and Hungary were overrepresented.

Initially, in putting together these two pieces of information, you might be tempted to conclude that because the highest frequency of the Tay-Sachs gene appeared in the same geographic region that produced the most cases of TB, the gene in fact offers no protection whatsoever. Indeed, this was precisely the mistaken conclusion of many researchers who had looked at these data before. But you have to pay careful attention to the numbers here: even at its highest frequency the Tay-Sachs gene was carried by far fewer people than would be infected by TB. What the statistics really indicate is that where TB is the biggest threat, natural selection produces the biggest response.

Think of it this way: You arrive at an island where you find that all the inhabitants of the north end wear suits of armor, while all the inhabitants of the south end wear only cloth shirts. You'd

be pretty safe in assuming that warfare is more prevalent in the north—and that war-related injuries account for far more deaths there than in the south. Thus, if the Tay-Sachs gene does indeed lend heterozygotes some protection against TB, you would expect to find the gene most often precisely where you find TB most often. Similarly, the sickle-cell gene reaches its highest frequencies in those parts of Africa where malaria is the biggest risk.

But you may believe there's still a hole in the argument: If Tay-Sachs heterozygotes are protected against TB, you may be asking, why is the gene common just in the Ashkenazim? Why did it not become common in the non-Jewish populations also exposed to TB in Austria, Hungary, and Czechoslovakia?

At this point we must recall the peculiar circumstances in which the Jews of Eastern Europe were forced to live. They were unique among the world's ethnic groups in having been virtually confined to towns for most of the past 2,000 years. Being forbidden to own land, Eastern European Jews were not peasant farmers living in the countryside, but businesspeople forced to live in crowded ghettos, in an environment where tuberculosis thrived.

Of course, until recent improvements in sanitation, these towns were not very healthy places for non-Jews either. Indeed, their populations couldn't sustain themselves: deaths exceeded births, and the number of dead had to be balanced by continued emigration from the countryside. For non-Jews, therefore, there was no genetically distinct urban population. For ghetto-bound Jews, however, there could be no emigration from the countryside; thus the Jewish population was under the strongest selection to evolve genetic resistance to TB.

Those are the conditions that probably led to Jewish TB resistance, whatever particular genetic factors prove to underlie it. I'd speculate that G_{M2} and related fats accumulate at slightly higher-than-normal levels in heterozygotes, although not at the lethal

levels seen in homozygotes. (The fat accumulation in heterozygotes probably takes place in the cell membrane, the cell's "armor.") I'd also speculate that the accumulation provides heterozygotes with some protection against TB, and that that's why the genes for Tay-Sachs, Gaucher's, and Niemann-Pick disease reached high frequencies in the Ashkenazim.

Having thus stated the case, let me make clear that I don't want to overstate it. The evidence is still speculative. Depending on how you do the calculation, the low frequency of TB deaths in Tay-Sachs grandparents either barely reaches or doesn't quite reach the level of proof that statisticians require to accept an effect as real rather than as one that's arisen by chance. Moreover, we have no idea of the biochemical mechanism by which fat accumulation might confer resistance against TB. For the moment, I'd say that the evidence points to some selective advantage of Tay-Sachs heterozygotes among the Ashkenazim, and that TB resistance is the only plausible hypothesis yet proposed.

For now Tay-Sachs remains a speculative model for the evolution of ethnic diseases. But it's already a proven model of what to do about them. Twenty years ago a test was developed to identify Tay-Sachs heterozygotes, based on their lower-than-normal levels of hexosaminidase A. The test is simple, cheap, and accurate: all I did was to donate a small sample of my blood, pay $35, and wait a few days to receive the results.

If that test shows that at least one member of a couple is not a Tay-Sachs heterozygotre, then any child of theirs can't be a Tay-Sachs homozygote. If both parents prove to be heterozygotes, there's a one-in-four chance of their child being a homozygote; that can then be determined by other tests performed on the mother early in pregnancy. If the results are positive, it's early enough for her to abort, should she choose to. That critical bit of knowledge has enabled parents who had gone through the agony of bearing a Tay-Sachs baby and watching him die to find the courage to try again.

The Tay-Sachs screening program launched in the United States in 1971 was targeted at the high-risk population: Ashkenazic Jewish couples of childbearing age. So successful has this approach been that the number of Tay-Sachs babies born each year in this country has declined tenfold. Today, in fact, more Tay-Sachs cases appear here in non-Jews than in Jews, because only the latter couples are routinely tested. Thus, what used to be the classic genetic disease of Jews is so no longer.

There's also a broader message to the Tay-Sachs story. We commonly refer to the United States as a melting pot, and in many ways that metaphor is apt. But in other ways we're not a melting pot, and we won't be for a long time. Each ethnic group has some characteristic genes of its own, a legacy of its distinct history. Tuberculosis and malaria are not major causes of death in the United States, but the genes that some of us evolved to protect ourselves against them are still frequent. Those genes are frequent only in certain ethnic groups, though, and they'll be slow to melt through the population.

With modern advances in molecular genetics, we can expect to see more, not less, ethnically targeted practice of medicine. Genetic screening for cystic fibrosis in European whites, for example, is one program that has been much discussed recently; when it comes, it will surely be based on the Tay-Sachs experience. Of course, what that may mean someday is more anxiety-ridden parents-to-be glowering at more dedicated genetics counselors. It will also mean fewer babies doomed to the agonies of diseases we may understand but that we'll never be able to accept.

Emerging Viruses

With environmental changes paving their way, armies of once-obscure viruses may be poised to launch an attack on unprepared humans.

John Langone

John Langone wrote about artificial hearts in the June 1986 issue of Discover.

In November 1989, when a batch of 200 cynomolgus monkeys shipped from the Philippines to Hazleton Research Products in Reston, Virginia, suddenly began dying in their cages, disease detectives at the Centers for Disease Control in Atlanta were understandably concerned. For one thing, the long-tailed macaques were important to biomedical research. For another, there were an awful lot of them in this country. Some 16,000 were brought here in 1989, 80 percent through Kennedy International Airport in New York City—not an especially cheery thought if whatever was killing the monkeys had arrived along with them.

Investigators obtained samples of the dead monkeys' tissues, put them under electron microscopes, and made a chilling discovery: the rodlike structures they observed bore a striking resemblance to Ebola virus, the cause of a dreaded hemorrhagic fever in humans. The disease is marked by vomiting and internal bleeding, and it often brings shock and death. Ebola, named for a river in Zaire, was responsible for three separate epidemics in Africa during the 1970s. In one, 98 percent of those infected became ill, and 88 percent died—quickly. Indeed, before the emergence of the AIDS virus, Ebola

was the most lethal virus known to humankind. But it had never before turned up anywhere in the world outside Africa.

As a precaution all the monkeys at Hazleton were destroyed. Over the next few months, however, monkeys quarantined in Texas began dying of the same fever. Then, this past April, what disease trackers feared might happen did: while performing an autopsy on a monkey, a lab worker at Hazleton cut his finger and developed an infection.

There is no treatment for Ebola; doctors could only isolate the worker and wait. The man never showed a high load of the virus in his blood, but within three weeks of becoming infected he was, as virologist Susan Fisher-Hoch of the Centers for Disease Control recalls, "full of brisk new antibodies to it."

Fortunately, neither this man nor three others at Hazleton who were also infected through contact with the animals became ill. Subsequent tests have revealed that although the monkey virus looks the same as Ebola, it is not genetically identical. Apparently this new version of Ebola, if that's what it is, does not replicate well in humans.

Reason to breathe easier? Not necessarily. "How close is close?" asks Fisher-Hoch. "It's not as pathogenic as Ebola, that's for sure. But it looks like Ebola, and it belongs to the same family. I don't think it's going to jump across the room at anybody, but any-

thing can happen, especially when you have blood contact."

The case of the Ebola-like virus is far more than just an object lesson for those who handle imported monkeys. More important, it is a warning that new armies of deadly viruses—although some of them are obscure and perhaps deceptively fragile—may be waiting for the opportunity to infect unsuspecting human populations. Indeed, there is a growing concern among virologists and infectious-disease specialists, universally jolted by the arrival of AIDS, that conditions may be ripe for similar surprises. "I wouldn't say we're in a state of panic," says Fisher-Hoch. "But there's much, much more out there than we know about."

Joshua Lederberg, winner of the 1958 Nobel Prize in Medicine and Physiology, best expresses the heightened concern. "It is still not comprehended widely that AIDS is a natural, almost predictable, phenomenon," he says. "It is not going to be a unique event. Pandemics are not acts of God but are built into the ecological relations between viruses, animal species, and the human species, and we had better understand that or we will rue it."

Lederberg's message starkly contradicts a cherished popular impression. Modern medicine and improved sanitation, we'd like to believe, have given us the upper hand over microbes. After all, many of the classic scourges—yellow fever, polio, bubonic plague, typhus—are now restricted to rather few geographic areas, and smallpox has been eradicated. But despite these advances, viral diseases remain the most prevalent of all human ailments. There are many hundreds, perhaps thousands, of viruses that cause illness in humans, ranging from acute respiratory and gastrointestinal afflictions to chronic hepatitis and genital herpes. Most viral diseases are not fatal. There are, however, a few quick killers like Ebola, and some that kill indirectly, like AIDS, by making the body vulnerable to other infections.

Many of the "emerging" viruses that concern Lederberg are recent additions to this list. Yet they are not new in the true sense of the word. They are either already infecting humans in remote areas or being carried about in animals, often tropical species, with little or no harm to the animals but with potentially disastrous consequences if transferred to humans. What's new about these viruses is that they've been given new opportunities to spread. As people encroach on the tropics, as cities grow and populations mingle, as humans, monkeys, and even mosquitoes crisscross the globe on airplanes, these obscure viruses can break out of their isolation. Again, the AIDS virus is a prime example. When first recognized in 1981, it was new only to the Western world. It presumably originated in central Africa, and it may have descended from a virus that existed in monkeys for as long as 50,000 years.

"These viruses have got to come from somewhere," says Lederberg wryly. "I don't think we're going to see many expressions of the fresh origin of life."

Ebola, and the similar Marburg virus—first identified in African green monkeys imported to Europe—are exceptionally potent. Fortunately they are also extremely rare. African fatalities of the 1970s Ebola epidemics numbered 452, and the total of known Marburg cases in humans is 39. But several other hemorrhagic viruses are making their rounds through animals and humans, and some are all too common. Korean hemorrhagic fever, for example, is a serious, chronic in-

fection caused by the Hantaan virus and spread by mice and rats. When humans contract Hantaan, they can develop severe internal bleeding and kidney failure. An estimated 3,000 United Nations soldiers came down with this infection during the Korean War; as many as 10 percent of them died.

Hantaan, at the moment, is generally confined to Asia, but in 1982 James Childs, a disease ecologist at the Johns Hopkins School of Hygiene and Public Health, isolated a close relative of Hantaan, called Seoul virus, in Baltimore's alley rats. No one knows when or how the virus first got here. But over the next few years investigators isolated Seoul virus from rats in Philadelphia, Houston, and New Orleans. In many other cities, including New York and San Francisco, rats had antibodies for the virus, meaning that they had been infected.

Many of the same human activities that threaten to disrupt the ecology of the planet also pave the way for epidemics.

Meanwhile, researchers at Johns Hopkins and the U.S. Army Medical Research Institute of Infectious Diseases at Fort Detrick, Maryland, began screening kidney-dialysis patients in eastern cities such as Baltimore, Detroit, and Washington, D.C., for antibodies to Seoul virus. "We know that the Seoul virus can cause an acute kidney disease," says Allan Watson, a kidney disease specialist at Johns Hopkins. "And there are now cases in Europe where people with the acute disease go on to develop chronic kidney disease." A similar pattern may be emerging in this country: "We found the prevalence of the antibodies in these patients to be much higher than we would expect in a normal population," says Watson.

This past year 15 Baltimore residents were found to have antibodies to Seoul virus. Fourteen of those 15 also

have high blood pressure, and seven have chronic kidney disease. According to James LeDuc, an infectious-disease specialist at Fort Detrick, these findings have "startling implications, the first recognition of what might be a new disease." LeDuc speculates that Seoul virus might also be contributing to the high rate of inner-city hypertension that clinicians have noted for the past ten years.

Another viral disease now lapping at our shores is dengue—a close relative of yellow fever that is also carried by mosquitoes. In its most common form dengue brings joint pain, headaches, and other flulike symptoms; in its severe, hemorrhagic form it can cause bleeding, prostration, shock, and death. Dengue is endemic in Asia and Africa. It is also common in South and Central America, where recent outbreaks have come close to the continental United States. In 1981 there was an epidemic of 344,000 cases in Cuba. During the past decade dengue has spread through the Caribbean Basin and beyond. In 1988 Ecuador had an outbreak of 400,000 cases (the milder kind) in just two to three months; from late 1989 to early 1990 Venezuela reported 9,000 cases, 2,000 of which were the severe kind; 70 proved fatal.

The hemorrhagic form of dengue is especially hard on children: mortality can reach 30 percent among infants less than one year old. When Lederberg was traveling through the Caribbean in January of this year, he noted several headlines about fatal cases, including one high school student. "It was startling to have a very healthy young person just felled within a matter of days," he says. Because the current epidemic is so close to U.S. territory, because the aggressive mosquito that carries the virus is well established in 17 states, and because there is no reliable vaccine, Lederberg is convinced that the United States is in grave danger of a good-size outbreak.

Dengue is no stranger to the U.S. mainland: in 1922 the virus infected perhaps 2 million people; the most recent epidemic in the continental United States was in 1945. Since then dengue has hung on at low levels as an import:

in 1989 doctors reported 95 Americans as having contracted a denguelike illness while traveling abroad, and 22 of those cases were confirmed as dengue. "I think we need very high vigilance about the detection of cases to be sure we isolate them so the disease doesn't spread further," says Lederberg. "We need to pay attention before it becomes a catastrophe."

Of course, no one can be certain whether Hantaan, dengue, some other emerging virus, or a new, unrecognized variant will become the next global scourge. "Everything depends on how we respond to it," says Lederberg. Explosive outbreaks of new infectious diseases have occurred regularly since antiquity, yet epidemics seem to catch people by surprise. "There will be more surprises," says Lederberg, "because our fertile imagination does not begin to match all the tricks that nature can play."

Epidemiologists can recite by rote the conditions that might prompt a virus to break out of the equilibrium in which it usually coexists with a host population: crowded living conditions, susceptible victims, a reasonably efficient means of transmission, low standards of medical care and education. There is, however, yet another factor that can tip the balance: human behavior that unwittingly helps the virus along. It now appears clear that many of the same human activities that threaten to disrupt the ecology of the planet—deforestation, dam building, intensive agriculture—also pave the way for epidemics.

Global warming, for example, could change the migration pattern of animals or the habitats of rodents and insects, enabling them to transport viruses to new regions. As virologist Stephen S. Morse of Rockefeller University explains it: "More often than not, what causes the emergence of these viruses and diseases is some human activity, some environmental or social change that promotes the transfer of viruses—call it viral traffic—to new hosts."

Viruses also, of course, help out their own cause. They do so through mutation and recombination, which means exchanging bits of their DNA or RNA with other viruses that infect the same host. This is the trickery they employ to exist; it enables them to outwit the formidable immunologic defenses a host erects when invaded. Influenza is a familiar example: one variant of the flu virus demonstrated the potency of genetic recombination in the 1918–19 epidemic that killed 20 million people worldwide. Most of the victims died from pneumonia when their lungs filled with fluid; many turned blue or purple and spat blood. Even healthy individuals could die within 48 hours of first feeling sick.

Because the flu virus is so variable, Lederberg classifies it as a perpetually emerging virus. And because it's so easily transmitted from person to person, he gives it the best odds of showing up as the next viral pandemic.

About 100 viruses transmitted through the bites of mosquitoes and ticks cause diseases, and at least 20 are capable of emerging in epidemic form.

Morse points out that influenza is also a good example of how humans speed up a virus's emergence. Even though most changes in the virus occur through random mutations, a new version often erupts by a quick reshuffling of genes between different strains. Humans have promoted such genetic exchanges through agricultural practices that put pigs, ducks, and farmers together, especially in China. And every major flu epidemic known has originated in South China.

The scenario goes like this. An avian flu virus passes from migratory birds and waterfowl, particularly ducks, to pigs. At the same time, human flu virus passes from the farmer to the pig, which becomes a "mixing vessel." (Pigs and humans, in fact, overlap considerably in the viruses each is susceptible to.) Once inside pigs the human and avian viruses exchange genes that code for key surface proteins on the virus called hemagglutinins, which trigger the immune response in humans. After what Morse calls "a trial run" in the local pigs, a new virus emerges in a form that can be passed back to humans. This variant might be more lethal than the original human virus, and because humans have never been exposed to it, they lack specific immunity—and a global pandemic catches fire.

Agriculture is giving a boost to other viruses beside old faithful influenza. Argentine hemorrhagic fever is a nasty example. Caused by the Junin virus, which is carried in a mouse called *Calomys musculinus,* this disease is a significant problem in South America. It does not pose an immediate threat to the United States, but it's a perfect example of how agriculture can change the ecology of a region's microbes.

C. musculinus thrives in cornfields. When Argentine farmers shifted from their traditional practice of crop mixing and began clearing the pampas to plant large crops of maize exclusively, they gave this little mouse a huge new habitat. At the same time herbicides dumped over the area to kill weeds reduced the diversity of the local flora and, consequently, the diversity of rodent species. *C. musculinus* eventually dominated. "The virus was always there, the mouse was always there," says Morse, "but what changed was the prevalence of that rodent and with it the virus."

Junin's range has grown from 6,000 square miles to 40,000, and 450 people a year are reportedly infected, many in the rural area surrounding Buenos Aires. "People become infected," says Morse, "after having walked someplace, touched something, or breathed somewhere the rodent has just run through, splashing virus as it urinated." The disease produces fever, sore throat, headache, and sometimes—like other hemorrhagic fevers—internal bleeding, shock, and death; and usually the survivors are left without hair on their head.

Korean hemorrhagic fever falls into the same ecological pattern. Carried by rodents, the Hantaan virus is especially prevalent during rice harvests, which put farmers in contact with rodent urine. Increased rice planting has provided more food for the field rodents as well as for burgeoning populations—and the incidence of Korean hemorrhagic fever has increased accordingly. Now, says Morse, there are 100,000 cases in China each year.

Closer to the United States, one of the newest emerging diseases linked to the spread of agriculture is Oropouche fever, a denguelike illness accompanied by diarrhea. Carried by the midge *Culicoides paranensis,* a biting gnat, this obscure disease was first spotted in Trinidad in the late 1950s, where the gnat bred in discarded cacao shells. With the rise of cacao as a cash crop in the Amazon region of Brazil, the gnat—probably already established there—was given more opportunities to bite humans. Then the disease hit Panama, just before the U.S. invasion, opening the possibility that GIs could come home with the virus.

Another viral highway that we've expanded over the years is standing water. As more water is tapped for irrigation, growing cities, and hydroelectric power, networks of reservoirs, ponds, and drainage ditches tend to spread on the landscape. "The basic equation," says Morse, "is more water equals more mosquitoes"—and more mosquito-borne diseases. About 100 arboviruses—those transmitted to humans chiefly through the bites of bloodsucking mosquitoes and ticks—cause diseases, and at least 20 are capable of emerging in epidemic form.

In the Americas dengue is the current front-runner. It was probably spread in the nineteenth century by the same mosquito that carried yellow fever, *Aedes aegypti,* which is still alive and well in the U.S. Gulf states. In fact, with the decline of mosquito eradication programs throughout the Americas in the 1960s and 1970s, *A. aegypti* has reestablished itself throughout most of its former range. Dengue is also transmitted by a very aggressive biter, *Aedes albopictus,* or Asian tiger mosquito, introduced into the United States in 1985. It got here in an unusual vehicle: hundreds of thousands of used

tires imported from Asia into Houston for recapping. In the tires were some eggs of the Asian mosquitoes—and wet tires make excellent incubators.

Often, though, mosquitoes don't need to smuggle their eggs; full-grown adults can simply hop a ride in the cabin or cargo hold of airplanes. It happens often enough to have spawned a parasitic disease called airport malaria. In 1989 there were five cases contracted by residents of Geneva who lived close to that city's international airport.

"This is why airplanes that travel this way are sprayed," says Lederberg. "Somebody comes aboard the plane with a can of pyrethrum and tries to kill the insects. It's not done very systematically." And no one, of course, yanks off virus-carrying passengers who have not yet become sick. "You can be in an African village where people may be dying like flies," says Lederberg, "And twenty-four hours later you're in downtown Los Angeles and coming down with Ebola or Lassa fever and you don't even know you have it."

Lassa fever, another rodent-borne disease, spreads not only through rodents but also directly from person to person. Although Lassa is fairly well confined to West Africa, it's one of those exotic tropical diseases, like Ebola, that merits close monitoring. With an incubation period of but a week or two, it could spread through a family or a hospital soon after being carried out of Africa. The virus causes a rash of symptoms—fever, muscle pains, chills, vomiting, dizziness, seizures, and many others—that are sometimes confused with other diseases. A failure to recognize Lassa quickly could be serious; mortality has reached 45 percent in some African outbreaks. From 1969 to 1976 eight cases of Lassa were confirmed in persons who had returned to the United States or Europe from Africa. Two died.

But despite its severe effects, Lassa is also a good example of why viruses tend not to emerge. Many of the viruses considered to be emerging, such as Lassa and Junin, are not spread among humans very easily, and Han-

taan has never been known to spread from person to person. Moreover, even though more contagious viruses, such as new strains of influenza, do spring out from time to time, they have not destroyed the species. "Very few very lethal diseases are readily transmissible from person to person," Lederberg acknowledges, "and the reason we know that is that we're here. We've built up defenses to deal with those things most of the time."

Viruses that infect humans have good reason for sparing our species: they need us to survive. A virus is essentially a packet of genes. Unlike the cells in our bodies, it contains no machinery to generate its own energy, grow, or reproduce. Instead, a virus must invade the host cells, commandeer the metabolic and reproductive machinery of those cells, and use it to produce endless copies of itself—but without doing too much damage to the host. It's against a virus's best interests to kill off large numbers of the species it infects.

The more lethal viruses haven't yet adapted well to their hosts. Also, they usually haven't evolved a good way of infecting the host. Even the AIDS virus, perceived by a fearful public early in the outbreak as capable of laying waste to humanity, is still not spread casually, and AIDS shows no signs of becoming a new Black Death. From the point of view of a virus it's better to lie low and replicate slowly in an many individuals as possible, perhaps with a minimum of symptoms. "That's the expected pattern of evolution," says Lederberg. With the AIDS virus, "all kinds of variants have appeared already. There's no proof, but there's at least a hint that it's becoming slightly less virulent."

So what's the worry? For one thing, the very uncertainties of viral evolution. Researchers still don't know the details of how viruses spread from animals to humans and vice versa. "We think we have a good general outline," says Lederberg, "but there's still a lot of work to be done. For example, we don't really know how Lassa fever is spread." Moreover, many of the viruses that now pose the greatest threat appear to mutate rapidly and unpredictably.

They'll certainly always be around: it's unlikely that humans will ever eradicate a virus that can fall back and regroup in an animal reservoir. Yellow fever may be under control, for example, but most efforts to eradicate its carrier mosquito are limited to urbanized areas. "You're not going to eradicate all the mosquitoes in the jungle," says Lederberg. So the yellow fever virus still lurks in jungle mosquitoes, and hence also in jungle primates, which presumably harbored the ancestor of the AIDS virus.

In that regard AIDS remains a frightening example of all the possibilities there are in viral evolution. "Here's a virus that is not that well adapted," says Lederberg, "and isn't smart enough to leave its host alive—although it is smart enough to leave the host alive for a long time. It's no accident you have this long latent period, and viruses that can do that are almost as good as the ones that leave their hosts completely intact."

Still, it's too early to be sure whether AIDS is an evolutionary fluke, or whether any other virus lurking on the fringes of our awareness may be capable of causing similar devastation. Howard Temin, a virologist at the University of Wisconsin and, like Lederberg, a Nobel Prize winner, doesn't feel that completely unknown viruses are worth worrying about. "I spend time worrying about the AIDS epidemic," he says, "not about the ones that might come along." And Temin suspects it's unlikely that another AIDS-like virus will show up. He believes it broke out of its isolation because of the social disruption and jet travel that followed World War II; if there were another odd virus ready to take off, we would have seen it already. "We've had

forty-five years," he points out, "and it hasn't appeared yet."

As for the known viruses, says Temin, "certainly with a population of two hundred fifty million mobile people we're going to have every disease. Whether they're going to be of any quantitative importance is another question. The AIDS virus is an unusual pathogen that's spread by sex and drugs; our normal control mechanisms do not work. These other viruses are spread by traditional ways; insects are a lot easier to control than sex and drugs."

All the same, earlier this year entomologist George Craig of Notre Dame collected some Asian tiger mosquitoes from a tire dump 40 miles south of St. Louis and sent them to the Centers for Disease Control in Fort Collins, Colorado. There investigators isolated a previously unknown virus—the first virus found in a North American *albopictus*. Is it dangerous? Bruce Francy, a Centers for Disease Control epidemiologist, says that although the virus is new, "several other related viruses have been recovered from mosquitoes in the United States. None are known to produce disease in humans; only one has been shown to produce encephalitis in horses. So we don't know for sure, but we're guessing it may not be a significant human pathogen. There are, however, some related viruses in South America that do produce disease in both humans and horses, such as Xingu virus and Fort Sherman virus."

If the North American virus does prove to be a harmless variant of its South American cousins, it will conform to recent trends. So far, most emerging viruses seem confined to developing countries and the tropics—where some now pose an overwhelming problem. And more continue to emerge. Earlier this year researchers

reported that they had isolated and sequenced the genetic material in what may be a relatively new disease in humans: hepatitis E. While the better known hepatitis A and B take an enormous toll in the Third World, hepatitis E, according to the World Health Organization, is also a huge threat. No hard figures are available as to its prevalence, because there is no easy way to test for it—a problem that may be remedied now that the viral genes have been isolated—but it may infect up to a million people a year and be responsible for more than half the cases of acute viral hepatitis in Asia.

International surveillance programs, therefore, are essential if we want to minimize unpleasant surprises. Donald Henderson, a specialist in public health at Johns Hopkins who directed the international campaign to eradicate smallpox, has called for the installation of clinics near tropical rain forests and in the densely populated outskirts of large cities to monitor patients for signs of unusual diseases. "For example, with AIDS," he says, "one would have detected an unusual number of patients with lesions on their skin, and this could have led to an early investigation."

But aside from early-warning programs—which Henderson estimates could cost $300 million annually—it's more a question of applying what is already known. As Morse put its, "I feel a lot more might have been done with the AIDS virus if we had paid more attention to other animal viruses. A lot had to be rediscovered. The epidemiology of AIDS could have been inferred from what we knew about hepatitis B. We need to build better bridges between the scientific disciplines and not—as we have through despoiling the environment—for the viruses."

Germ Wars

Beset by controversy, the U.S. military is using genetic engineering to design defenses against biological weapons

Melissa Hendricks

In 17 years as an Army virologist at Fort Detrick in Frederick, Md., Neil Levitt found his work a risky business. On several occasions, he says, his supervisors issued him a gas mask to screen out toxic fumes emitted by a faulty ventilation system. In another incident, he recalls, a malfunctioning exhaust hood blew radioactive iodine onto his face. And once he discovered that several liters of a debilitating virus has inexplicably disappeared from a lab freezer.

"There is reason to believe that at least one nation, USSR, continued the development of an offensive biological weapons capability after signing the treaty."

—1987 report to Army by scientific advisers assessing BDRP

Levitt, who worked for the Department of Defense's Biological Defense Research Program (BDRP), says he repeatedly asked officials overseeing his work to investigate the safety violations. But the Army denied some of his requests and ignored others, he says, leading him to resign in 1986. With the

Foundation on Economic Trends, a Washington, D.C.-based environmental action organization, Levitt sued the Department of Defense (DOD) for violating national environmental law. In an out-of-court settlement of that suit, the DOD agreed to conduct environmental impact studies of its biological warfare research facilities (SN: 2/28/87, p. 132).

Levitt's lawsuit helped spotlight and expand a long-running but largely low-key controversy among some biological scientists over military germ research. While the upfront issues center on safety, larger questions of national defense and international relations are so intertwined in the dispute they seem almost inseparable.

Critics of the BDRP contend that "accidents waiting to happen" at DOD-funded laboratories require a revamping of the nation's biological warfare program. Inadequate safety enforcement risks the well-being of scientists in the labs and of residents living nearby, they argue. But behind the immediate personal fears and concerns for public health, they acknowledge, lie more complex issues of national security and international treaty.

In the preliminary draft of its environmental impact statement on the overall BDRP, forced by Levitt's suit and released in January 1988, the DOD says the program poses no significant risks to researchers or the public; falls within the allowances of the 1972 Bio-

logical Weapons Convention treaty; and represents a vital defense against potential biological warfare threats. While information concerning those threats is classified, Army science advisers stated in a report issued last year that "there is reason to believe that at least one nation, USSR, continued the development of an offensive biological weapons capability after signing the treaty."

"It's like testing a vest against bullets. You first need to have the bullets."

—epidemiologist and BDRP critic Jay Jacobson

The Biological Weapons Convention treaty, signed by 111 nations including the United States and the Soviet Union, prohibits the development, production and stockpiling of biological weapons except for defensive purposes. However, it "does not preclude research into those offensive aspects of biological agents necessary to determine what defensive measures are required," according to a 1969 statement issued by then-National Security Adviser Henry Kissinger.

This exception troubles Levitt and others, who view offensive and defensive research as indistinguishable, says Jay Jacobson, an infectious-disease specialist and epidemiologist at the

University of Utah School of Medicine in Salt Lake City: "It's like testing a vest against bullets. You first need to have the bullets." Intensifying complaints by critics in recent years has been the BDRP's use of genetic engineering—a technology unanticipated by the drafters of the treaty. Molecular biologist Keith Yamamoto of the University of California, San Francisco, notes that scientists can now create microorganisms that can cause deadly diseases for which no cures exist. "Using gene cloning destroys the distinction between offense and defense, and gives a loophole in the 1972 treaty," Yamamoto says.

"Using gene cloning destroys the distinction between offense and defense."

—molecular biologist and BDRP opponent Keith Yamamoto

Senate subcommittee hearings this past summer evaluated the safety of biological and chemical warfare research facilities. Testimony included Levitt's and that of Jeremy Rifkin, director of the Foundation on Economic Trends. Rifkin, best known for his outspoken opposition to genetic engineering, accused the DOD of failing to update safety policies as it expanded its budget for research on disease-causing organisms from about $16 million in 1980 to about $90 million in 1986.

The biological weapons issue has sparked debate in other political, scientific and public circles. During the past few years, the Army has sought to scale up its biological warfare research facility at the Dugway (Utah) Proving Grounds. But nearby residents have protested the facility ever since the Army accidentally released nerve chemicals there in 1968, killing thousands of sheep. Following a lawsuit filed against the DOD by Rifkin, the Army agreed earlier this year to back down on its plans for expanding the

facility. Moreover, more than 600 biological researchers have signed pledges to refuse DOD funds for their work, and a bill is pending in Congress to implement the Biological Weapons Convention treaty as U.S. law. Supporters contend a domestic law would be more effective at deterring violators than the existing treaty.

Biological weapons existed for centuries prior to the 1972 treaty. The Greeks and Romans poisoned drinking water with decaying corpses 2,000 years ago. During World War II, the Japanese experimented on prisoners of war with plague, anthrax, smallpox and other diseases. But not until this decade have scientists gained the capacity to design novel biological weapons surreptitiously and with ease. The nature of genetic engineering makes it almost impossible for one nation to verify whether another is complying with the treaty, says Col. David Huxsoll, Commander of the U.S. Army Medical Research Institute of Infectious Diseases (USAMRIID) at Fort Detrick, the BDRP's leading medical research facility. He and other military planners say the United States must defend against the possibility of terrorists or hostile nations manipulating genes to build weapons.

The military says its strategy is to defend against as many perceived threats as possible. For example, DOD-sponsored scientists are seeking defenses against viruses that cause yellow fever, Rift Valley fever, Korean hemorrhagic fever and dengue fever; bacteria causing botulism, anthrax and plague; various snake-venom and animal toxins; and several parasitic organisms. The plans call for the development of drugs and vaccines capable of deterring several related biological weapons rather than only a single agent. One way to do this, says Leonard Smith of USAMRIID, is to find a common means of attack shared by a group of agents and to learn which proteins participate in the attack. Then, the theory goes, scientists could create a vaccine designed to make the body produce antibodies against those common proteins. Investigating a dozen toxins from several snake spe-

cies, Smith has found several that appear to target a single protein at the junction where nerve signals are transmitted between cells. "This provides hope for finding a single vaccine against several different toxins," he says.

In similar work, John Middlebrook of USAMRIID has examined several related bacterial and snake-venom toxins to find a common "neutralizing epitope," a section of a toxin protein at which an antibody can block the toxin's activity. Among 14 or 15 different toxins studied so far, he has identified one antibody that neutralizes as many as four different toxins.

"Compare the recombinant anthrax protein to a car with its motor removed. The car lacking a motor looks identical to a car with a motor but it does not run."

—BDRP biochemist Donald Robertson

Parallel efforts in virology seek to create vaccines against several different genetic varieties of one virus. Joel Dalrymple of USAMRIID is attempting to improve the existing vaccine against the virus causing Rift Valley fever, a disease common in sub-Saharan Africa and spread to humans by mosquitoes. The vaccine now routinely given to U.S. military personnel has drawbacks: It is expensive, requires three injections and may not work against all 33 to 38 varieties of the virus. Dalrymple and his co-workers have identified two proteins in the virus' outer coat, one of which, G2, appears to induce immunity in mice. They are now producing antibodies to various pieces of G2 to see which best protect the mice against Rift Valley fever. The researchers hope that cloning the genes coding for those protein segments will lead to a more effective vaccine.

Still another technique uses a harmless "carrier" virus to transport into the human body immunity-inducing pieces from the protein coats of several different viruses. As a first step in building such a "polyvalent" vaccine, Dalrymple is examining the alphaviruses, which can cause fever, arthritis and death, and are found mostly outside of the United States. He is focusing on three different species of alphavirus to determine which genes to include in the polyvalent vaccine.

If successful, such efforts could benefit civilians as well as the Armed Forces. But skeptics contend the military's research goals are unrealistic. Even if BDRP scientists produced a vaccine effective against many different viruses, they say, enemy scientists could mutate an agent's genes to create an entirely new organism against which the drug or vaccine would not work. "Nature does this herself: A virus changes its clothes and comes back wearing a different coat," notes Yamamoto. "The military cannot make an infinite number of vaccines to an infinite number of agents."

BDRP scientists maintain that their goals, though far off, are attainable. "I won't accept the criticism that the number of viruses out there is overwhelming and too numerous to make a vaccine," Dalrymple says. "It is possible to make a vaccine against all alphaviruses causing human disease." He won't stop making vaccines against single strains of alphavirus while waiting for this to happen, he adds.

In more basic research, DOD-supported scientists seek to identify which proteins and genes of various biological agents are responsible for causing disease symptoms, and which might be prime targets for drugs and vaccines. Lt. Col. Martin Crumrine of US-AMRIID, Donald Robertson of Brigham Young University in Provo, Utah, and their collaborators are studying *Bacillus anthracis,* the bacterium that

Activists Target Chemical Weapons

Flushed with the success of its lawsuits against the Army's biological weapons programs, the Washington, D.C.-based Foundation on Economic Trends last week sued U.S. Department of Defense (DOD) officials in an effort to shut down the nation's chemical weapons program. The suit contends the DOD has failed to document the safety of its chemical warfare program as required by the National Environmental Policy Act. DOD's program includes basic research, production of new chemical weapons and dismantling of older ones.

Under the act's regulations, organizations performing activities that may significantly affect the environment must first prepare environmental impact statements. According to the Foundation's lawsuit, the military has failed to prepare such statements for its chemical warfare program.

This year marks the first since 1969 that the DOD has produced any new chemical weapons. But the budget for chemical warfare research has grown steadily in the past decade, and there is evidence that safety precautions have not kept pace. This past June, for example, an in-house assessment of chemical safety released by the Army's Inspector General found that "chemical safety has slipped through a crack." It says the Army "suffers from a lack of published policy guidelines, inadequate staffing, no systematic program of oversight, and a less than clear statement of chemical safety responsibilities."

A July 1988 report by the U.S. General Accounting Office further criticized the nation's chemical warfare program for its failure to take into consideration, when choosing research locations, such factors as environmental conditions at laboratory sites and proximity to residential areas or public facilities. It also noted "numerous deficiencies" in emergency plans for chemical accidents.

Many of the deficiencies noted in the Inspector General's report have been rectified, and others are being resolved, according to Army spokesman Maj. Richard Bridges. "We are going to do everything in our power to make sure our installations and the communities surrounding them are afforded the safest possible practices," Bridges says. "And we have no intention whatsoever of injuring the public or our soldiers, our most precious commodity."

He notes that staff positions have been filled and safety regulations are being drafted, adding that budget restrictions and attention to details have slowed implementation of some government recommendations. He declines to comment on specifics of the Foundation's lawsuit. However, he says, "I cannot say with 100 percent certainty that every single environmental impact statement that is required for every installation that the Army owns is complete, is current, is on file."

The Foundation's suit asks the U.S. District Court for the District of Columbia to halt all chemical weapons research and production pending completion of appropriate environmental statements. The suit also seeks to halt the dismantling of older, obsolete weapons—an ongoing process the Army plans to complete by 1994. Millions of pounds of nerve gas are stored near major airports, schools and shopping malls, according to legal documents the Foundation filed. The suit contends that without proper environmental assessments, the scheduled disposal may create an even greater hazard than does storage.

The DOD sponsors chemical weapons research at dozens of government and private institutions across the country. A total of 11 sites in Alabama, California, Illinois, Maryland, Missouri, New York, Ohio and Pennsylvania handle "neat," or full-strength, chemical warfare agents. Dozens of other facilities conduct research on dilute versions.

—*R. Weiss*

causes anthrax. Anthrax is endemic in parts of Africa and elsewhere, but only a few cases of the disease occur each year in the United States, usually in workers who contract it from woolly animals such as sheep or goats. Anthrax symptoms include skin ulcers, gastrointestinal pains and severe and sometimes fatal pneumonia.

"If the United States makes a vaccine against a biological warfare agent, it provokes other countries to make other biological weapons."

—epidemiologist and BDRP critic Jay Jacobson

Bacillus anthracis produces three toxin proteins. The existing vaccine contains one of the proteins, called protective antigen, which induces antibody production in the immunized host but is slow to take effect and requires repeated immunizations. Crumrine has cloned the protective antigen gene into *Escherichia coli* and *Bacillus subtilus* bacteria. If all goes well, he says, the bacteria will produce large quantities of protective antigen in a form suitable for use as a vaccine, which should be easier to produce and should work better than the existing vaccine. His preliminary experiments indicate that the protective antigen produced by *B. subtilus* protects guinea pigs against anthrax without harming the animals.

Using a different strategy, Robertson is selectively mutating *B. anthracis* genes. He hopes to destroy the toxicity but not the overall chemical structure of the proteins for which the genes code. The resulting mutated and harmless bacteria, when used as a vaccine, would "fool" the human immune system into beefing up its defenses against *B. anthracis.* "Compare the recombinant anthrax protein to a car with its motor removed," Robertson explains. "The car lacking a motor looks identical to a car with a motor, but it does not run."

Although Robertson's and Crumrine's methods are essentially those used by molecular biologists to create vaccines against influenza, the AIDS virus, hepatitis B and other infectious agents, there are those who oppose military sponsorship of such studies. Critics say the knowledge acquired through such research—better understanding of a bacterium's genetic makeup, the function of each piece of each gene, its preferred growing conditions and ways to clone and produce its toxins—could be used to produce toxic proteins of a more dangerous nature.

"By separating and distinguishing parts of the molecule that make it infectious from the antibody-causing parts, scientists could make toxins that would have no antibody-eliciting section," Yamamoto says. Agents altered in this way could be used only offensively, he contends.

Another factor troubling some people is that the basic research often involves the transfer of hazardous genes into genetically altered varieties of bacteria that live naturally in humans. Microbiologist Richard Novick, director of the Public Health Research Institute in New York City, says he "could see how this research could easily be perverted to build incapacitating agents." Novick, a civilian scientist, in the 1960s refused a DOD proposal that he introduce penicillin-resistance genes into a pneumonia-causing bacterium. "This would have been a disservice to the human population," says Novick. In the early 1980s, he again turned down DOD funds, this time for his studies of *Staphylococcus* bacteria, whose toxins attack the human gut and are a leading cause of food poisoning.

Novick and Yamamoto describe scenarios in which recombinant DNA techniques could lead to the creation of more dangerous toxins. By linking one toxin gene onto another toxin gene, they say, scientists could form "double-edged toxins" that could injure a cell in two ways. For example, one toxin could poison a cell while a second toxin inactivates the cell's enzyme normally responsible for degrading the first toxin. They also envision scientists attaching a toxin to another protein whose job is penetrating certain cells, as a means of selectively poisoning those cells. Such "coupled toxins" already are being studied as a means of fighting cancer and AIDS (SN: 12/3/88, p. 358).

Military scientists argue that their biological warfare research will not result in such frightening scenarios. They say they work at incapacitating potentially hazardous agents, rather than turning them into weapons. In defensive research, USAMRIID's Huxsoll explains, scientists look at a virus' chemical nature, its size and structure. They learn what it infects, how to cripple it and how to grow it in limited, laboratory quantities. On the other hand, he says, scientists making a weapon would look at how to stabilize the virus, make it more potent and disseminate it, and how to grow it in large quantities.

"If I could build a vaccine and put it in the literature, it would be a deterrent to any evil person thinking to put out these agents as weapons."

—BDRP virologist Joel Dalrymple

Military scientists add that biological defense research often ends up benefiting public health efforts in areas neglected by other research efforts. Michael Buchmeier of Scripps Clinic in La Jolla, Calif., a recipient of both DOD and National Institutes of Health funds for his research on the often deadly Lassa virus, says: "It is difficult to get money to study diseases such as Lassa fever. We've gone to major companies and been refused funds. One agency with a good track record is the Army." Buchmeier says Lassa fever is a substantial public health problem in African countries, such as Sierra Leone, where it accounts for approximately 30 percent of the hospital deaths and a substantial number of miscarriages.

Critics contend that such militarily supported research has other international consequences. Growing and working with biological agents within an Army-supported research facility not only draws the nation closer to using those agents as weapons, but also leads other countries to suspect the United States is performing offensive research, they argue.

"If the United States makes a vaccine against a biological warfare agent, it provokes other countries to make other biological weapons," Jacobson says. "This leads to an escalation of weapons, as is occurring in the nuclear arms race." Shifting the DOD's biomedical research to civilian agencies, such as the National Institutes of Health and the Centers for Disease Control, critics contend, would reduce what Rifkin terms a microbiological version of "missile-gap paranoia."

With such a dichotomy of opinions, a modified biological defense effort acceptable to both sides seems unlikely. However, at this summer's Senate hearings, subcommittee chairman Carl Levin and Army representatives agreed that DOD-sponsored laboratories should abide by the same safety guidelines as the National Institutes of Health and the Centers for Disease Control. Both critics and some biological warfare researchers are increasingly discussing the necessity of an open research program, a sort of "global defense," as Jacobson calls it.

Dalrymple explains why the military may support such a defense: "If I could build a vaccine and put it in the literature, it would be a deterrent to any evil person thinking to put out these agents as weapons."

Biomedical ethicist Thomas Murray, of Case Western University School of Medicine in Cleveland, cites another reason for openness. He believes people are afraid of biotechnology because they are aware that groups or individuals with mixed motives might create dangerous organisms, or that well-meaning researchers might do so unintentionally. "Fears," he says, "are seriously exacerbated by secrecy."

Racial Odyssey

Boyce Rensberger

The human species comes in an artist's palette of colors: sandy yellows, reddish tans, deep browns, light tans, creamy whites, pale pinks. It is a rare person who is not curious about the skin colors, hair textures, bodily structures and facial features associated with racial background. Why do some Africans have dark brown skin, while that of most Europeans is pale pink? Why do the eyes of most "white" people and "black" people look pretty much alike but differ so from the eyes of Orientals? Did one race evolve before the others? If so, is it more primitive or more advanced as a result? Can it be possible, as modern research suggests, that there is no such thing as a pure race? These are all honest, scientifically worthy questions. And they are central to current research on the evolution of our species on the planet Earth.

Broadly speaking, research on racial differences has led most scientists to three major conclusions. The first is that there are many more differences among people than skin color, hair texture and facial features. Dozens of other variations have been found, ranging from the shapes of bones to the consistency of ear wax to subtle variations in body chemistry.

The second conclusions is that the overwhelming evolutionary success of the human species is largely due to its great genetic variability. When migrating bands of our early ancestors reached a new environment, at least a few already had physical traits that gave them an edge in surviving there. If the coming centuries bring significant environmental changes, as many believe they will, our chances of surviving them will be immeasurably enhanced by our diversity as a species.

There is a third conclusion about race that is often misunderstood. Despite our wealth of variation and despite our constant, everyday references to race, no one has ever discovered a reliable way of distinguishing one race from another. While it is possible to classify a great many people on the basis of certain physical features, there are no known feature or groups of features that will do the job in all cases.

Skin color won't work. Yes, most Africans from south of the Sahara and their descendants around the world have skin that is darker than that of most Europeans. But there are millions of people in India, classified by some anthropologists as members of the Caucasoid, or "white," race who have darker skins than most Americans who call themselves black. And there are many Africans living in sub-Sahara Africa today whose skins are no darker than the skins of many Spaniards, Italians, Greeks or Lebanese.

What about stature as a racial trait? Because they are quite short, on the average, African Pygmies have been considered racially distinct from other dark-skinned Africans. If stature, then, is a racial criterion, would one include in the same race the tall African Watusi and the Scandinavians of similar stature?

The little web of skin that distinguishes Oriental eyes is said to be a particular feature of the Mongoloid race. How, then, can it be argued that the American Indian, who lacks this epicanthic fold, is Mongoloid?

Even more hopeless as racial markers are hair color, eye color, hair form, the shapes of noses and lips or any of the other traits put forth as typical of one race or another.

NO NORMS

Among the tall people of the world there are many black, many white and many in between. Among black people of the world there are many with kinky hair, many with straight or wavy hair, and many in between. Among the broad-nosed, full-lipped people of the world there are many with dark skins, many with light skins and many in between.

How did our modern perceptions of race arise? One of the first to attempt a scientific classification of peoples was Carl von Linné, better known as Linnaeus. In 1735, he published a classification that remains the standard today. As Linnaeus saw it there were four races, classifiable geographically and by skin color. The names Linnaeus gave them were *Homo sapiens Africanus nigrus* (black African human being), *H. sapiens Americanus rube-*

scens (red American human being), *H. sapiens Asiaticus fuscusens* (brownish Asian human being), and *H. sapiens Europaeus albescens* (white European human being). All, Linnaeus recognized, were members of a single human species.

A species includes all individuals that are biologically capable of interbreeding and producing fertile offspring. Most matings between species are fruitless, and even when they succeed, as when a horse and a donkey interbreed and produce a mule, the progeny are sterile. When a poodle mates with a collie, however, the offspring are fertile, showing that both dogs are members of the same species.

Even though Linnaeus's system of nomenclature survives, his classifications were discarded, especially after voyages of discovery revealed that there were many more kinds of people than could be pigeonholed into four categories. All over the world there are small populations that don't fit. Among the better known are:

- The so-called Bushmen of southern Africa, who look as much Mongoloid as Negroid.
- The Negritos of the South Pacific, who do look Negroid but are very far from Africa and have no known links to that continent.
- The Ainu of Japan, a hairy aboriginal people who look more Caucasoid than anything else.
- The Lapps of Scandinavia, who look as much like Eskimos as like Europeans.
- The aborigines of Australia, who often look Negroid but many of whom have straight or wavy hair and are often blond as children.
- The Polynesians, who seem to be a blend of many races, the proportions differing from island to island.

To accommodate such diversity, many different systems of classification have been proposed. Some set up two or three dozen races. None has ever satisfied all experts.

CLASSIFICATION SYSTEM

Perhaps the most sweeping effort to impose a classification upon all the peoples of the world was made by the American anthropologist Carleton Coon. He concluded there are five basic races, two of which have major subdivisions: Caucasoids; Mongloids; full-size Australoids (Australian aborigines); dwarf Australoids (Negritos—Andaman Islanders and similar peoples); full-size Congoids (African Negroids); dwarf Congoids (African Pygmies); and Capoids (the so-called Bushmen and Hottentots).

In his 1965 classic, *The Living Races of Man,* Coon hypothesized that before A.D. 1500 there were five pure races—five centers of human population that were so isolated that there was almost no mixing.

Each of these races evolved independently, Coon believed, diverging from a pre-*Homo sapiens* stock that was essentially the same everywhere. He speculated that the common ancestor evolved into *Homo sapiens* in five separate regions at five different times, beginning about 35,000 years ago. The populations that have been *Homo sapiens* for the shortest periods of time, Coon said, are the world's "less civilized" races.

The five pure races remained distinct until A.D. 1500; then Europeans started sailing the world, leaving their genes—as sailors always have—in every port and planting distant colonies. At about the same time, thousands of Africans were captured and forcibly settled in many parts of the New World.

That meant the end of the five pure races.. But Coon and other experts held that this did not necessarily rule out the idea of distinct races. In this view, there *are* such things as races; people just don't fit into them very well anymore.

The truth is that there is really no hard evidence to suggest that five or any particular number of races evolved independently. The preponderance of evidence today suggests that as traits typical of fully modern people arose in any one place, they spread quickly to all human populations. Advances in intelligence were almost certainly the fastest to spread. Most anthropologists and geneticists now believe that human

beings have always been subject to migrating and mixing. In other words, there probably never were any such things as pure races.

Race mixing has not only been a fact of human history but is, in this day of unprecedented global mobility, taking place at a more rapid rate than ever. It is not farfetched to envision the day when, generations hence, the entire "complexion" of major population centers will be different. Meanwhile, we can see such changes taking place before our eyes, for they are a part of everyday reality.

HYBRID VIGOR

Oddly, those who assert scientific validity for their notions of pure and distinct races seem oblivious of a basic genetic principle that plant and animal breeders know well: too much inbreeding can lead to proliferation of inferior traits. Crossbreeding with different strains often produces superior combinations and "hybrid vigor."

The striking differences among people may very well be a result of constant genetic mixing. And as geneticists and ecologists know, in diversity lies strength and resilience.

To understand the origin and proliferation of human differences, one must first know how Darwinian evolution works.

Evolution is a two-step process. Step one is mutation: somehow a gene in the ovary or testes of an individual is altered, changing the molecular configuration that stores instructions for forming a new individual. The children who inherit that gene will be different in some way from their ancestors.

Step two is selection: for a racial difference, or any other evolutionary change to arise, it must survive and be passed through several generations. If the mutation confers some disadvantage, the individual dies, often during embryonic development. But if the change is beneficial in some way, the individual should have a better chance of thriving than relatives lacking the advantage.

DISEASE ORIGINS

The gene for sickle cell anemia, a disease found primarily among black people, appears to have evolved because its presence can render its bearer resistant to malaria. Such a trait would have obvious value in tropical Africa.

A person who has sickle cell anemia must have inherited genes for the disease from both parents. If a child inherits only one sickle cell gene, he or she will be resistant to malaria but will not have the anemia. Paradoxically, inheriting genes from both parents does not seem to affect resistance to malaria.

In the United States, where malaria is practically nonexistent, the sickle cell gene confers no survival advantage and is disappearing. Today only about 1 out of every 10 American blacks carries the gene.

Many other inherited diseases are found only in people from a particular area. Tay-Sachs disease, which often kills before the age of two, is almost entirely confined to Jews from parts of Eastern Europe and their descendants elsewhere. Paget's disease, a bone disorder, if found most often among those of English descent. Impacted wisdom teeth are a common problem among Asians and Europeans but not among Africans. Children of all races are able to digest milk because their bodies make lactase, the enzyme that breaks down lactose, or milk sugar. But the ability to digest lactose in adulthood is a racially distributed trait.

About 90 percent of Orientals and blacks lose this ability by the time they reach adulthood and become quite sick when they drink milk.

Even African and Asian herders who keep cattle or goats rarely drink fresh milk. Instead, they first treat the milk with fermentation bacteria that break down lactose, in a sense predigesting it. They can then ingest the milk in the form of yogurt or cheese without any problem.

About 90 percent of Europeans and their American descendants, on the other hand, continue to produce the enzyme throughout their lives and can drink milk with no ill effects.

NATURAL SELECTION

If a new trait is beneficial, it will bring reproductive success to its bearer. After several generations of multiplication, bearers of the new trait may begin to outnumber nonbearers. Darwin called this natural selection to distinguish it from the artificial selection exercised by animal breeders.

Skin color is the human racial trait most generally thought to confer an evolutionary advantage of this sort. It has long been obvious in the Old World that the farther south one goes, the darker the skin color. Southern Europeans are usually somewhat darker than northern Europeans. In North Africa, skin colors are darker still, and, as one travels south, coloration reaches its maximum at the Equator. The same progressions holds in Asia, with the lightest skins to the north. Again, as one moves south, skin color darkens, reaching in southern India a "blackness" equal to that of equatorial Africans.

This north-south spectrum of skin color derives from varying intensities of the same dark brown pigment called melanin. Skin cells simply have more or less melanin granules to be seen against a background that is pinkish because of the underlying blood vessels. All races can increase their melanin concentration by exposure to the sun.

What is it about northerly latitudes in the Northern Hemisphere that favors less pigmentation and about southerly latitudes that favors more? Exposure to intense sunlight is not the only reason why people living in southerly latitudes are dark. A person's susceptibility to rickets and skin cancer, his ability to withstand cold and to see in the dark may also be related to skin color.

The best-known explanation says the body can tolerate only a narrow range of intensities of sunlight. Too much causes sunburn and cancer, while too little deprives the body of vitamin D, which is synthesized in the skin under the influence of sunlight. A dark complexion protects the skin from the harmful effects of intense sunlight. Thus, albinos born in equatorial regions have a high rate of skin cancer. On the other hand, dark skin in northerly latitudes screens out sunlight needed for the synthesis of vitamin D. Thus, dark-skinned children living in northern latitudes had high rates of rickets—a bone-deforming disease caused by a lack of vitamin D—before their milk was routinely fortified. In the sunny tropics, dark skin admits enough light to produce the vitamin.

Recently, there has been some evidence that skin colors are linked to differences in the ability to avoid injury from the cold. Army researchers found that during the Korean War blacks were more susceptible to frostbite than were whites. Even among Norwegian soldiers in World War II, brunettes had a slightly higher incidence of frostbite than did blonds.

EYE PIGMENTATION

A third link between color and latitude involves the sensitivity of the eye to various wavelengths of light. It is known that dark-skinned people have more pigmentation in the iris of the eye and at the back of the eye where the image falls. It has been found that the less pigmented the eye, the more sensitive it is to colors at the red end of the spectrum. In situations illuminated with reddish light, the northern European can see more than a dark African sees.

It has been suggested that Europeans developed lighter eyes to adapt to the longer twilights of the North and their greater reliance on firelight to illuminate caves.

Although the skin cancer-vitamin D hypothesis enjoys wide acceptance, it may well be that resistance to cold, possession of good night vision and other yet unknown factors all played roles in the evolution of skin colors.

Most anthropologists agree that the original human skin color was dark brown, since it is fairly well established that human beings evolved in the tropics of Africa. This does not, however, mean that the first people were Negroids, whose descendants, as they moved north, evolved into light-skinned Caucasoids. It is more likely that the skin color of various populations changed several times from dark to light and back as people moved from one region to another.

Consider, for example, that long before modern people evolved, *Homo erectus* had spread throughout Africa, Europe and Asia. The immediate ancestor of *Homo sapiens, Homo erectus,* was living in Africa 1.5 million years ago and in Eurasia 750,000 years ago. The earliest known forms of *Homo sapiens* do not make their appearance until somewhere between 250,000 and 500,000 years ago. Although there is no evidence of the skin color of any hominid fossil, it is probable that the *Homo erectus* population in Africa had dark skin. As subgroups spread into northern latitudes, mutations that reduced pigmentation conferred survival advantages on them and lighter skins came to predominate. In other words, there were probably black *Homo erectus* peoples in Africa and white ones in Europe and Asia.

Did the black *Homo erectus* populations evolve into today's Negroids and the white ones in Europe into today's Caucasoids? By all the best evidence, nothing like this happened. More likely, wherever *Homo sapiens* arose it proved so superior to the *Homo erectus* populations that it eventually replaced them everywhere.

If the first *Homo sapiens* evolved in Africa, they were probably dark-skinned; those who migrated northward into Eurasia lost their pigmentation. But it is just as possible that the first *Homo sapiens* appeared in northern climes, descendants of white-skinned *Homo erectus.* These could have migrated southward toward Africa, evolving darker skins. All modern races, incidentally, arose long after the brain had reached its present size in all parts of the world.

North-south variations in pigmentation are quite common among mammals and birds. The tropical races tend to be darker in fur and feather, the desert races tend to be brown, and those near the Arctic Circle are lighter colored.

There are exceptions among humans. The Indians of the Americas, from the Arctic to the southern regions of South America, do not conform to the north-south scheme of coloration. Though most think of Indians as being reddish-brown, most Indians tend to be relatively light skinned, much like their presumed Mongoloid ancestors in Asia. The ruddy complexion that lives in so many stereotypes of Indians is merely what years of heavy tanning can produce in almost any light-skinned person. Anthropologists explain the color consistency as a consequence of the relatively recent entry of people into the Americas—probably between 12,000 and 35,000 years ago. Perhaps they have not yet had time to change.

Only a few external physical differences other than color appear to have adaptive significance. The strongest cases can be made for nose shape and stature.

WHAT'S IN A NOSE

People native to colder or drier climates tend to have longer, more beak-shaped noses than those living in hot and humid regions. The nose's job is to warm and humidify air before it reaches sensitive lung tissues. The colder or drier the air is, the more surface area is needed inside the nose to get it to the right temperature or humidity. Whites tend to have longer and beakier noses than blacks or Orientals. Nevertheless, there is great variation within races. Africans in the highlands of East Africa have longer noses than Africans from the hot, humid lowlands, for example.

Stature differences are reflected in the tendency for most northern peoples to have shorter arms, legs and torsos and to be stockier than people from the tropics. Again, this is an adaptation to heat or cold. One way of reducing heat loss is to have less body surface, in relation to weight or volume, from which heat can escape. To avoid overheating, the most desirable body is long limbed and lean. As a result, most Africans tend to be lankier than northern Europeans. Arctic peoples are the shortest limbed of all.

Hair forms may also have a practical role to play, but the evidence is weak. It has been suggested that the more tightly curled hair of Africans insulates the top of the head better than does straight or wavy hair. Contrary to expectation, black hair serves better in this role than white hair. Sunlight is absorbed and converted to heat at the outer surface of the hair blanket; it radiates directly into the air. White fur, common on Arctic animals that need to absorb solar heat, is actually transparent and transmits light into the hair blanket, allowing the heat to form within the insulating layer, where it is retained for warmth.

Aside from these examples, there is little evidence that any of the other visible differences among the world's people provide any advantage. Nobody knows, for example, why Orientals have epicanthic eye folds or flatter facial profiles. The thin lips of Caucasoids and most Mongoloids have no known advantages over the Negroid's full lips. Why should middle-aged and older Caucasoid men go bald so much more frequently than the men of other races? Why does the skin of Bushmen wrinkle so heavily in the middle and later years? Or why does the skin of Negroids resist wrinkling so well? Why do the Indian men in one part of South America have blue penises? Why do Hottentot women have such unusually large buttocks?

There are possible evolutionary explanations for why such apparently useless differences arise.

One is a phenomenon known as sexual selection. Environmentally adaptive traits arise, Darwin thought, through natural selection—the environment itself chooses who will thrive or decline. In sexual selection, which Darwin also suggested, the choice belongs to the prospective mate.

In simple terms, ugly individuals will be less likely to find mates and reproduce their genes than beautiful specimens will. Take the blue penis as an example. Women might find it unusually attractive or perhaps believe it to be endowed with special powers. If so, a man born with a blue penis will find many more opportunities to reproduce his genes than his ordinary brothers.

Sexual selection can also operate when males compete for females. The moose with the larger antlers or the lion with the more imposing mane will stand a better chance of discouraging less well-endowed males and gaining access to females. It is possible that such a process operated among Caucasoid males, causing them to become markedly hairy, especially around the face.

ATTRACTIVE TRAITS

Anthropologists consider it probable that traits such as the epicanthic fold or the many regional differences in facial features were selected this way.

Yet another method by which a trait can establish itself involves accidental selection. It results from what biologists call genetic drift.

Suppose that in a small nomadic band a person is born with perfectly parallel fingerprints instead of the usual loops, whorls or arches. That person's children would inherit parallel fingerprints, but they would confer no survival advantages. But if our family decides to strike out on its own, it will become the founder of a new band consisting of its own descendants, all with parallel fingerprints.

Events such as this, geneticists and anthropologists believe, must have oc-

curred many times in the past to produce the great variety within the human species. Among the apparently neutral traits that differ among populations are:

Ear Wax
There are two types of ear wax. One is dry and crumbly and the other is wet and sticky. Both types can be found in every major population, but the frequencies differ. Among northern Chinese, for example, 98 percent have dry ear wax. Among American whites, only 16 percent have dry ear wax. Among American blacks the figure is 7 percent.

Scent Glands
As any bloodhound knows, every person has his or her own distinctive scent. People vary in the mixture of odoriferous compounds exuded through the skin—most of it coming from specialized glands called apocrine glands. Among whites, these are concentrated in the armpits and near the genitals and anus. Among blacks, they may also be found on the chest and abdomen. Orientals have hardly any apocrine glands at all. In the words of the Oxford biologist John R. Baker, "The Europids and Negrids are smelly, the Mongoloids scarcely or not at all." Smelliest of all are northern European, or so-called Nordic, whites. Body odor is rare in Japan. It was once thought to indicate a European in the ancestry and to be a disease requiring hospitalization.

Blood Groups
Some populations have a high percentage of members with a particular blood group. American Indians are overwhelmingly group O—100 percent in some regions. Group A is most common among Australian aborigines and the Indians in western Canada. Group B is frequent in northern India, other parts of Asia and western Africa.

Advocates of the pure-race theory once seized upon blood groups as possibly unique to the original pure races. The proportions of groups found today,

they thought, would indicate the degree of mixing. It was subsequently found that chimpanzees, our closest living relatives, have the same blood groups as humans.

Taste
PTC (phenylthiocarbamide) is a synthetic compound that some people can taste and other cannot. The ability to taste it has no known survival value, but it is clearly an inherited trait. The proportion of persons who can taste PTC varies in different populations: 50 to 70 percent of Australian aborigines can taste it, as can 60 to 80 percent of all Europeans. Among East Asians, the percentage is 83 to 100 percent, and among Africans, 90 to 97 percent.

Urine
Another indicator of differences in body chemistry is the excretion of a compound known as BAIB (beta-amino-isobutyric acid) in urine. Europeans seldom excrete large quantities, but high levels of excretion are common among Asians and American Indians. It had been shown that the differences are not due to diet.

No major population has remained isolated long enough to prevent any unique genes from eventually mixing with those of neighboring groups. Indeed, a map showing the distribution of so-called traits would have no sharp boundaries, except for coastlines. The intensity of a trait such as skin color, which is controlled by six pairs of genes and can therefore exist in many shades, varies gradually from one population to another. With only a few exceptions, every known genetic possibility possessed by the species can be found to some degree in every sizable population.

EVER-CHANGING SPECIES

One can establish a system of racial classification simply by listing the features of populations at any given moment. Such a concept of race is, however, inappropriate to a highly mobile and ever-changing species such as *Homo sapiens*. In the short view, races may seem distinguishable, but in biology's long haul, races come and go. New ones arise and blend into neighboring groups to create new and racially stable populations. In time, genes from these groups flow into other neighbors, continuing the production of new permutations.

Some anthropologists contend that at the moment American blacks should be considered a race distinct from African blacks. They argue that American blacks are a hybrid of African blacks and European whites. Indeed, the degree of mixture can be calculated on the basis of a blood component known as the Duffy factor.

In West Africa, where most of the New World's slaves came from, the Duffy factor is virtually absent. It is present in 43 percent of American whites. From the number of American blacks who are now "Duffy positive" it can be calculated that whites contributed 21 percent of the genes in the American black population. The figure is higher for blacks in northern and western states and lower in the South. By the same token, there are whites who have black ancestors. The number is smaller because of the tendency to identify a person as black even if only a minor fraction of his ancestors were originally from Africa.

The unwieldiness of race designations is also evident in places such as Mexico where most of the people are, in effect, hybrids of Indians (Mongoloid by some classifications) and Spaniards (Caucasoid). Many South American populations are tri-hybrids—mixtures of Mongoloid, Caucasoid and Negroid. Brazil is a country where the mixture has been around long enough to constitute a racially stable population. Thus, in one sense, new races have been created in the United States, Mexico and Brazil. But in the long run, those races will again change.

Sherwood Washburn, a noted anthropologist, questions the usefulness of racial classification: "Since races are open systems which are intergrading, the number of races will depend on the purpose of the classification. I think we should require people who propose a classification of races to state in the first place why they wish to divide the human species."

The very notion of a pure race, then, makes no sense. But, as evolutionists know full well, a rich genetic diversity within the human species most assuredly *does*.

Primates

Primates are fun. They are active, intelligent, colorful, emotionally expressive, and unpredictable. In other words, observing them is like holding up an opaque mirror to ourselves. The image may not be crystal clear or, indeed, what some would consider flattering, but it is certainly familiar enough to be illuminating.

Primates are, of course, but one of many orders of mammals that adaptively radiated into the variety of ecological niches vacated at the end of the Age of Reptiles about 65 million years ago. Whereas some mammals took to the sea (cetaceans), and some took to the air (chiroptera, or bats), primates are characterized by an arboreal or forested adaptation. Whereas some mammals can be identified by their food-getting habits, such as the meat-eating carnivores or the herbivorous perissodactyls and artiodactyls, primates have a penchant for eating almost anything and are best described as omnivorous. In taking to the trees, however, primates did not simply develop a full-blown set of distinguishing characteristics that set them off easily from other orders of mammals, the way the rodent order can be readily identified by its gnawing set of front teeth. Rather, each primate seems to represent degrees of anatomical, biological, and behavioral characteristics on a continuum of "progress" with respect to the particular traits we humans happen to be interested in. So, for example, we find in our closest relatives *degrees* of erectness in posture, manual dexterity, intellectual ability, and so on.

None of this is meant to imply, of course, that the living primates are our ancestors. Since the prosimians, monkeys, and apes are our contemporaries, they are no more our ancestors than we are theirs and, as living end-products of evolution, we have all descended from a common stock in the distant past.

So, if we are interested primarily in our own evolutionary past, why study primates at all? Because, by the criteria we have set up as significant milestones in the evolution of humanity, an inherent reflection of our own bias, they have not evolved as far as we have. They and their environments, therefore, may represent glimmerings of the evolutionary stages and ecological circumstances through which our own ancestors may have gone. For example, Wray Herbert shows us in "Lucy's Uncommon Forebear" that the best model for a common ancestor would be one with the locomotor flexibility to speciate "into both an arboreal African ape and a highly specialized human biped," and the pygmy chimpanzee seems to best approximate that model. What we stand to gain from studying the pygmy chimpanzee is an educated guess as to how our own ancestors might have appeared and behaved as semierect creatures before becoming bipedal. Aside from being a pleasure to observe, then, living primates can teach us something about our past.

Another reason for studying primates is that they allow us to test certain notions too often taken for granted. For instance, in "These Are Real Swinging Primates," by Shannon Brownlee, we find that, contrary to expectations, sexual competitiveness is not necessarily incompatible with gregariousness and cooperation among troop members. In a similar way, the research of Barbara Smuts, recounted in "What Are Friends For?" reveals that friendship bonds, as illustrated by the olive baboons of East Africa, have little if anything to do with a sexual division of labor or even sexual exclusivity between a pair-bonded male and female. In both articles, authored by women whose research is impeccable, there is the challenge to the traditional male-oriented idea that reproductive strategies among primates are solely determined by males and for males. If nothing else, these articles show that relationships between the sexes are subject to wide ecological variation, the kinds of answers obtained depend upon the kinds of questions asked, and that we have to be very careful about generalizing from any one particular study. We may, if we are not careful, draw conclusions that say more about our own skewed perspectives than about that which we claim to understand.

Still another benefit of studying the living primates is that they provide us with perspectives that the bones and stones of the fossil hunters will never reveal: a sense of the richness and variety of social patterns that must have existed in the primate order for so many tens of millions of years. In addition to the articles by Brownlee and Smuts, for example, we have the comparative surveys conducted by Jared Diamond ("Everything *Else* You Always Wanted to Know About Sex . . . But That We Were Afraid You'd Never Ask") and James Shreeve ("Machiavellian Monkeys"). Although these articles generate more questions than they answer, especially regarding human sexuality, they could not have been written without the broad range of primate studies that have recently been carried out.

Finally, there is a sense of urgency in the study of primates as we contemplate the dreaded possibility of their imminent extinction. We have already lost 14 species of lemurs in the past thousand years (most of which were larger than the contemporary forms), and the fate of most other free-ranging primates is in the balance—efforts to rehabilitate some of them into the wild (see "Suburban Chimp") notwithstanding. It is with considerable irony that future generations may come to envy us as having been among the first and last people to be able to observe our

closest relatives in their natural habitats. If for no other reason, we need to collect as much information as we can about primates because they are still with us.

Looking Ahead: Challenge Questions

How does human sexuality differ from that of other creatures?

How and why do the reproductive strategies of male and female primates differ?

How is it possible for the muriqui monkeys to be sexually competitive and yet gregarious and cooperative?

Why is friendship important to olive baboons and what implications does this have for the origins of pair-bonding in hominid evolution?

What is the role of deception among primates and how might it have led to greater intelligence?

Under what circumstances does divorce become common in the human species?

To what extent is chimpanzee survival in the wild a matter of learning rather than instinct?

What do you think the hypothetical common ancestor of chimpanzees and humans might have looked and acted like?

"Everything *Else* You Always Wanted to Know About Sex . . . But That We Were Afraid You'd Never Ask"

Jared Diamond

Among the various species of apes and man, which has the biggest penis?

And why?

Why do men have much smaller testes than chimpanzees?

Why are men bigger than women?

Why are humans the only social animals that prefer copulating in private?

Why don't human females, unlike almost all other female mammals, have easily recognized days of fertility, with sexual receptivity confined largely to those intervals?

If your answer to the first question was the gorilla, you're wrong. The correct reply is man. If you gave intelligent answers to the remaining questions, publish them; scientists are still debating rival theories.

The six questions illustrate the difficulty of explaining the most obvious facts of our sexual anatomy and physiology. Part of the problem is our hangups about sex: scientists didn't begin to study it seriously until recently, and they still have trouble being objective. Another difficulty is that they can't do controlled experiments on sexual practices, as they can on our intake of cholesterol or our tooth-brushing habits. Finally, our sex organs didn't just evolve in isolation: they're an outgrowth of our social habits, which in turn stem from the way we once obtained food. Given knowledge of how an animal feeds, a biologist can often predict its mating system and genital anatomy. Hence if we want to understand how human sexuality got to be the way it is, we have to begin by exploring the evolution of our diet and our society.

From the vegetarian preferences of our ape ancestors, we diverged within the last several million years to become social carnivores who eat meat as well as vegetables. Yet our teeth and claws remained relatively harmless, like those of apes, not the jagged instruments of true carnivores like the tiger. Our hunting prowess depended on large brains instead. By acting in coordinated groups, using shrewd tactics and primitive weaponry, our ancestors killed large, dangerous prey and regularly shared food with each other. And while the human child was acquiring the skills to become a hunter-gatherer, it was fed by both parents for years after weaning. In contrast, apes obtain their own food as soon as they are weaned. Gorilla, chimpanzee, and gibbon fathers offer protection only to their young; orangutan fathers provide nothing beyond their sperm.

The social system we've developed to accommodate our un-apelike nurturing habits seems utterly normal to us, but it's bizarre by ape standards and virtually unique among animals. Adult orangutans are essentially solitary. Adult gibbons live in separate, monogamous, male-female pairs, while gorillas live in polygamous harems of several adult females, usually dominated by a single adult male. Our closest kin, the chimpanzees, are fairly promiscuous; they exist in communities of dispersed females, attended by a group of adult males. By contrast, human societies, like human food habits, resemble those of lions and wolves: we live in bands containing many adult males and many adult females. Furthermore—and here we diverge even from the social carnivores and are most like colonies of sea birds—our males and females pair off with each other. The pairing is more or less monogamous in most modern political states, but it's still mildly polygynous among most surviving hunter-gatherer bands, like the !Kung San of the Kalahari desert, which may provide clues to how people lived over the last million years. By mildly polygynous, I mean that most hunter-gatherer men can support only one wife, but a few successful men have several. (I'll discuss the "science" of extramarital sex by and by.)

How does this social organization shape the bodies of men and women? Consider the fact that adult men are slightly bigger than woman of their age (on average, about eight per cent taller and 20 per cent heavier). A zoologist from outer space would take one look at my wife, who's 5'8", next to me (5'10"), and would instantly conclude, if the evolutionary rules on his planet were the same as ours, that we belonged to a mildly polygynous species. How could he guess mating practices from relative body size? He would know that among mammals, the greater the male's size advantage over the female, the larger the harem size. Male and female gibbons are the same size, and they are monogamous. Male gorillas weigh nearly twice as much as females, and have harems containing three to six females. But the greatest weight advantage belongs to the male southern elephant seal, whose three tons entitle him to as many as 48 wives. In a monogamous species, every male can win a female, so the males don't need overpowering size. But only a few males can get the females in a very polygynous species. Hence, the bigger the harem, the fiercer the competition among males is likely to be and the more important it is for a male to be able to ward off competing males. Size obviously helps. With our bigger males and occasional polygyny, humans fit this pattern: males are just slightly bigger than females. (However, at some point in human evolution male intelligence and personality came to count for more than size: male basketball players and football linemen don't seem to have more wives than male jockeys or coxwains.)

The males and females of polygynous species tend to have more marked differences in secondary sexual characteristics, which also play a role in attracting mates and dominating rivals. For instance, male and female gibbons look alike at a distance, while male gorillas (befitting their polygyny) are easily recognized by their crested heads and silver-haired backs. Humans fall somewhere in between. Here, too, our anatomy reflects our mild polygyny. The external differences between men and women aren't nearly as marked as sex-related differences in gorillas or orangutans, but the zoologist from outer space could probably distinguish men and women by the body and facial hair of men, men's unusually large penises (of which more soon), and the large breasts of women even before their first pregnancy (in this we are unique among primates).

Now to the genitals themselves: the combined weight of the testes in the average man is about an ounce and a half, compared to an ounce and a quarter for a 450-pound male gorilla. But macho human males really have nothing to boast about: their testes are put to shame by the four-ounce testes of a 100-pound male chimpanzee. Why is the chimp so well endowed?

For an answer, we turn to one of the triumphs of modern physical anthropology, the Theory of Testis Size. By weighing the testes of 33 primate species, British scientists were able to identify two trends: males of species that copulate more often need bigger testes, and those of promiscuous species in which several males routinely copulate in quick sequence with one female need especially big testes (reason: the male that injects the most semen has the best chance of fertilizing the egg). What about the tiny-testicled gorilla? In fact, his modest testes are perfectly adequate for his modest needs. Even for a male with a harem of several females, the sex act is a rare treat; it occurs only a few times a year. That is because a female gorilla doesn't resume sexual activity until three to four years after giving birth, and even then is receptive for only a couple of days a month (until she becomes pregnant again).

The sex life of a male orangutan may be only slightly more demanding. But the male chimp lives in the simian equivalent of sexual nirvana. He has almost daily opportunities to copulate. That, plus his need to outdo other males in semen output if he is to fertilize the profligate female, explains his need for giant testes. Human males make do with medium-sized testes, because the average man copulates more often than a gorilla or an orangutan but less often than a chimp. In addition, the typical human female in an average menstrual cycle doesn't force several males into a sperm competition to fertilize her.

From this triumph of scientific sexual exegesis, we now descend to a glaring failure: the inability of twentieth-century science to formulate an adequate Theory of Penis Length. The erect penis averages one and a quarter inches in a gorilla, an inch and a half in an orangutan, three inches in a chimp, and six inches in a man. Visual conspicuousness similarly varies: a gorilla's penis can hardly be seen even when erect because of its black color, whereas the chimp's erect pink penis stands out boldly against the bare white skin behind it. The flaccid penis isn't even visible in apes. Why does the human male need a penis that is larger and more conspicuous than that of any other primate? Doesn't it represent an evolutionary waste—an expenditure of protoplasm that could be better devoted to, say, expanding the cerebral cortex or improving the fingers?

Biologists usually reply by citing distinctive features of human coitus that they suppose might be served by a long penis: our frequent use of the face-to-face "missionary" position, our acrobatic variety in intercourse, and the supposedly long duration of our coital bouts. None of these explanations survives close scrutiny. The face-to-face position is also the one preferred by orangutans and pygmy chimps, and is occasionally used by gorillas. Orangs mix face-to-face copulation with dorso-ventral (à la canines) and sideways positions. What's more, they copulate hanging from tree branches, a feat that vies with or even surpasses our ingenious and often exacting gyrations. As for the duration of human intercourse, studies have shown that coitus lasts on average about four minutes in Americans. This is much longer than the performance of gorillas (one minute) or chimps (eight seconds), but is only a fraction that of orangutans (15 minutes).

A popular alternative theory for the long penis is that it evolved as an organ of display, like a peacock's tail or a lion's mane. This explanation really begs the question: What type of display, and to whom? Proud male anthropologists unhesitatingly answer: an attraction display, to women. It's hard to decide whether this answer is correct—or just wishful thinking by men. Many women say that they are "turned on" more by a man's voice, legs, shoulders, and buttocks than by his penis.

Another possible role for a large penis is as a threat or status display vis-à-vis other men. This explanation is supported by the phallic art that men create for men, and the widespread male obsession with penis size. Evolution of the human penis was limited by the length of the vagina: a penis would damage a women if it were significantly larger. However, I can guess what the penis would look like if this practical constraint were removed and if men could design themselves. It would resemble the penis sheaths (phallocarps) used as everyday male attire in some areas of New Guinea where I do field work. Phallocarps vary in length (up to two feet), diameter (up to four inches), shape (curved or straight), the angle made with the wearer's body, and decoration (for example, a tuft of fur at the end). Each man has a wardrobe of several sizes and shapes. Western male anthropologists interpret the phallocarp as something worn for modesty or concealment, to which my wife had a succinct rebuttal: "The most immodest display of modesty I've ever seen!"

If these aspects of human sexual anatomy are a puzzlement, so are our sexual activities, which must be considered freakish by any decent mammalian standards. Most mammals are sexually inactive most of the time, copulating only when the female is in heat, or estrus—that is, when she's ovulating and therefore capable of being fertilized. Female mammals apparently "know" when they're ovulating, for they solicit copulation at those times by presenting their genitals towards the males. Lest a male

be particularly dense, many female primates go farther: the area around the vagina, and in some species the buttocks and breast, swells up and turns red, pink, or blue. This visual advertisement of female availability affects male monkeys in the same way that *Playboy* centerfolds affect male humans. In the presence of females with brightly swollen genitals, male monkeys stare much more often at the female's genitals, develop higher testosterone levels, attempt to copulate more often, and penetrate more quickly and after fewer pelvic thrusts than in the presence of females who aren't displaying themselves.

The human sexual cycle is different. A woman's receptivity is more or less constant, year round. Numerous studies have tried to determine whether receptivity varies at all through a woman's monthly cycle, but scientists still don't agree on an answer.

Indeed, the period of human ovulation is so well concealed that we didn't have accurate scientific information on its timing until fairly recently. Until the 1930s, many doctors thought that women could conceive at any point in their cycle, or even that conception was most likely at the time of menstruation. In contast to the male baboon, who has only to scan his surroundings for brightly swollen females, the human male hasn't the foggiest notion of which females around him are ovulating. A woman herself may learn to recognize sensations associated with ovulation, but this "rhythm method" is tricky, even with the help of thermometers and ratings of vaginal mucus quality. Besides, it's based on hard-won, modern book knowledge—not on the innate sense of sexual readiness that drives female mammals of other species.

The human female's concealed ovulation, constant receptivity, and brief fertile period in each menstrual cycle ensure that most copulations take place at the wrong time for conception. Worse still, menstrual cycle length varies more between women, or from cycle to cycle in a given woman, than among most other mammals. As a result, even young newlyweds who make love at maximum frequency and without contraceptives have only a 28 per cent probability of

conception per menstrual cycle. Animal breeders would be in despair if a prize cow had such low fertility.

In these days of growing human overpopulation, one of the most paradoxical tragedies, in my view, is the Roman Catholic church's insistence that copulation has conception as its only natural purpose, and that the rhythm method is the only proper means of birth control. These claims would be valid for gorillas and most other mammals, but not for us. In no species besides man has the purpose of copulation become so unrelated to conception, or the rhythm method so unsuited by contraception.

As a way of achieving fertilization, sex for us is a huge waste of time. Had we retained a proper estrous cycle like other mammals, our ancestors could have devoted much more time to butchering mastodons than to the sexual chase. And females could thereby have fed more babies and outcompeted neighboring clans whose females no longer advertised estrus. Thus, the most hotly debated problem in the evolution of human reproduction is why we ended up concealing ovulation, and what good all our mis-timed copulations do us.

A related paradox is that of concealed copulation. Promiscuous or monogamous, all other group-living animals have sex in public. Paired sex gulls mate in the midst of the colony; a female chimpanzee may mate consecutively with five or more males in each other's presence. Why are we unique in our strong preference for privacy?

Biologists are currently arguing over at least six different theories to explain the origin of concealed ovulation and copulation. Interestingly, the theories often turn out to be a reflection of the gender and outlook of their proponents:

1. Theory preferred by many traditional male anthropologists

Concealed ovulation and copulation both evolved to enhance cooperation and reduce aggression among male hunters. How could cavemen have brought off the teamwork needed to spear a mammoth if they'd been fighting for the public favors of a cavewoman in estrus? The implicit message: women's physiology is important chiefly for its effect on bonds between men, the real movers of society. However, one can broaden this theory to make it less blatantly sexist: visible estrus and public sex would disrupt human society by affecting female/female and male/female as well as male/male bonds.

2. Theory preferred by many other traditional male anthropologists

Concealment cements the bonds between a particular man and woman, thereby laying the foundations of the human family. A woman remains sexually attractive and receptive so that she can satisfy a man sexually all the time, bind him to her, and reward him for his help in rearing her baby. The message: women evolved to make men happy. Left unexplained is why pairs of gibbons, whose unwavering devotion to monogamy should make them role models for the Moral Majority, remain constantly together even though they have sex only every few years.

3. Theory of a more modern male anthropologist

Donald Symons, of the University of California at Santa Barbara, notes that a male chimpanzee which kills a small animal is more likely to share the meat with an estrous female than with a nonestrous female. This suggests to him that human females may have evolved the ability to be in a constant state of estrus to ensure a frequent meat supply from male hunters. Another possibility, Symons says, is that women in most hunter-gatherer societies, even though they have little say in choosing a husband, by being constantly attractive could privately seduce a superior male and secure his genes for her children. Symons's theories, while still male-oriented, at least view women as cleverly pursuing their own goals.

4. Theory of a male biologist and a female biologist

If a man could recognize signs of ovulation, say Richard Alexander and Katherine Noonan, he could use that knowledge to fertilize his wife and then safely go off philandering the rest of the time. Hence women evolved concealed ovulation to force men into marriage by exploiting male paranoia about fatherhood. Not knowing the time of ovula-

tion, a man must copulate with his wife often to have a chance of fertilizing her, and that leaves him less time to dally with other women. The wife benefits, but so does the husband. He gains confidence in the paternity of his children, and he needn't worry that his wife will suddenly attract many competing men by turning bright red on a particular day. At last, we have a theory seemingly grounded in sexual equality.

5. Theory of a feminist sociobiologist

Sarah Hrdy, of the University of California at Davis, was impressed by the frequency with which many male primates kill infants not their own. The bereaved mother is thereby induced to come into estrus again, and often mates with the murderer, thus increasing his output of progeny. (Such violence has been common in human history: male conquerors kill the vanquished men and children but spare the women.) As a counter-measure, Hrdy says, women evolved concealed ovulation to manipulate men by confusing the issue of paternity. A woman who distributed her favors widely would thereby enlist many men to help feed (or at least not to kill) her infant, since many men could suppose themselves to be the infant's father. Right or wrong, Hrdy's theory transfers sexual power to women.

6. Theory of a female zoologist

At seven and a half pounds, the average human newborn weighs about twice as much as a newborn gorilla, but the 200-pound gorilla mother is much heavier than the average human mother. Because the human newborn is so much larger in relation to its mother, human birth is exceptionally painful and dangerous. Until the advent of modern medicine, women often died in childbirth, whereas I've never heard of this happening to a female gorilla or chimpanzee. Once humans evolved enough intelligence to associate conception with copulation, estrous women could choose to avoid copulating at the time of ovulation in order to spare themselves the pain and peril of childbirth. But such women would leave fewer descendants than women who couldn't detect their ovulation. Thus, where male anthropologists saw concealed ovulation as something evolved by women for men

(Theories 1 and 2), Nancy Burley, of the University of Illinois, sees it as a trick that natural selection evolved to deceive women.

Which, if any, of these six theories is correct? Not only are biologists uncertain; it's only in recent years that concealed ovulation, as well as questions involving human testes and penis size, has begun to receive serious attention. Even more tantalizing is why a subject about which we're so obsessed is the one we understand the least. Many of our explanations have scarcely advanced beyond the level of cocktail-party speculation.

The meagreness of data is nowhere more apparent than in the study of adultery. People have reason to lie when asked whether they've committed adultery, which makes it difficult for serious scholars to get accurate information about this important subject. One of the few available sets of hard facts emerged as a totally unexpected byproduct of a medical study performed nearly half a century ago for a different reason.

I recently learned of the findings, which have never been revealed until now, from the distinguished medical scientist who ran the study. (Since he doesn't want to be identified, I'll call him Dr. X.) In the 1940s Dr. X was studying the genetics of human blood groups, which are molecules acquired only by inheritance. Each of us has dozens of blood group substances on our red blood cells, and each substance must come from either our mother or father. Dr. X's research plan was straightforward: go to an obstetrics ward of a respectable U.S. hospital; collect blood samples from 1,000 newborn babies and their parents; identify the individual blood groups; and then use standard genetic reasoning to deduce the inheritance patterns.

To Dr. X's shock, the blood groups revealed that almost ten per cent of the babies were the products of adultery. Proof of their illegitimacy came from the discovery that they had one or more blood groups that were lacking in both alleged parents. There could be no question of mistaken maternity: the blood samples were drawn from the babies soon after they emerged from their mothers. A blood group present in a baby but absent in its undoubted mother could only have come from its father. Thus, absence of that blood group from the mother's husband as well showed conclusively that the baby had been sired by some other man. The true incidence of adulterous sex was probably considerably higher than ten per cent, since many blood group substances now used in paternity tests were not known in the 1940s, and because intercourse doesn't necessarily result in conception.

Since the 1940s, the myth that marital infidelity is rare in the U.S. has been exploded by a long succession of surveys, beginning with the Kinsey Report. Nevertheless, even liberated Americans of the 1980s are still profoundly ambivalent about adultery. It's thought of as exciting: no soap opera could get high ratings without it. And it has few rivals as a basis of jokes. Yet we often use humor to deal with painful subjects. Certainly, in the course of history, adultery has had few rivals as a cause of murder and human misery.

What makes a married person decide to seek extramarital sex—or shun it when it's available? Because scientists have theories about almost everything else, it isn't surprising that they've also got a theory of extramarital sex (abbreviated EMS, and not to be confused with premarital sex = PMS or premenstrual syndrome = PMS). With many species of animals the problem of EMS never arises, because they don't opt for "marriage" in the first place. A female Barbary ape (a species of macaque monkey) in heat copulates promiscuously with every adult male in her troop, averaging one copulation per 17 minutes. However, some mammals and most bird species prefer marriage. That is, a male and a female form a lasting pair bond to provide care or protection to their offspring. Once there's marriage, there's also the possibility of what sociobiologists euphemistically term the pursuit of a "mixed reproductive strategy"—MRS, or in plain English, both monogamous and extramarital sex.

Married animals vary enormously in the degree to which they mix their reproductive strategies. There appears to be no recorded instance of EMS in gibbons, whereas snow geese indulge in it regularly. Human societies similarly vary. To explain all this variation, sociobiologists have found it useful to apply game theory, whereby life is considered an evolutionary contest whose winners are those players leaving the largest number of offspring.

The problem for the animal is to figure out what strategy is most likely to win: rigid fidelity, pure promiscuity, or MRS. It quickly becomes apparent that the best strategy is not the same for males and females of the same species. This is because of two profound differences in their reproductive biology: the minimum effort that's required and the risk of being cuckolded.

For human males, the minimum effort needed to sire an offspring is the act of copulation, a very small expenditure of time and energy. The man who sires a baby by one woman one day is biologically capable of siring a baby by another woman the next. For women, however, the minimum effort consists of copulation plus pregnancy plus (throughout most of human history) several years of nursing—a vast commitment of time and energy. A man can have far more children than a woman. A nineteenth century visitor to the court of the Nizam of Hyderabad, a polygynous Indian potentate, reported that four of the Nizam's wives gave birth within eight days, and that nine more births were anticipated the following week. The record number of offspring for a man is 888, set by Emperor Moulay Ismail "the Blood-thirsty" of Morocco, in the early eighteenth century, while the record for a woman is only 69 (an eighteenth century Muscovite who gave birth only to twins, triplets, and quadruplets). Few women have topped 20 children, a mark easily achieved by men in polygynous societies.

If the sole objective is achieving the greatest number of offspring, a man stands to gain much more from EMS or polygamy than a woman. In the sole polyandrous society for which I could find data, the Tre-ba of Tibet, women with two husbands average fewer children, not more, than women with one husband. In the nineteenth century,

Mormon men realized big benefits from polygyny: men with one wife averaged only seven children, but men with two or three wives averaged 16 and 20, respectively. Polygynous Mormon men averaged 2.4 wives and 15 children, while polygynous Mormon church leaders averaged five wives and 25 children. Similarly, among the polygynous Temne people of Sierra Leone, a man's average number of children increases from 1.7 to 7 as his number of wives increases from one to five.

The other sexual asymmetry relevant to reproductive strategy involves confidence that one really is the biological parent of one's putative offspring. A cuckholded animal deceived into rearing offspring not its own has lost the game—its genes aren't passed on—to another player, the real parent, whose genes are. Barring a switch of babies in the hospital nursery, women can't be betrayed in this way: they usually see their babies born. Nor can there be cuckoldry of males in species practicing external fertilization. For instance, some male fish watch the female shed eggs, then immediately deposit sperm on them and scoop them up to care for them, secure in their paternity. But men and other male animals practicing internal fertilization run a greater risk. All the would-be father knows for sure is that his sperm went in, and eventually an offspring came out. Only observation of the female throughout her whole fertile period can exclude the possibility that some other male's sperm also entered and did the fertilizing.

In the past, the Nayar society of southern India had an extreme solution to this simple asymmetry. The Nayar women freely took many lovers, depriving husbands of any confidence in their paternity. To make the best of a bad situation, a Nayar man didn't live with his wife or care for her children. He lived with his sisters instead, and tended their children. These nieces and nephews were sure to share some of his genes. . . .

[S]urveys show that men are more interested in EMS than women are; that men are more inclined to seek a variety of partners; that women's motives for EMS are more likely to be marital dissatisfaction and/or a desire for a new lasting relationship; and that men are less selective in taking on casual partners than women. Among the New Guinea highlanders with whom I work, the men say they seek EMS because sex with their own wives inevitably becomes boring, even if they have several wives, while the women who seek it do so mainly because their husbands cannot satisfy them (often because of old age). In the debriefing questionnaires that several hundred young Americans filled out for a computer dating service, women expressed stronger partner preferences than men did: they cared more about intelligence, status, dancing ability, or a particular religion or race. The only category in which men were more selective was physical attractiveness. After a date, two and a half times as many men as women expressed a strong romantic attraction to their computer-selected partners, which means the women were choosier than the men.

Our attitudes toward EMS are also revealed in laws and behavior. Some particularly hypocritical and sadistic features of human societies stem from two fundamental difficulties that men face in seeking EMS. First, a man who pursues a MRS is trying to have it both ways: sex with other men's wives, while denying other men sex with his own wife (or wives). Thus, some men inevitably gain at the expense of other men. Second, there's a realistic biological basis for men's widespread paranoia about being cuckolded.

Adultery laws provide a clear example of how men have dealt with these dilemmas. Until recently, such laws have existed essentially to secure a man's confidence in the paternity of his children, not for the benefit of the wife. They define adultery by the woman's marital status; the man's is irrelevant. EMS by a married woman is considered an offense against her husband, who's commonly entitled to damages—often violent revenge, or else divorce with refund of the bride price. EMS by a married man isn't considered an offense against his wife, however. If his partner in adultery is married, the offense is against her husband; if unmarried, against her father or brothers (because her value as a prospective bride is reduced).

No criminal law against male infidelity even existed until a French statute of 1810, and that only forbade a married man to keep a concubine in his conjugal house against his wife's wishes. Even today, courts in the U.S. and England often reduce a homicide charge to manslaughter or else acquit altogether when a husband kills an adulterous wife or her lover caught in the act.

Perhaps the most elaborate system to uphold confidence of paternity was that maintained by Chinese emperors, especially during the T'ang Dynasty (618-907). A team of court ladies kept records of menstruation dates for each of the emperor's hundreds of wives and concubines, so that he could copulate on a day likely to result in fertilization. The dates of intercourse were also recorded, and commemorated by a silver ring on the woman's left leg.

Preoccupation with paternity continues. In some cultures it involves limiting sexual access to wives, or to daughters or sisters who would command a high bride price if delivered as virgins. Women may be closely chaperoned or even held under virtual house arrest. The same objective underlies the code of "honor and shame" widespread in Mediterranean countries (translation: EMS for me but not for you). Stronger measures include the barbaric mutilations euphemistically and misleadingly termed female circumcision. These consist of removal of the clitoris or most of the external female genitals to reduce female interest in sex, marital or otherwise. Men bent on certainty invented mechanical contrivances, called chastity belts, and infibulation—suturing a woman's labia majora nearly shut, so as to make intercourse impossible. An infibulated wife can be de-infibulated for childbirth or for insemination after each child is weaned, and can be re-infibulated when the husband takes a long trip. Female circumcision and infibulation are still practiced in 23 countries today, from Africa through Arabia to Indonesia.

When all else fails, murder is available as a last resort. Sexual jealousy is one of the commonest causes of homicide in many U.S. cities, and in a number of other countries as well. Usually, the murderer is a husband and the victim his adulterous wife or her lover; or else the lover kills the husband. Until the formation of centralized political states provided soldiers with loftier motives for combat, sexual jealousy loomed large in human history as a cause of war. It was Paris's seduction (abduction? rape?) of Helen, Menelaus's wife, that provoked the Trojan War. In the modern New Guinea highlands, only disputes over ownership of pigs rival those over sex in triggering war.

Asymmetric adultery laws, and all the other means of ensuring paternity, serve as ways for males to promote their genes. As studies of apes illustrate, some of the tactics used by human males are shared with many animals, including jealous murder, infanticide, rape, inter-group warfare, and adultery itself. Some male snakes, worms, and insects achieve the same result as human infibulators by plugging up a female's vagina after copulating with her.

Sociobiologists have had considerable success at understanding the markedly different sexual strategies in animal species. It's no longer controversial to contend that natural selection causes animals to evolve behaviorally, as well as anatomically, for the purpose of maximizing the number of their descendants. But no theory has caused bitterer division among contemporary biologists than the suggestion that natural selection has likewise molded our *social* behavior. Many of the practices I've discussed are considered barbaric by modern Western society. Yet some biologists are outraged not only by the practices themselves but also by sociobiological explanations of their evolution.

Like any other science, sociobiology is open to abuse. People have never lacked for pretexts, scientific and otherwise, to justify the subjugation or killing of other people. Even Darwinian evolution has been twisted to this end. Sociobiological explanations of human sexuality are sometimes seen as seeking to justify men's abuse of women, and are analogous to the biological justifications advanced for whites' treatment of blacks or the Nazis' treatment of Jews. In the critiques of sociobiology, two fears recur: that an evolutionary basis for abhorrent behavior would seem to justify it; and that a genetic basis for the behavior would imply the futility of attempts at change.

Neither fear warrants a blanket condemnation of sociobiology. We can seek to understand how something arose, regardless of whether we consider it admirable or abominable. Also, we aren't mere slaves to our evolved characteristics, not even to genetically acquired ones. Modern civilization is fairly successful at thwarting ancient practices like infanticide and murder, and modern medicine sometimes succeeds at thwarting our genes when they cause disease. Our objections to infibulation aren't based on the outcome of evolutionary or genetic debates. We condemn it because the mutilation of one person by another is ethically loathsome.

In short, we've evolved, like other animals, to win at a single game: to leave as many descendants as possible. Much of the legacy of this strategy is still buried in our psyches. But we've also chosen to pursue loftier, ethical goals, which may conflict with our ingrained Darwinian ones. The ability to make a moral choice between them represents our most radical break with other animals.

Machiavellian Monkeys

The sneaky skills of our primate cousins suggest that we may owe our great intelligence to an inherited need to deceive.

James Shreeve

This is a story about frauds, cheats, liars, faithless lovers, incorrigible con artists, and downright thieves. You're gonna love 'em.

Let's start with a young rascal named Paul. You'll remember his type from your days back in the playground. You're minding your own business, playing on the new swing set, when along comes Paul, such a little runt that you hardly notice him sidle up to you. All of a sudden he lets out a scream like you've run him through with a white-hot barbed harpoon or something. Of course the teacher comes running, and the next thing you know you're being whisked inside with an angry finger shaking in our face. That's the end of recess for you. But look out the window: there's Paul, having a great time on *your* swing. Cute kid.

Okay, you're a little older now and a little smarter. You've got a bag of chips stashed away in your closet, where for once your older brother won't be able to find them. You're about to open the closet door when he pokes his head in the room. Quickly you pretend to be fetching your high tops; he gives you a look but he leaves. You wait a couple of minutes, lacing up the sneakers in case he walks back in, then you dive for the chips. Before you can get the bag open, he's over your shoulder, snatching it out of your hands. "Nice try, punk," he says through a mouthful,

"but I was hiding outside your room the whole time."

This sort of trickery is such a common part of human interaction that we hardly notice how much time we spend defending ourselves against it or perpetrating it ourselves. What's so special about the fakes and cheaters here, however, is that they're not human. Paul is a young baboon, and your big brother is, well, a chimpanzee. With some admittedly deceptive alterations of scenery and props, the situations have been lifted from a recent issue of *Primate Report.* The journal is the work of Richard Byrne and Andrew Whiten, two psychologists at the University of St. Andrews in Scotland, and it is devoted to cataloging the petty betrayals of monkeys and apes as witnessed by primatologists around the world. It is a testament to the evolutionary importance of what Byrne and Whiten call Machiavellian intelligence—a facility named for the famed sixteenth-century author of *The Prince,* the ultimate how-to guide to prevailing in a complex society through the judicious application of cleverness, deceit, and political acumen.

Deception is rife in the natural world. Stick bugs mimic sticks. Harmless snakes resemble deadly poisonous ones. When threatened, blowfish puff themselves up and cats arch their backs and bristle their hair to seem bigger than they really are. All these animals could be said to practice deception because they fool other animals—usu-

ally members of other species—into thinking they are something that they patently are not. Even so, it would be overreading the situation to attribute Machiavellian cunning to a blowfish, or to accuse a stick bug of being a lying scoundrel. Their deceptions, whether in their looks or in their actions, are programmed genetic responses. Biology leaves them no choice but to dissemble: they are just being true to themselves.

The kind of deception that interests Byrne and Whiten—what they call tactical deception—is a different kettle of blowfish altogether. Here an animal has the mental flexibility to take an "honest" behavior and use it in such a way that another animal—usually a member of the deceiver's own social group—is misled, thinking that a normal, familiar state of affairs is under way, while, in fact, something quite different is happening.

Take Paul, for example. The real Paul is a young chacma baboon that caught Whiten's attention in 1983, while he and Byrne were studying foraging among the chacma in the Drakensberg Mountains of southern Africa. Whiten saw a member of Paul's group, an adult female named Mel, digging in the ground, trying to extract a nutritious plant bulb. Paul approached and looked around. There were no other baboons within sight. Suddenly he let out a yell, and within seconds his mother came running, chasing the startled Mel over a small cliff. Paul then took the bulb for himself.

In this case the deceived party was Paul's mother, who was misled by his scream into believing that Paul was being attacked, when actually no such attack was taking place. As a result of her apparent misinterpretation Paul was left alone to eat the bulb that Mel had carefully extracted—a morsel, by the way, that he would not have had the strength to dig out on his own.

If Paul's ruse had been an isolated case, Whiten might have gone on with his foraging studies and never given it a second thought. But when he compared his field notes with Byrne's, he noticed that both their notebooks were sprinkled with similar incidents and had been so all summer long. After they returned home to Scotland, they boasted about their "dead smart" baboons to their colleagues in pubs after conferences, expecting them to be suitably impressed. Instead the other researchers countered with tales about their own shrewd vervets or Machiavellian macaques.

"That's when we realized that a whole phenomenon might be slipping through a sieve," says Whiten. Researchers had assumed that this sort of complex trickery was a product of the sophisticated human brain. After all, deceitful behavior seemed unique to humans, and the human brain is unusually large, even for primates—"three times as big as you would expect for a primate of our size," notes Whiten, if you're plotting brain size against body weight.

But if primates other than humans deceived one another on a regular basis, the two psychologists reasoned, then it raised the extremely provocative possibility that the primate brain, and ultimately the human brain, is an instrument crafted for social manipulation. Humans evolved from the same evolutionary stock as apes, and if tactical deception was an important part of the lives of our evolutionary ancestors, then the sneakiness and subterfuge that human beings are so manifestly capable of might not be simply a result of our great intelligence and oversize brain, but a driving force behind their development.

To Byrne and Whiten these were ideas worth pursuing. They fit in with a theory put forth some years earlier

---

Suddenly Paul let out a yell, and his mother came running, chasing Mel over a small cliff.

---

by English psychologist Nicholas Humphrey. In 1976 Humphrey had eloquently suggested that the evolution of primate intelligence might have been spurred not by the challenges of environment, as was generally thought, but rather by the complex cognitive demands of living with one's own companions. Since then a number of primatologists had begun to flesh out his theory with field observations of politically astute monkeys and apes.

Deception, however, had rarely been reported. And no wonder: If chimps, baboons, and higher primates generally are skilled deceivers, how could one ever know it? The best deceptions would by their very nature go undetected by the other members of the primate group, not to mention by a human stranger. Even those ruses that an observer could see through would have to be rare, for if used too often, they would lose their effectiveness. If Paul always cried wolf, for example, his mother would soon learn to ignore his ersatz distress. So while the monkey stories swapped over beers certainly suggested that deception was widespread among higher primates, it seemed unlikely that one or even a few researchers could observe enough instances of it to scientifically quantify how much, by whom, when, and to what effect.

Byrne and Whiten's solution was to extend their pub-derived data base with a more formal survey. In 1985 they sent a questionnaire to more than 100 primatologists working both in the field and in labs, asking them to report back any incidents in which they felt their subjects had perpetrated decep-

tion on one another. The questionnaire netted a promising assortment of deceptive tactics used by a variety of monkeys and all the great apes. Only the relatively small-brained and socially simple lemur family, which includes bush babies and lorises, failed to elicit a single instance. This supported the notion that society, sneakiness, brain size, and intelligence are intimately bound up with one another. The sneakier the primate, it seemed, the bigger the brain.

Byrne and Whiten drew up a second, much more comprehensive questionnaire in 1989 and sent it to hundreds more primatologists and animal behaviorists, greatly increasing the data base. Once again, when the results were tallied, only the lemur family failed to register a single case of deception.

All the other species, however, represented a simian rogues' gallery of liars and frauds. Often deception was used to distract another animal's attention. In one cartoonish example, a young baboon, chased by some angry elders, suddenly stopped, stood on his hind legs, and stared at a spot on the horizon, as if he noticed the presence of a predator or a foreign troop of baboons. His pursuers braked to a halt and looked in the same direction, giving up the chase. Powerful field binoculars revealed that no predator or baboon troop was anywhere in sight.

Sometimes the deception was simply a matter of one animal hiding a choice bit of food from the awareness of those strong enough to take it away. One of Jane Goodall's chimps, for example, named Figan, was once given some bananas after the more dominant members of the troop had wandered off. In the excitement, he uttered some loud "food barks"; the others quickly returned and took the bananas away. The next day Figan again waited behind the others and got some bananas. This time, however, he kept silent, even though the human observers, Goodall reported, "could hear faint choking sounds in his throat."

Concealment was a common ruse in sexual situations as well. Male monkeys and chimpanzees in groups have fairly strict hierarchies that control their access to females. Animals at the top of the order intimidate those lower down, forcing them away from females. Yet one researcher reported seeing a male stump-tailed macaque of a middle rank leading a female out of sight of the more dominant males and then mating with her silently, his climax unaccompanied by the harsh, low-pitched grunts that the male stump-tailed normally makes. At one point during the tryst the female turned and stared into his face, then covered his mouth with her hand. In another case a subordinate chimpanzee, aroused by the presence of a female in estrus, covered his erect penis with his hand when a dominant male approached, thus avoiding a likely attack.

In one particularly provocative instance a female hamadryas baboon slowly shuffled toward a large rock, appearing to forage, all the time keeping an eye on the most dominant male in the group. After 20 minutes she ended up with her head and shoulders visible to the big, watchful male, but with her hands happily engaged in the elicit activity of grooming a favorite subordinate male, who was hidden from view behind the rock.

Baboons proved singularly adept at a form of deception that Byrne and Whiten call "using a social tool." Paul's scam is a perfect example: he fools his mother into acting as a lever to pry the plant bulb away from the adult female, Mel. But can it be said unequivocally that he intended to deceive her? Perhaps Paul had simply learned through trial and error that letting out a yell brought his mother running and left him with food, in which case there is no reason to endow his young baboon intellect with Machiavellian intent. How do we know that Mel didn't actually threaten Paul in some way that Byrne and Whiten, watching, could not comprehend? While we're at it, how do we know that any of the primate deceptions reported here were really deliberate, conscious acts?

"It has to be said that there is a whole school of psychology that would

deny such behavior even to humans," says Byrne. The school in question—strict behaviorism—would seek an explanation for the baboons' behavior not by trying to crawl inside their head but by carefully analyzing observable behaviors and the stimuli that might be triggering them. Byrne and Whiten's strategy against such skepticism was to be hyperskeptical themselves. They accepted that trial-and-error learning or simple conditioning, in which an animal's actions are reinforced by a reward, might account for a majority of the incidents reported to them—even when they believed that tactical deception was really taking place. But when explaining things "simply" led to a maze of extraordinary coincidences and tortuous logic, the evidence for deliberate deception seemed hard to dismiss.

Society, sneakiness, brain size, and intelligence are intimately bound up with one another.

Paul, for instance, *might* have simply learned that screaming elicits the reward of food, via his mother's intervention. But Byrne witnessed him using the same tactic several times, and in each case his mother was out of sight, able to hear his yell but not able to see what was really going on. If Paul was simply conditioned to scream, why would he do so only when his mother could not see who was—or was not—attacking her son?

Still, it is possible that she was not intentionally deceived. But in at least one other, similar case there is virtually no doubt that the mother was responding to a bogus attack, because the alleged attacker was quite able to verbalize his innocence. A five-year-old male chimp named Katabi, in the process of weaning, had discovered that the best way to get his reluctant mother to suckle him was to convince her he needed reassurance. One day Katabi approached a human observer—Japanese primatologist Toshisada Nish-

ida—and began to screech, circling around the researcher and waving an accusing hand at him. The chimp's mother and her escort immediately glared at Nishida, their hair erect. Only by slowly backing away from the screaming youngster did Nishida avoid a possible attack from the two adult chimps.

"In fact I did nothing to him," Nishida protested. It follows that the adults were indeed misled by Katabi's hysterics—unless there was some threat in Nishida unknown even to himself.

"If you try hard enough," says Byrne, "you can explain every single case without endowing the animal with the ability to deceive. But if you look at the whole body of work, there comes a point where you have to strive officiously to deny it."

The cases most resistant to such officious denials are the rarest—and the most compelling. In these interactions the primate involved not only employed tactical deception but clearly understood the concept. Such comprehension would depend upon one animal's ability to "read the mind" of another: to attribute desires, intentions, or even beliefs to the other creature that do not necessarily correspond to its own view of the world. Such mind reading was clearly evident in only 16 out of 253 cases in the 1989 survey, all of them involving great apes.

For example, consider Figan again, the young chimp who suppressed his food barks in order to keep the bananas for himself. In his case, mind reading is not evident: he might simply have learned from experience that food barks in certain contexts result in a loss of food, and thus he might not understand the nature of his own ruse, even if the other chimps are in fact deceived.

But contrast Figan with some chimps observed by Dutch primatologist Frans Plooij. One of these chimps was alone in a feeding area when a metal box containing food was opened electronically. At the same moment another chimp happened to approach. (Sound familiar? It's your older brother again.) The first chimp quickly closed the metal box (that's you hiding your chips), walked away, and sat down, looking around as if nothing had happened. The second chimp departed, but after going some distance away he hid behind a tree and peeked back at the first chimp. When the first chimp thought the coast was clear, he opened the box. The second chimp ran out, pushed the other aside, and ate the bananas.

Chimp One might be a clever rogue, but Chimp Two, who counters his deception with a ruse of his own, is the true mind reader. The success of his ploy is based on his insight that Chimp One was trying to deceive *him* and on his ability to adjust his behavior accordingly. He has in fact performed a prodigious cognitive leap—proving himself capable of projecting himself into another's mental space, and becoming what Humphrey would call a natural psychologist.

Niccolò Machiavelli might have called him good raw material. It is certainly suggestive that only the great apes—our closest relatives—seem capable of deceits based on such mind reading, and chimpanzees most of all. This does not necessarily mean that chimps are inherently more intelligent: the difference may be a matter of social organization. Orangutans live most of their lives alone, and thus they would not have much reason to develop such a complex social skill. And gorillas live in close family groups, whose members would be more familiar, harder to fool, and more likely to punish an attempted swindle. Chimpanzees, on the other hand, spend their lives in a shifting swirl of friends and relations, where small groups constantly form and break apart and reform with new members.

"What an opportunity for lying and cheating!" muses Byrne. Many anthropologists now believe that the social life of early hominids—our first non-ape ancestors—was much like that of chimps today, with similar opportunities to hone their cognitive skills on one another. Byrne and Whiten stop just short of saying that mind reading is the key to understanding the growth of human intelligence. But it would be disingenuous to ignore the possibility. If you were an early hominid who could comprehend the subjective impressions of others and manipulate them to your own ends, you might well have a competitive advantage over those less psychosocially nimble, perhaps enjoying slightly easier access to food and to the mating opportunities that would ensure your genetic survival.

Consider too how much more important your social wits would be in a world where the targets of your deceptions were constantly trying to outsmart *you*. After millennia of intrigue and counterintrigue, a hominid species might well evolve a brain three times bigger than it "should" be—and capable of far more than deceiving other hominids. "The ability to attribute other intentions to other people could have been an enormous building block for many human achievements, including language," says Whiten. "That this leap seems to have been taken by chimps and possibly the other great apes puts that development in human mentality quite early."

So did our intellect rise to its present height on a tide of manipulation and deceit? Some psychologists, even those who support the notion that the evolution of intelligence was socially driven, think that Byrne and Whiten's choice of the loaded adjective *Machiavellian* might be unnecessarily harsh.

"In my opinion," says Humphrey, "the word gives too much weight to the hostile use of intelligence. One of the functions of intellect in higher primates and humans is to keep the social unit together and make it able to successfully exploit the environment. A lot of intelligence could better be seen as driven by the need for cooperation and compassion." To that, Byrne and Whiten only point out that cooperation is itself an excellent Machiavellian strategy—sometimes.

The Scottish researchers are not, of course, the first to have noticed this. "It is good to appear clement, trustworthy, humane, religious, and honest, and also to be so," Machiavelli advised his aspiring Borgia prince in 1513. "But always with the mind so disposed that, when the occasion arises not to be so, you can become the opposite."

These Are Real Swinging Primates

There's a good evolutionary reason why the rare muriqui of Brazil should heed the dictum 'Make love, not war'

Shannon Brownlee

When I first heard of the muriqui four years ago, I knew right away that I had to see one. This is an unusual monkey, to say the least. To begin with, it's the largest primate in South America; beyond that, the males have very large testicles. We're talking gigantic, the size of billiard balls, which means that the 30-pound muriqui has *cojones* that would look more fitting on a 400-pound gorilla.

But it wasn't prurience that lured me to Brazil. My interest in the muriqui was intellectual, because more than this monkey's anatomy is extraordinary. Muriqui society is untroubled by conflict: troops have no obvious pecking order; males don't compete overtly for females; and, most un-monkeylike, these monkeys almost never fight.

The muriqui is also one of the rarest monkeys in the world. It lives in a single habitat, the Atlantic forest of southeastern Brazil. This mountainous region was once blanketed with forest from São Paulo to Salvador (*see map*), but several centuries of slash-and-burn agriculture have reduced it to fragments.

In 1969 Brazilian conservationist Alvaro Coutinho Aguirre surveyed the remaining pockets of forest and estimated that 2,000 to 3,000 muriquis survived. His data were all but ignored until Russell Mittermeier, a biologist, trained his sights on the muriquis ten years later. Known as Russel of the

Apes to his colleagues, Mittermeier, and American, directs the primate program for the World Wildlife Fund. He hopscotches from forest to forest around the world looking for monkeys in trouble and setting up conservation plans for them. In 1979 he and Brazilian zoologist Celio Valle retraced Aguirre's steps and found even fewer muriquis. Today only 350 to 500 are left, scattered among four state and national parks and six other privately held plots.

In 1981 Karen Strier, then a graduate student at Harvard, approached Mittermeier for help in getting permission to observe the muriqui. He took her to a coffee plantation called Montes Claros, near the town of Caratinga, 250 miles north of Rio de Janeiro. Over the next four years she studied the social behavior of the muriqui there—and came up with a provocative theory about how the monkey's unconventional behavior, as well as its colossal testicles, evolved. She reasoned that the evolution of both could be explained, at least in part, by the muriquis' need to avoid falling out of trees.

Last June I joined Strier, now a professor at Beloit (Wis.) College, on one of her periodic journeys to Montes Claros—clear mountains, in Portuguese. We arrived there after a disagreeable overnight bus trip over bad roads. As we neared the plantation, I found it difficult to believe there was a forest—much less a monkey—within miles. Through the grimy windows of the bus

I saw hillsides stripped down to russet dirt and dotted with spindly coffee plants and stucco farmhouses. There wasn't anything taller than a banana tree in sight. As the bus lurched around the last curve before our stop the forest finally appeared, an island of green amid thousands of acres of coffee trees and brown pastures.

Strier was eager to start looking for the muriquis—"There's a chance we won't see them the whole four days you're here," she said—so no sooner had we dropped our bags off at a cottage on the plantation than we set out along a dirt road into the forest. The trees closed around us—and above us, where they gracefully arched to form a vault of green filigree. Parrots screeched; leaves rustled; a large butterfly flew erratically by on transparent wings. By this time Strier had guided me onto a steep trail, along which she stopped from time to time to listen for the monkeys.

They appeared soon enough, but our first meeting was less than felicitous. After we had climbed half a mile, Strier motioned for me to stop. A muffled sound, like that of a small pig grunting contentedly, came from up ahead. We moved forward a hundred yards. Putting a finger to her lips, Strier sank to her haunches and looked up.

I did the same; twelve round black eyes stared back at me. A group of six muriquis squatted, silent, 15 feet above in the branches, watching us intently.

They began to grunt again. A sharp smell with undertones of cinnamon permeated the air. A light rain began to fall. I held out my palm to catch a drop. It was warm.

"Hey, this isn't rain!" I said.

Strier grinned and pointed to her head. "That's why I wear a hat," she said.

My enthusiasm for the muriquis waned slightly after that. We left them at dusk and retired to the cottage, where Strier described her arrival at Montes Claros four years earlier. Mittermeier acted as guide and interpreter during the first few days of her pilot study. He introduced her to the owner of the 5,000-acre plantation, Feliciano Miguel Abdala, then 73, who had preserved the 2,000-acre forest for more than 40 years. His is one of the only remaining tracts of Atlantic forest, and he agreed to let Strier use it as the site of her study. Then Mittermeier introduced her to the muriquis, assuring her they would be easy to see.

They weren't, and observing them closely is a little like stargazing on a rainy night: not only do you run the risk of getting wet, but you can also spend a lot of time looking up and never see a thing. Mittermeier was adept at spotting the monkeys in the forest, and helped Strier acquire this skill.

But brief glimpses of the monkeys weren't enough. "My strategy was to treat them like baboons, the only other species I'd ever studied," she says. "I thought I couldn't let them out of my sight." She tried to follow on the ground as they swung along in the trees. "They went berserk," she says. They threw branches, shrieked, urinated on her—or worse—and fled.

Even after the muriquis grew accustomed to her, keeping up with them wasn't easy. They travel as much as two miles a day, which is tough for someone picking her way through thick growth on the forest floor. As Strier and a Brazilian assistant learned the muriquis' habitual routes and daily patterns, they cleared trails. These helped, but the muriquis could still travel much faster than she could. "I've often thought the thing to have would be a jet

pack," Strier says. "It would revolutionize primatology. Your National Science Foundation grant would include binoculars, pencils, and a jet pack."

Observing muriquis is like stargazing on a rainy night. You may get wet, and you can spend hours looking and seeing nothing.

The monkeys move by brachiating, swinging hand over hand from branch to branch, much like a child on a jungle gym. Only one other group of monkeys brachiates; the rest clamber along branches on all fours. The muriquis' closest relatives are two other Latin American genera, the woolly monkeys and the spider monkeys—hence woolly spider monkey, its English name. But the muriqui is so unlike them that it has its own genus, *Brachyteles,* which refers to its diminutive thumb, an adaptation for swinging through the trees. Its species name is *arachnoides,* from the Greek for spider, which the muriqui resembles when its long arms, legs, and tail are outstretched.

Brachiating is a specialization that's thought to have evolved because it enables primates to range widely to feed on fruit. Curiously, though, muriquis have a stomach designed for digesting leaves. Strier found that their diet consists of a combination of the two foods. They eat mostly foliage, low-quality food for a monkey, but prefer flowers and fruits, like figs and the *caja manga,* which is similar to the mango. Year after year they return to certain trees when they bloom and bear fruit. The rest of the time the muriquis survive on leaves by passing huge quantities of them through their elongated guts, which contain special bacteria to help them digest the foliage. By the end of the day their bellies are so distended with greenery that even the males look pregnant.

We returned to the trail the next morning just after dawn. Condensation

trickled from leaves; howler monkeys roared and capuchins cooed and squeaked; a bird sang with the sweet, piercing voice of a piccolo. Then Strier had to mention snakes. "Watch out for snakes," she said blithely, scrambling on all fours up a steep bank. I followed her, treading cautiously.

The muriquis weren't where we had left them the day before. Strier led me along a ridge through a stand of bamboo, where a whisper of movement drifted up from the slope below. Maybe it was just the wind, but she thought it was the muriquis, so we sat down to wait. After a couple of hours, she confessed, "This part of research can get kind of boring."

By noon the faint noise became a distinct crashing. "That's definitely them," she said. "It's a good thing they're so noisy, or I'd never be able to find them." The monkeys, perhaps a dozen of them, swarmed uphill, breaking branches, chattering, uttering their porcine grunts as they swung along. At the crest of the ridge they paused, teetering in indecision while they peered back and forth before settling in some legume trees on the ridgetop. We crept down out of the bamboo to within a few feet of them, so close I noticed the cinnamon scent again—only this time I kept out of range.

Each monkey had its own feeding style. One hung upside down by its tail and drew the tip of a branch to its mouth; it delicately plucked the tenderest shoots with its rubbery lips. Another sat upright, grabbing leaves by the handful and stuffing its face. A female with twins—"Twins have never been seen in this species," Strier whispered as she excitedly scribbled notes—ate with one hand while hanging by the other and her tail. Her babies clung to the fur on her belly.

I had no trouble spotting the males. Their nether parts bulged unmistakably—blue-black or pink-freckled, absurd-looking monuments to monkey virility. I asked Strier what sort of obscene joke evolution was playing on the muriquis when it endowed them thus.

We were about to consider this question when a high-pitched whinnying began a few hundred yards away. Immediately a monkey just overhead pulled itself erect and let out an ear-splitting shriek, which set the entire troop to neighing like a herd of nervous horses. Then they took off down into the valley.

Strier and I had to plunge pell-mell into the underbrush or risk losing them for the rest of the day. "They're chasing the other troop," she said as we galloped downhill. A group of muriquis living on the opposite side of the forest had made a rare foray across the valley.

The monkeys we were observing swung effortlessly from tree to tree; we wrestled with thorny vines, and fell farther and farther behind. An impenetrable thicket forced us to backtrack in search of another route. By the time we caught up to the muriquis, they were lounging in a tree, chewing on unripe fruit and chuckling in a self-satisfied sort of way. The intruding troop was nowhere to be seen. "They must have scared the hell out of those other guys," said Strier, laughing.

Tolerance of another troop is odd behavior for monkeys, but not so odd as the fact that they never fight among themselves.

Such confrontations occur infrequently; muriquis ordinarily tolerate another troop's incursions. Strier thinks they challenge intruders only when there's a valuable resource to defend—like the fruit tree they were sitting in.

Tolerance of another troop is odd behavior for monkeys, but not as odd as the fact that members of a muriqui troop never fight among themselves. "They're remarkably placid," said Strier. "They wait in line to dip their hands into water collected in the bole of a tree. They have no apparent pecking order or dominance hierarchy. Males and females are equal in status, and males don't squabble over fe-

males." No other primate society is known to be so free of competition, not even that of gorillas, which have lately gained a reputation for being the gentle giants of the primate world.

Strier's portrayal of the muriqui brought to mind a bizarre episode that Katharine Milton, an anthropologist at the University of California at Berkeley, once described. While studying a troop of muriquis in another patch of the Atlantic forest, she observed a female mating with a half a dozen males in succession; that a female monkey would entertain so many suitors came as no surprise, but Milton was astonished at the sight of the males lining up behind the female "like a choo-choo train" and politely taking turns copulating. They continued in this manner for two days, stopping only to rest and eat, and never even so much as bared their teeth.

Primates aren't known for their graciousness in such matters, and I found Milton's report almost unbelievable. But Strier confirms it. She says that female muriquis come into heat about every two and a half years, after weaning their latest offspring, and repeatedly copulate during that five- to seven-day period with a number of males. Copulations, "cops" in animal-behavior lingo, last as long as 18 minutes, and average six, which for most primates (including the genus *Homo,* if Masters and Johnson are correct) would be a marathon. Yet no matter how long a male muriqui takes, he's never harassed by suitors-in-waiting.

Strier has a theory to explain the muriqui's benignity, based on a paper published in 1980 by Richard Wrangham, a primatologist at the University of Michigan. He proposed that the social behavior of primates could in large part be predicted by what the females eat.

This isn't a completely new idea. For years primatologists sought correlations between ecological conditions and social structure, but few patterns emerged—until Wrangham's ingenious insight that environment constrains the behavior of each sex differently. Specifically, food affects the sociability of females more than males.

Wrangham started with the generally accepted premise that both sexes in every species have a common aim: to leave as many offspring as possible. But each sex pursues this goal in its own way. The best strategy for a male primate is to impregnate as many females as he can. All he needs, as Wrangham points out, is plenty of sperm and plenty of females. As for the female, no matter how promiscuous she is, she can't match a male's fecundity. On average, she's able to give birth to only one offspring every two years, and her success in bearing and rearing it depends in part upon the quality of food she eats. Therefore, all other things being equal, male primates will spend their time cruising for babes, while females will look for something good to eat.

Wrangham's ingenious insight: the social behavior of primates can in large part be predicted by what the females eat.

Wrangham perceived that the distribution of food—that is, whether it's plentiful or scarce, clumped or evenly dispersed—will determine how gregarious the females of a particular species are. He looked at the behavior of 28 species and found that, in general, females forage together when food is plentiful and found in large clumps—conditions under which there's enough for all the members of the group and the clumps can be defended against outsiders. When clumps become temporarily depleted, the females supplement their diet with what Wrangham calls subsistence foods. He suggest that female savanna baboons, for example, live in groups because their favorite foods, fruits and flowers, grow in large clumps that are easy to defend. When these are exhausted they switch to seeds, insects, and grasses. The females form long-lasting relationships within their groups, and establish stable dominance hierarchies.

Chimpanzees provide an illustration of how females behave when their food isn't in clumps big enough to feed everybody. Female chimps eat flowers, shoots, leaves, and insects, but their diet is composed largely of fruits that are widely scattered and often not very plentiful. They may occasionally gather at a particularly abundant fruit tree, but when the fruit is gone they disperse to forage individually for other foods. Members of the troop are constantly meeting at fruit trees, splitting up, and gathering again.

These two types of female groups, the "bonded" savanna baboons and "fissioning" chimps, as Wrangham calls them, pose very different mating opportunities for the males of their species. As a consequence, the social behavior of the two species is different. For a male baboon, groups of females represent the perfect opportunity for him to get cops. All he has to do is exclude other males. A baboon troop includes a clan of females accompanied by a number of males, which compete fiercely for access to them. For baboons there are few advantages to fraternal cooperation, and many to competition.

Male chimpanzees fight far less over females than male baboons do, principally because there's little point—the females don't stick together. Instead, the males form strong alliances with their fellows. They roam in gangs looking for females in heat, and patrol their troop's borders against male interlopers.

Wrangham's theory made so much sense, Strier says, that it inspired researchers to go back into the field with a new perspective. She saw the muriqui as an excellent species for evaluating the model, since Wrangham had constructed it before anyone knew the first thing about this monkey. His idea would seem all the more reasonable if it could predict the muriqui's behavior.

It couldn't, at least not entirely. Strier has found that the females fit Wrangham's predictions: they stick together and eat a combination of preferred and subsistence foods, defending the preferred from other troops. But the males don't conform to the theory. "Considering that the females are foraging together, there should be relatively low pressure on the males to cooperate," she says. "It's odd: the males should compete, but they don't."

She thinks that limitations on male competition may explain muriqui behavior. First, the muriquis are too big to fight in trees. "I think these monkeys are at about the limit of size for rapid brachiation," she says. "If they were bigger, they couldn't travel rapidly through the trees. They fall a lot as

it is, and it really shakes them up. I've seen an adult fall about sixty feet, nearly to the ground, before catching hold of a branch. That means that whatever they fight about has got to be worth the risk of falling out of a tree."

Moreover, fighting may require more energy than the muriquis can afford. Milton has estimated the caloric value of the food eaten by a muriqui each day and compared it to the amount of energy she would expect a monkey of that size to need. She concluded that the muriqui had little excess energy to burn on combat.

The restriction that rapid brachiation sets on the muriqui's size discourages competition in more subtle ways, as well. Given that muriquis are polygynous, the male should be bigger than the female, as is almost invariably the case among other polygynous species—but he's not. The link between larger males and polygyny is created by sexual selection, an evolutionary force that Darwin first recognized, and which he distinguished from natural selection by the fact that it acts exclusively on one sex. Sexual selection is responsible for the manes of male lions, for instance, and for the large canines of male baboons.

In a polygynous society, the advantages to being a large male are ob-

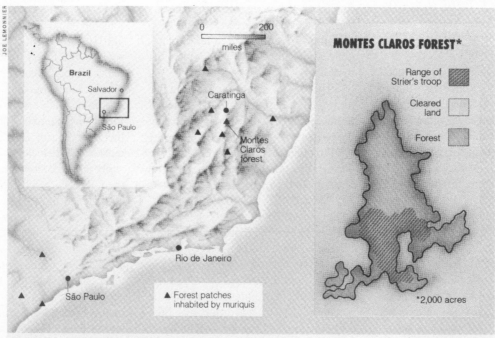

The 350 to 500 surviving muriquis live in ten patches of the Atlantic forest of southeastern Brazil.

vious: he who's biggest is most likely to win the battles over females—and pass on his genes for size. But sexual selection's push toward large males has been thwarted in the muriqui, says Strier. Any competitive benefits greater size might bring a male would be offset in part by the excessive demands on his energy and the costs of falling out of trees.

She believes that the constraints on the males' size have had a profound effect on the muriquis' social behavior. Most important, says Strier, with males and females being the same size, the females can't be dominated, which means they can pick their mates. Most female primates aren't so fortunate: if they copulate with subordinate males, they risk being attacked by dominant ones. But a female muriqui in heat can easily refuse a suitor, simply by sitting down or by moving away.

The size of the males has a profound effect on muriqui behavior. For one thing, they are simply too big to fight in trees.

Fighting not only doesn't help the male muriqui in his quest for cops; it may even harm his chances, since females can shun an aggressive male. Strier believes that females may also be responsible for the male muriquis' canine teeth not being oversized. As a rule, the male's canines are the same size as the female's only in monogamous primate species, but over the generations female muriquis may have mated more readily with males whose teeth were no bigger than their own. In sum, Strier thinks, for a male muriqui the costs of competing are far outweighted by the benefits of avoiding it.

But he has the means to vie for reproductive success and still come across as Mr. Nice Guy: his sperm. Sperm competition, as it's called, is a hot new idea in sociobiology, originally proposed to explain male bonding

in chimpanzees, and, as Milton was the first to suggest, it may explain why the muriqui has such enormous testicles.

The competition is something like a game of chance. Imagine a bucket with a hole in the bottom just big enough for a marble to pass through. People gather round, each with a handful of marbles. They drop their marbles in the bucket, mix them up, and one comes out the bottom. Whoever owns that marble is the winner.

In the sperm competition among male muriquis, the bucket is a female, the marbles are sperm, and winning means becoming a father. No male can be sure it will be his sperm that impregnates a female, since she mates with a number of his fellows. His chances are further complicated by the fact that the female muriqui, like all New World monkeys, gives no visible indication of ovulation; there may be nothing that signals the male (or the female) when during her heat that occurs. So it's to the male's advantage to continue mating as often as the female will have him.

This may sound like monkey heaven, but it puts the male on the horns of a dilemma. If he copulates as often as possible, he could run low on sperm just when the female is ovulating. On the other hand, if he refrains from copulating to save sperm, he may miss his chance at procreating altogether. Selection may have come to his aid, Strier reasons, by acting on his testicles.

Here's a plausible scenario. Suppose a male came along that could produce more sperm than the average muriqui because his testicles were bigger than average. That male would clean up in the reproductive arena. The ratio of testicle size to body weight has been correlated with high sperm count and repeated copulation over a short period in other mammals, and bigger testicles probably also increase the percentage of viable and motile sperm.

If the muriqui's testicles are anything like those of other species, then a male with extra big ones has a slight reproductive advantage. Like a player with more marbles to put in the bucket, a male that can produce more and

better sperm has a better than average chance of impregnating females and passing on this advantageous trait to his sons. Just as important, the outsized organs probably don't cost him much in metabolic energy. Thus, over generations, the muriqui's testicles have grown larger and larger.

Strier's theory has five years of data behind, it, and it's the kind of theory that will stimulate researchers to reexamine their ideas about other species. Yet it isn't her only concern; she concentrates equally on the muriqui's uncertain future. On our last day in the forest we watched the monkeys cross a six-foot gap in the canopy 60 feet above us. One by one they stood poised for a moment on the end of a branch before launching themselves. Strier counted them as they appeared in silhouette against a grey sky. The total was 33, including the twins. "They're up from twenty-two in 1982," she said. "That's a very fast increase."

The muriquis at Montes Claros make up almost one-tenth of the total population of the species, and they're critical to its survival—as are all the other isolated and widely separated troops. Each group's genetic pool is limited, and eventually the troops could suffer inbreeding depression, a decline in fecundity that often appears in populations with little genetic variability.

Strier and Mittermeier predict that one day muriquis will have to be managed, the way game species are in the U.S. They may be transported between patches of forest to provide some gene flow. But that's a dangerous proposition now. There are too few muriquis to risk it, and none has ever bred or survived for long in captivity. "Before my study, conservationists would probably have moved males between forests," Strier says. "That would've been a mistake. I have tentative evidence that in a natural situation the females may be the ones that do the transferring between groups."

For now, though, she thinks the biggest concern isn't managing the monkeys but preventing their habitat from disappearing. Preserving what remains of the Atlantic forest won't be easy, and no one knows this better than Feliciano Miguel Abdala, the man responsible for there being any forest at all at Montes Claros.

Abdala has little formal education, but he's rich; he owns nine plantations besides Montes Claros. His family lives in relative splendor in Caratinga, but he likes to spend the weekdays here. His house is just beyond the edge of the forest, and sunlight filters through the bougainvillea vine entwining the front porch. Chickens can be seen through the cracks in the floorboards, scratching in the dirt under the house. Electric cords are strung crazily from the rafters, and a bare bulb dangles in the center of his office. Abdala removes his straw hat decorously and places it on a chair before sitting at his desk.

Abdala bought the 5,000 acres of Montes Claros in 1944. The region was barely settled then, and smoke still rose from the great burning heaps of slash left from clearing the forest. Abdala's land included one of the last stands of trees. I ask him why he saved it. "I am a conservationist," he says. "For a long time the local people thought I was crazy because I wouldn't cut the forest. I told them not to shoot the monkeys, and they stopped. Now all my workers are crazy, too."

I ask Abdala about his plans for his forest. He rubs his head distractedly and says, vaguely. "I hope it will continue."

Abdala believes the government should buy Montes Claros—plantation and rain forest—to create a nature reserve. He'll probably maintain the forest as long as he lives, but the land is quite valuable, and his heirs might not share his lofty sentiments.

As important as the muriquis have become to understanding social systems, and as much as U.S. conservationists may wish to see these monkeys preserved, Strier thinks that in the end it's up to the Brazilians to save them. She's expecting a three-year grant from the National Science Foundation; part of the money will go toward allowing her to observe the monkeys in other forest patches, watching for variation in their behavior as a test of her ideas. Studies like hers will be critical not only for proving theories but also for ensuring that plans for managing the muriquis will work. The rest of the money will permit her to train seven Brazilian graduate students, because she says, "the future of the muriqui lies with the Brazilians."

What Are Friends For?

Among East African baboons, friendship means companions, health, safety . . . and, sometimes, sex

Barbara Smuts

Virgil, a burly adult male olive baboon, closely followed Zizi, a middle-aged female easily distinguished by her grizzled coat and square muzzle. On her rump Zizi sported a bright pink swelling, indicating that she was sexually receptive and probably fertile. Virgil's extreme attentiveness to Zizi suggested to me—and all rival males in the troop—that he was her current and exclusive mate.

Zizi, however, apparently had something else in mind. She broke away from Virgil, moved rapidly through the troop, and presented her alluring sexual swelling to one male after another. Before Virgil caught up with her, she had managed to announce her receptive condition to several of his rivals. When Virgil tried to grab her, Zizi screamed and dashed into the bushes with Virgil in hot pursuit. I heard sounds of chasing and fighting coming from the thicket. Moments later Zizi emerged from the bushes with an older male named Cyclops. They remained together for several days, copulating

often. In Cyclops's presence, Zizi no longer approached or even glanced at other males.

Primatologists describe Zizi and other olive baboons (*Papio cynocephalus anubis*) as promiscuous, meaning that both males and females usually mate with several members of the opposite sex within a short period of time. Promiscuous mating behavior characterizes many of the larger, more familiar primates, including chimpanzees, rhesus macaques, and gray langurs, as well as olive, yellow, and chacma baboons, the three subspecies of savanna baboon. In colloquial usage, promiscuity often connotes wanton and random sex, and several early studies of primates supported this stereotype. However, after years of laboriously recording thousands of copulations under natural conditions, the Peeping Toms of primate fieldwork have shown that, even in promiscuous species, sexual pairings are far from random.

Some adult males, for example, typically copulate much more often than

others. Primatologists have explained these differences in terms of competition: the most dominant males monopolize females and prevent lower-ranking rivals from mating. But exceptions are frequent. Among baboons, the exceptions often involve scruffy, older males who mate in full view of younger, more dominant rivals.

A clue to the reason for these puzzling exceptions emerged when primatologists began to question an implicit assumption of the dominance hypothesis—that females were merely passive objects of male competition. But what if females were active arbiters in this system? If females preferred some males over others and were able to express these preferences, then models of mating activity based on male dominance alone would be far too simple.

Once researchers recognized the possibility of female choice, evidence for it turned up in species after species. The story of Zizi, Virgil, and Cyclops is one of hundreds of examples of female primates rejecting the sexual advances of particular males and enthusiastically cooperating with others. But what is the basis for female choice? Why might they prefer some males over others?

This question guided my research on the Eburru Cliffs troop of olive baboons, named after one of their favorite sleeping sites, a sheer rocky outcrop rising several hundred feet above the floor of the Great Rift Valley, about 100 miles northwest of Nairobi, Kenya. The 120 members of Eburru Cliffs spent their days wandering through open grassland studded with occasional acacia thorn trees. Each night they retired to one of a dozen sets of cliffs that provided protection from nocturnal predators such as leopards.

Most previous studies of baboon sexuality had focused on females who, like Zizi, were at the peak of sexual receptivity. A female baboon does not mate when she is pregnant or lactating, a period of abstinence lasting about eighteen months. The female then goes into estrus, and for about two weeks out of every thirty-five-day cycle, she mates. Toward the end of this two week period she may ovulate, but usually the female undergoes four or five estrous cycles before she conceives. During pregnancy, she once again resumes a chaste existence. As a result, the typical female baboon is sexually active for less than 10 percent of her adult life. I thought that by focusing on the other 90 percent, I might learn something new. In particular, I suspected that routine, day-to-day relationships between males and pregnant or lactating (nonestrous) females might provide clues to female mating preferences.

Nearly every day for sixteen months, I joined the Eburru Cliffs baboons at their sleeping cliffs at dawn and traveled several miles with them while they foraged for roots, seeds, grass, and occasionally, small prey items, such as baby gazelles or hares (see "Predatory Baboons of Kekopey," *Natural History,* March 1976). Like all savanna baboon troops, Eburru Cliffs functioned as a cohesive unit organized around a core of related females, all of whom were born in the troop. Unlike the females, male savanna baboons

leave their natal troop to join another where they may remain for many years, so most of the Eburru Cliffs adult males were immigrants. Since membership in the troop remained relatively constant during the period of my study, I learned to identify each individual. I relied on differences in size, posture, gait, and especially, facial features. To the practiced observer, baboons look as different from one another as human beings do.

As soon as I could recognize individuals, I noticed that particular females tended to turn up near particular males again and again. I came to think of these pairs as friends. Friendship among animals is not a well-documented phenomenon, so to convince skeptical colleagues that baboon friendship was real, I needed to develop objective criteria for distinguishing friendly pairs.

I began by investigating grooming, the amiable simian habit of picking through a companion's fur to remove dead skin and ectoparasites (see "Little Things That Tick Off Baboons," *Natural History,* February 1984). Baboons spend much more time grooming than is necessary for hygiene, and previous research had indicated that it is a good measure of social bonds.

Although eighteen adult males lived in the troop, each nonestrous female performed most of her grooming with just one, two, or occasionally, three males. For example, of Zizi's twenty-four grooming bouts with males, Cyclops accounted for thirteen, and a second male, Sherlock, accounted for all the rest. Different females tended to favor different males as grooming partners.

Another measure of social bonds was simply who was observed near whom. When foraging, traveling, or resting, each pregnant or lactating female spent a lot of time near a few males and associated with the others no more often than expected by chance. When I compared the identities of favorite grooming partners and frequent companions, they overlapped almost completely. This enabled me to develop a formal definition of friendship: any male that scored high on both

grooming and proximity measures was considered a friend.

Virtually all baboons made friends; only one female and the three males who had most recently joined the troop lacked such companions. Out of more than 600 possible adult female-adult male pairs in the troop, however, only about one in ten qualified as friends; these really were special relationships.

Several factors seemed to influence which baboons paired up. In most cases, friends were unrelated to each other, since the male had immigrated from another troop. (Four friendships, however, involved a female and an adolescent son who had not yet emigrated. Unlike other friends, these related pairs never mated.) Older females tended to be friends with older males; younger females with younger males. I witnessed occasional May-December romances, usually involving older females and young adult males. Adolescent males and females were strongly rule-bound, and with the exception of mother-son pairs, they formed friendships only with one another.

Regardless of age or dominance rank, most females had just one or two male friends. But among males, the number of female friends varied greatly from none to eight. Although high-ranking males enjoyed priority of access to food and sometimes mates, dominant males did not have more female friends than low-ranking males. Instead it was the older males who had lived in the troop for many years who had the most friends. When a male had several female friends, the females were often closely related to one another. Since female baboons spend a lot of time near their kin, it is probably easier for a male to maintain bonds with several related females at once.

When collecting data, I focused on one nonestrous female at a time and kept track of her every movement toward or away from any male; similarly, I noted every male who moved toward or away from her. Whenever the female and a male moved close enough to exchange intimacies, I wrote down exactly what happened. When foraging together, friends tended to remain a few yards apart. Males more often wandered away from females than the reverse, and females, more often than males, closed the gap. The female behaved as if she wanted to keep the male within calling distance, in case she needed his protection. The male, however, was more likely to make approaches that brought them within actual touching distance. Often, he would plunk himself down right next to his friend and ask her to groom him by holding a pose with exaggerated stillness. The female sometimes responded by grooming, but more often, she exhibited the most reliable sign of true intimacy: she ignored her friend and simply continued whatever she was doing.

In sharp contrast, when a male who was not a friend moved close to a female, she dared not ignore him. She stopped whatever she was doing and held still, often glancing surreptitiously at the intruder. If he did not move away, she sometimes lifted her tail and presented her rump. When a female is not in estrus, this is a gesture of appeasement, not sexual enticement. Immediately after this respectful acknowledgement of his presence, the female would slip away. But such tense interactions with nonfriend males were rare, because females usually moved away before the males came too close.

These observations suggest that females were afraid of most of the males in their troop, which is not surprising: male baboons are twice the size of females, and their canines are longer and sharper than those of a lion. All Eburru Cliffs males directed both mild and severe aggression toward females. Mild aggression, which usually involved threats and chases but no body contact, occurred most often during feeding competition or when the male redirected aggression toward a female after losing a fight with another male. Females and juveniles showed aggression toward other females and juveniles in similar circumstances and occasionally inflicted superficial wounds. Severe aggression by males, which involved body contact and sometimes biting, was less common and also more puzzling, since there was no apparent cause.

An explanation for at least some of these attacks emerged one day when I was watching Pegasus, a young adult male, and his friend Cicily, sitting together in the middle of a small clearing. Cicily moved to the edge of the clearing to feed, and a higher-ranking female, Zora, suddenly attacked her. Pegasus stood up and looked as if he were about to intervene when both females disappeared into the bushes. He sat back down, and I remained with him. A full ten minutes later, Zora appeared at the edge of the clearing; this was the first time she had come into view since her attack on Cicily. Pegasus instantly pounced on Zora, repeatedly grabbed her neck in his mouth and lifted her off the ground, shook her whole body, and then dropped her. Zora screamed continuously and tried to escape. Each time, Pegasus caught her and continued his brutal attack. When he finally released her five minutes later she had a deep canine gash on the palm of her hand that made her limp for several days.

This attack was similar in form and intensity to those I had seen before and labeled "unprovoked." Certainly, had I come upon the scene after Zora's aggression toward Cicily, I would not have understood why Pegasus attacked Zora. This suggested that some, perhaps many, severe attacks by males actually represented punishment for actions that had occurred some time before.

Whatever the reasons for male attacks on females, they represent a serious threat. Records of fresh injuries indicated that Eburru Cliffs adult females received canine slash wounds from males at the rate of one for every female each year, and during my study, one female died of her injuries. Males probably pose an even greater threat to infants. Although only one infant was killed during my study, observers in Botswana and Tanzania have seen recent male immigrants kill several young infants.

Protection from male aggression, and from the less injurious but more frequent aggression of other females and juveniles, seems to be one of the main advantages of friendship for a female baboon. Seventy times I observed an adult male defend a female or her offspring against aggression by another troop member, not infrequently a high-ranking male. In all but six of these cases, the defender was a friend. Very few of these confrontations involved actual fighting; no male baboon, subordinate or dominant, is anxious to risk injury by the sharp canines of another.

Males are particularly solicitous guardians of their friends' youngest infants. If another male gets too close to an infant or if a juvenile female plays with it too roughly, the friend may intervene. Other troop members soon learn to be cautious when the mother's friend is nearby, and his presence provides the mother with a welcome respite from the annoying pokes and prods of curious females and juveniles obsessed with the new baby. Male baboons at Gombe Park in Tanzania and Amboseli Park in Kenya have also been seen rescuing infants from chimpanzees and lions. These several forms of male protection help to explain why females in Eburru Cliffs stuck closer to their friends in the first few months after giving birth than at any other time.

The male-infant relationship develops out of the male's friendship with the mother, but as the infant matures, this new bond takes on a life of its own. My co-worker Nancy Nicolson found that by about nine months of age, infants actively sought out their male friends when the mother was a few yards away, suggesting that the male may function as an alternative caregiver. This seemed to be especially true for infants undergoing unusually early or severe weaning. (Weaning is generally a gradual, prolonged process, but there is tremendous variation among mothers in the timing and intensity of weaning. See "Mother Baboons," *Natural History,* September 1980). After being rejected by the mother, the crying infant often approached the male friend and sat huddled against him until its whimpers subsided. Two of the infants in Eburru Cliffs lost their mothers when they were still quite young. In each case, their bond with the mother's friend subsequently intensified, and—perhaps as a result—both infants survived.

A close bond with a male may also improve the infant's nutrition. Larger than all other troop members, adult males monopolize the best feeding sites. In general, the personal space surrounding a feeding male is inviolate, but he usually tolerates intrusions by the infants of his female friends, giving them access to choice feeding spots.

Although infants follow their male friends around rather than the reverse, the males seem genuinely attached to their tiny companions. During feeding, the male and infant express their pleasure in each other's company by sharing spirited, antiphonal grunting duets. If the infant whimpers in distress, the male friend is likely to cease feeding, look at the infant, and grunt softly, as if in sympathy, until the whimpers cease. When the male rests, the infants of his female friends may huddle behind him, one after the other, forming a "train," or, if feeling energetic, they may use his body as a trampoline.

When I returned to Eburru Cliffs four years after my initial study ended, several of the bonds formed between males and the infants of their female friends were still intact (in other cases, either the male or the infant or both had disappeared). When these bonds involved recently matured females, their long-time male associates showed no sexual interest in them, even though the females mated with other adult males. Mothers and sons, and usually maternal siblings, show similar sexual inhibitions in baboons and many other primate species.

The development of an intimate relationship between a male and the infant of his female friend raises an obvious question: Is the male the infant's father? To answer this question definitely we would need to conduct genetic analysis, which was not possible for these baboons. Instead, I estimated paternity probabilities from observations of the temporary (a few hours or days) exclusive mating relationships, or consortships, that estrous females form with a series of different males. These estimates were apt to be fairly accurate, since changes in the female's sexual swelling allow one to pinpoint the timing of conception to within a few days. Most females consorted with only two or three males during this period, and these males were termed likely fathers.

In about half the friendships, the male was indeed likely to be the father of his friend's most recent infant, but in the other half he was not—in fact, he had never been seen mating with the female. Interestingly, males who were friends with the mother but not likely fathers nearly always developed a relationship with her infant, while males who had mated with the female but were not her friend usually did not. Thus friendship with the mother, rather than paternity, seems to mediate the development of male-infant bonds. Recently, a similar pattern was documented for South American capuchin monkeys in a laboratory study in which paternity was determined genetically.

These results fly in the face of a prominent theory that claims males will invest in infants only when they are closely related. If males are not fostering the survival of their own genes by caring for the infant, then why do they do so? I suspected that the key was female choice. If females preferred to mate with males who had already demonstrated friendly behavior, then friendships with mothers and their infants might pay off in the future when the mothers were ready to mate again.

To find out if this was the case, I examined each male's sexual behavior with females he had befriended before they resumed estrus. In most cases, males consorted considerably more often with their friends than with other females. Baboon females typically mate with several different males, including both friends and nonfriends, but prior friendship increased a male's probability of mating with a female above what it would have been otherwise.

This increased probability seemed to reflect female preferences. Females occasionally overtly advertised their disdain for certain males and their desire for others. Zizi's behavior, described above, is a good example. Virgil was not one of her friends, but Cyclops was. Usually, however, females expressed preferences and aversions more subtly. For example, Delphi, a petite adolescent female, found herself pursued by Hector, a middle-aged adult male. She did not run away or refuse to mate with him, but whenever he wasn't watching, she looked around for her friend Homer, an adolescent male. When she succeeded in catching Homer's eye, she narrowed her eyes and flattened her ears against her skull, the friendliest face one baboon can send another. This told Homer she would rather be with him. Females expressed satisfaction with a current consort partner by staying close to him, initiating copulations, and not making advances toward other males. Baboons are very sensitive to such cues, as indicated by an experimental study in which rival hamadryas baboons rarely challenged a male-female pair if the female strongly preferred her current partner. Similarly, in Eburru Cliffs, males were less apt to challenge consorts involving a pair that shared a long-term friendship.

Even though females usually consorted with their friends, they also mated with other males, so it is not surprising that friendships were most vulnerable during periods of sexual activity. In a few cases, the female consorted with another male more often than with her friend, but the friendship survived nevertheless. One female, however, formed a strong sexual bond with a new male. This bond persisted after conception, replacing her previous friendship. My observations suggest that adolescent and young adult females tend to have shorter, less stable friendships than do older females. Some friendships, however, last a very long time. When I returned to Eburru Cliffs six years after my study began, five couples were still together. It is possible that friendships occasionally last for life (baboons probably live twenty to thirty years in the wild), but it will require longer studies, and some very patient scientists, to find out.

By increasing both the male's chances of mating in the future and the likelihood that a female's infant will survive, friendship contributes to the reproductive success of both partners. This clarifies the evolutionary basis of friendship-forming tendencies in baboons, but what does friendship mean to a baboon? To answer this question we need to view baboons as sentient beings with feelings and goals not unlike our own in similar circumstances. Consider, for example, the friendship between Thalia and Alexander.

The affair began one evening as Alex and Thalia sat about fifteen feet apart on the sleeping cliffs. It was like watching two novices in a singles bar. Alex stared at Thalia until she turned and almost caught him looking at her. He glanced away immediately, and then she stared at him until his head began to turn toward her. She suddenly became engrossed in grooming her toes. But as soon as Alex looked away, her gaze returned to him. They went on like this for more than fifteen minutes, always with split-second timing. Finally, Alex managed to catch Thalia looking at him. He made the friendly eyes-narrowed, ears-back face and smacked his lips together rhythmically. Thalia froze, and for a second she looked into his eyes. Alex approached, and Thalia, still nervous, groomed him. Soon she calmed down, and I found them still together on the cliffs the next morning. Looking back on this event months later, I realized that it marked the beginning of their friendship. Six years later, when I returned to Eburru Cliffs, they were still friends.

If flirtation forms an integral part of baboon friendship, so does jealousy. Overt displays of jealousy, such as chasing a friend away from a potential rival, occur occasionally, but like humans, baboons often express their emotions in more subtle ways. One evening a colleague and I climbed the cliffs and settled down near Sherlock, who was friends with Cybelle, a middle-aged female still foraging on the ground below the cliffs. I observed Cybelle while my colleague watched Sherlock, and we kept up a running commentary. As long as Cybelle was feeding or interacting with females, Sherlock was relaxed, but each time she approached another male, his body would stiffen, and he would stare intently at the scene below. When Cybelle presented politely to a male who had recently tried to befriend her, Sherlock even made threatening sounds under his breath. Cybelle was not in estrus at the time, indicating that male baboon jealousy extends beyond the sexual arena to include affiliative interactions between a female friend and other males.

Because baboon friendships are embedded in a network of friendly and antagonistic relationships, they inevitably lead to repercussions extending beyond the pair. For example, Virgil once provoked his weaker rival Cyclops into a fight by first attacking Cyclops's friend Phoebe. On another occasion, Sherlock chased Circe, Hector's best friend, just after Hector had chased Antigone, Sherlock's friend.

In another incident, the prime adult male Triton challenged Cyclops's possession of meat. Cyclops grew increasingly tense and seemed about to abandon the prey to the younger male. Then Cyclops's friend Phoebe appeared with her infant Phyllis. Phyllis wandered over to Cyclops. He immediately grabbed her, held her close, and threatened Triton away from the prey. Because any challenge to Cyclops now involved a threat to Phyllis as well, Triton risked being mobbed by Phoebe and her relatives and friends. For this reason, he backed down. Males frequently use the infants of their female friends as buffers in this way. Thus, friendship involves costs as well as benefits because it makes the participants vulnerable to social manipulation or redirected aggression by others.

Finally, as with humans, friendship seems to mean something different to each baboon. Several females in Eburru Cliffs had only one friend. They were devoted companions. Louise and Pandora, for example, groomed their friend Virgil and no other male. Then there was Leda, who, with five friends, spread herself more thinly than any other female. These contrasting patterns of friendship were associated with striking personality differences. Louise and Pandora were unobtrusive females who hung around quietly with Virgil and their close relatives. Leda seemed to be everywhere at once, playing with infants, fighting with juveniles, and making friends with males. Similar differences were apparent among the males. Some devoted a great deal of time and energy to cultivating friendships with females, while others focused more on challenging other males. Although we probably will never fully understand the basis of these individual differences, they contribute immeasurably to the richness and complexity of baboon society.

Male-female friendships may be widespread among primates. They have been reported for many other groups of savanna baboons, and they also occur in rhesus and Japanese Macaques, capuchin monkeys, and perhaps in bonobos (pygmy chimpanzees). These relationships should give us pause when considering popular scenarios for the evolution of male-female relationships in humans. Most of these scenarios assume that, except for mating, males and females had little to do with one another until the development of a sexual division of labor, when, the story goes, females began to rely on males to provide meat in exchange for gathered food. This, it has been argued, set up new selection pressures favoring the development of long-term bonds between individual males and females, female sexual fidelity, and as paternity certainty increased, greater male investment in the offspring of these unions. In other words, once women began to gather and men to hunt, presto—we had the nuclear family.

This scenario may have more to do with cultural biases about women's economic dependence on men and idealized views of the nuclear family than with the actual behavior of our hominid ancestors. The nonhuman primate evidence challenges this story in at least three ways.

First, long-term bonds between the sexes can evolve in the absence of a sexual division of labor of food sharing. In our primate relatives, such relationships rest on exchanges of social, not economic, benefits.

Second, primate research shows that highly differentiated, emotionally intense male-female relationships can occur without sexual exclusivity. Ancestral men and women may have experienced intimate friendships long before they invented marriage and norms of sexual fidelity.

Third, among our closest primate relatives, males clearly provide mothers and infants with social benefits even when they are unlikely to be the fathers of those infants. In return, females provide a variety of benefits to the friendly males, including acceptance into the group and, at least in baboons, increased mating opportunities in the future. This suggests that efforts to reconstruct the evolution of hominid societies may have overemphasized what the female must supposedly do (restrict her mating to just one male) in order to obtain male parental investment.

Maybe it is time to pay more attention to what the male must do (provide benefits to females and young) in order to obtain female cooperation. Perhaps among our ancestors, as in baboons today, sex and friendship went hand in hand. As for marriage—well, that's another story.

Suburban Chimp

She's a scientific heroine who has the chance to be free—if she can survive

Eugene Linden

Back in 1973, when Eugene Linden wrote *Apes, Men, and Language,* he was an enthusiastic twenty-five-year-old convinced that the ape-language experiments at the Institute for Primate Studies in Norman, Oklahoma, would herald a whole new era in interspecies communication. He believed that by teaching apes to use sign language, scientists would also learn more about the nature of language and intelligence itself. But today Linden finds himself involved in a painful reexamination of the talking apes of the Seventies.

Indeed, many people have begun to debate the experiments' validity. Some researchers, for instance, contend that forcing captive animals to submit to the whims of man undermines the very notion of communication. Others argue that the idea of apes having the capacity for language is so preposterous it should not be investigated at all.

Linden's primary concern, however, is the apes themselves. Today, following the decline of the sign-language studies of the last decade, the Oklahoma apes seem to be on the move—to cages in other primate centers, to AIDS laboratories, to zoos. "Wherever they have gone," Linden says, "all of the chimps still live, to use Jane Goodall's phrase, 'in the shadow of man.' Their various journeys are a pilgrim's progress through an ambiguous moral and scientific terrain in which chimpanzees encounter and con-

tend with the embodiments of the various aspects of man's relationship with our animal nature. Some of these involuntary pilgrims will pay with their lives for our uncertainty about who we are. Apart from any moral questions," Linden adds, "the sagas of some of these animals provide stories of devoted, intelligent, and marvelously strong individuals who have had to deal with challenges for which evolution has not fully prepared them."

Lucy, a captive-born chimp reared as part of a human family by Maurice and Jane Temerlin, became the focus of Linden's most recent book. During Lucy's first 11 years she lived in an attractive ranch house bordered by an expanse of lawns and gardens. Lucy had a sibling (the Temerlins' teenage son Steve) and a pet cat. Her standard of living was considerably higher than that of many of the people who worked with her. At a certain point, though, the Temerlins found they could no longer keep the rambunctious Lucy at home. So they asked the independent, legendarily stubborn Janis Carter, already caring for Lucy on a daily basis, to help rehabilitate the suburban chimp in the wild. What follows is part of Lucy's saga.

Janis happened to arrive at a moment when the Temerlins were beginning to wonder about Lucy's future. Lucy was 11 years old in 1975, and the Temerlins' house and furnishings offered about the same resistance to Lucy that a house of balsa wood might offer

to an exuberant human adolescent. Moreover, the Temerlins could envision a day in the future when their tenuous dominance over Lucy might break down utterly. What could they do if one day Lucy simply refused to obey them? And besides, the Temerlins wanted to live a normal life again. Like so many others who dealt with chimps on a day-to-day basis, they found themselves worn out by the climate of demands that follows from the mere fact of having a chimpanzee around the house.

Although Jane Temerlin does not remember precisely, she says that in late 1976 or early 1977 she and her husband heard about Stella Brewer's work in rehabilitating chimps in the wild. "Once we heard that it might be possible to give Lucy a life in the wild," says Jane Temerlin, "we began to think seriously about the prospect." The reaction around the university was "guarded at best," she says. "People did not come out and say the idea was nutty, but they let us know that they thought it was nearly impossible."

Still, the Temerlins had to do something. Lucy was not only full-grown but, as Jane puts it, "reproductively needy" (meaning that she developed explicit crushes on people). If they did not come to some decision soon, they feared she would be forever denied the possibility of a normal life with other chimps.

When first approached, Stella Brewer was reluctant to take Lucy on, and with good reason. Lucy was fully grown and had no previous experience with the wild. There were no precedents for rehabilitating a fully grown chimpanzee, and Lucy certainly was not a prime candidate for life in the wild by any standard. She had been born and raised in the United States and in pampered upper-middle-class circumstances. Lucy slept on a mattress, sipped soda, developed schoolgirl crushes, and would sit in the living room during the afternoon and leaf through magazines. She was a regular little Private Benjamin.

Even worse, she had little experience with other chimpanzees. Finally, Stella Brewer did not have the prior relationship with Lucy necessary to give her dominance over the chimp.

The communications between the Brewers and the Temerlins occurred not long after Janis Carter had begun working with Lucy. "Janis had developed a good relationship with Lucy," says Jane Temerlin, "which was unusual because she had not been with Lucy for long and because Lucy was full-grown. She shared our concern about Lucy—we would have long talks—and when we asked her whether she would consider the possibility of going with Lucy to Africa, she jumped at the chance."

The offer to have someone accompany Lucy and ease the transition ultimately caused Stella Brewer to change her mind. For the Temerlins, who could see no attractive alternative destiny for Lucy at home, it seemed like a worthwhile gamble. At least Lucy would have a chance to lead the life nature had crafted for her.

Still, it was in retrospect a somewhat haphazard expedition. The idea that Lucy, the fastidious, toilet-trained chimpanzee princess, could make it in the wild stretched the odds to the limit. And despite Janis's relationship with the chimp and her willingness to accompany Lucy, there was little in her background to suggest that Janis was prepared for the rigors she would face. She did not even like camping!

And indeed, the first few months of the experience seemed to bear out all those who felt that the plan was ill conceived. The Temerlins returned to the United States after about a week, but Janis says she could see almost from the moment she arrived that there was no possibility she would return in a few weeks as planned. For one thing, according to Janis, the Brewers were totally unprepared for their arrival. They had made no provision for Lucy and her chimpanzee friend, Marianne, also under Janis's care; and so, at Abuko Reserve (Lucy's first home in Africa), the two chimps were transferred to steel cages that were far more primitive than anything in use at the Institute for Primate Studies. Lucy went into a decline from the moment she arrived and within weeks was an emaciated, hairless wreck—the kind of picture that might show up as the alarmist photo on the cover of a radical animals' rights publication. Because it was feared that once she left her cage no one would be able to get her back into it, the cage could not be properly cleaned, and her circumstances degenerated rapidly into utter squalor.

'Lucy slept on a mattress, sipped soda, had schoolgirl crushes, and would sit in the living room all afternoon leafing through magazines. She was a regular little Private Benjamin.'

Marianne fared a little better. She had not led a life as privileged as Lucy's, and the transition, while traumatic, was still less stressful than it was for Lucy.

Nor did Janis make any headway in her efforts to help Lucy to learn the ways of a wild chimp. "I would give her netto [a sweet, edible seed pod], and she would throw it away," Janis recalled later on. She tried everything to teach Lucy wild behavior. She would sign to her, talk to her, and in general try to bring the wilds to her. But given the circumstances, it is little wonder that these early lessons bore little fruit. Abuko Reserve is right on the outskirts of Banjul, the capital of

The Gambia, well served by roads and frequently visited by tourists and locals. The complex where Lucy and Marianne were kept was a zoolike series of cages. While there remained the promise that Lucy might eventually move to a more secluded area, the immediate reality was that though Lucy was in Africa, she was in a zoo—and not a zoo that compared favorably with zoos in the United States.

To all appearances the effort was a dismal failure. Janis's health was suffering as well. Concerned about her welfare, the Temerlins wrote Janis and encouraged her to come home. After supporting Janis for a year, they began to feel financial strains, and they greatly reduced her support. There was reason to believe that Janis Carter would soon return to the United States. But she didn't.

I kept hearing reports about Lucy's life in Africa. Although most of these reports stressed the hazards Lucy and Janis faced and the inappropriateness of trying to educate a suburbanite like Lucy for the wilds, I still felt that perhaps what Janis was doing offered the only glimmer of hope for captive chimps.

And so I went to The Gambia in July 1982 to visit Janis Carter and to see for myself how things were working out. At the point I visited The Gambia, Janis was dividing her time between Banjul and the Baboon Islands, a more remote preserve she had found for the chimps. From her account it appeared that her first years in The Gambia had been only slightly less difficult than Lucy's. She had spent her time in Abuko living in an eight-foot-square tree house in the reserve. While there she learned what she could about which plants and fruits were edible and which were not and when various plants and trees bore fruit. It was while she was in Abuko that she had an unfortunate run-in with safari ants. Safari ants are a distinctive feature of the African landscape. They march in columns, and woe to any edible thing that happens to be in their path. In this case it was Janis. One night, asleep within the customary protection of mosquito netting, she woke to find that strands of her hair had fallen through the netting and that ants had begun to climb over her body. She looked around the room to discover that she and her entire room were virtually carpeted with the ants. She knew that safari ants had killed Buddha, a favorite adult male chimp at Abuko, and intimations of her own mortality passed through her mind. She saw little spiders jumping around that were being eaten alive. She ripped off her ant-covered nightclothes and then had to climb down the ladder, also covered with ants. When she tried to brush them out of her hair, the ants bit into her scalp. Her inability to get at them brought her close to the edge of panic, and naked, she ran the mile to the Brewers' house, where together they killed the remaining ants with alcohol. It was an experience she remembered five years later with a shudder.

Apart from Janis's traumas, progress in teaching Lucy to adapt was slow to the point of being virtually unnoticeable.

Finally, after some time in Abuko, Janis moved Lucy, Marianne, and some other, younger chimps (former captives also awaiting repatriation to the forests) upriver to the Baboon Islands. And the move put Janis and her chimps in a setting that was much closer to what Janis had envisioned when she left the states for Africa. On Baboon Island there was the possibility that Lucy might pull herself together.

Dash, the oldest male, was only five when they moved to the island in May 1979. The dominant figure was Janis, and the dominant chimp was Lucy, a female. She would not have been the dominant chimp if there had been an adult male around or even a strange adult female, but the only other large chimp in the group was Marianne, who was several years Lucy's junior. Lucy certainly did not dominate by reason of her knowledge of life in the bush. During the first year on Baboon Island, she would surely have been glad to exchange her new life for a motel room.

Janis's home on the island was a cage built by some obliging commandos from the British armed forces who were on bush maneuvers nearby when Janis first moved to Baboon Island. And so she lived in the cage while the chimps slept outdoors. The evidence is that at first the chimps would have loved to reverse this situation. They would sleep on top of her cage, and when they were frightened, which was not infrequently, they would relieve themselves on Janis. She quickly took care to get something to protect her from the various elements, and she also took steps to encourage the chimps to sleep elsewhere.

Although she had the cage, at first Janis spent a good deal of time sleeping outside with the chimps. She wanted to teach them quickly about living in trees. This is where chimps ordinarily sleep, and it is also a lot safer for them than sleeping on the ground.

She built a platform in a nearby tree and would bend branches and leaves into a nest. The platform served as a halfway house in getting Lucy and Marianne off the ground. Before too long Lucy began to sleep in trees, but she would sleep in the fork of sturdy branches rather than out among the leaves, like the other chimps. So far as I know, Janis has been unable to get the earthbound Lucy to move beyond her safe but uncomfortable fork hostels. Although the other chimps have learned to build nests out among the leaves, unlike wild chimps they will use a nest more than once, a practice that quickly leads to some squalid accommodations.

Moreover, Janis could not force the chimps to move each night for sanitary reasons. Since she had had to teach them by example, she would have had to risk her own neck in attempting to build a new nest in a high place every day. It was a risk she could not afford to take, for if she had fallen and broken a bone or two she would have had only the chimps to provide her with the necessary first aid.

Teaching by example meant eating all the foods the chimps should eat and hoping that they would emulate her. When she saw an edible leaf Janis would imitate chimp food barks and point the way. If the leaves were in a tree, Janis would climb to a low branch and enthusiastically munch on the leaves, making satisfied grunts to let the chimps know that they were missing out on a real treat.

While Lucy eventually began to eat wild-grown foods that Janis had gathered for her, she resisted gathering food herself.

For the first year Lucy clung to her relationship with Janis. She would not groom other chimps, and she would not drink from the river. "Lucy saw me drinking from a bottle," says Janis, "and that's what she wanted to do."

'When she saw an edible leaf Janis would imitate chimp barks and point the way. If the leaves were in a tree, Janis would climb to a branch and munch on them, making satisfied grunts.'

Lucy's first big breakthrough came when she learned to gather the leaves and flowers of the baobab tree. Even more important, she eventually learned to crack the baobab fruit. According to Janis, "It was as if everybody else knew it was her first time because they all stopped what they were doing and watched."

But despite small victories, progress was slow, and Janis remembers that even after a year on the island she was still thinking that perhaps she had made a mistake in bringing Lucy there and that all her efforts might have been for naught. At the time Janis was severely stretched financially, and she felt stretched in every other way as well. At this low point the chimps did something that infuriated Janis but that turned out to be a turning point in Lucy's adaptation to the wild.

What they did was to tear down the back of Janis's cage. "This may sound sick," Janis recalls, "but I was so mad at the ungratefulness, I remember thinking, *They're not going to have any more food; they can either make it or not make it.*

"Lucy got pathetically thin. She would just sit there and sign all the time: Food . . . drink . . . Jan come out . . . Lucy's hurt. She would whine and start pulling out her hair. It was so hard to ignore it, and what I finally had to do was to stop her from having visual contact with me. I made her go back and sit behind the cage. I'd say, 'I don't want to see you.' So she would go back around the corner there, back where she could barely, barely see me. Then she would slowly move up until I was in view. This went on for six days. And finally I decided I had to go out and help her be miserable, and so I would go out with the group, and she still wouldn't go away from the cage. It got to the point where I thought she might not have the strength to go on, and I started going shorter distances.

"Then one day she just broke. I was at my absolute wits' end. I didn't think she was going to eat a leaf. I didn't think she was going to do anything, and we had fight after fight after fight. We fell asleep on the ground next to each other—we weren't having contact with each other—and when I woke up it was as though she had decided during her nap that she was going to start

trying. She sat up and picked a leaf within arm's reach and handed it to me to eat it, and I ate it and then shared it with her. After that she started trying. I don't know how much longer she could have gone on, or myself, either. I was at my absolute limit."

Janis describes her role as that of a psychologist who has to break down barriers before behavior can change. Her total repudiation of Lucy succeeded where her cajolings had failed. From this point on Lucy made steady progress, learning from Janis as well as from the wilder chimps.

A year after my visit Lucy became very ill. I had put Janis in touch with Jim Mahoney of the Laboratory for Experimental Medicine and Surgery in Primates, and he flew over to examine Lucy and the other chimps. His secondary purpose was to see whether Janis's approach was a viable alternative to the grim destiny facing chimps in laboratories in the United States.

When Mahoney saw Lucy she was extremely thin and weak. He diagnosed the illness as chronic anemia, possibly brought on by hookworm.

Because the chimps are on a fairly small island they tend to follow regular paths through the bush, and this increases the likelihood of hookworm. Without treatment Mahoney feels that Lucy would have been dead in a matter of weeks. The treatment consisted of two transfusions and a diet supplement.

During the six days Lucy spent in captivity Mahoney says that she began to revert to her dependent state. Mahoney also says that the health crisis threw Janis into a profound depression about whether Lucy and the other chimps might ever be free.

Jim Mahoney came back from his trip impressed with the effort Janis had put into habituating her charges to the wild but daunted by the prospect of doing what she had done for more than a limited number of chimps. Lucy, he adds, was not a proper candidate for rehabilitation because of her extreme identification with people. On the other hand, whatever her future, Lucy has for a few years lived the life of a chimp in the wild—something only she and Marianne out of 1,700 captive chimps in America have had a chance to do.

Lucy's Uncommon Forebear

The first systematic studies of pygmy chimpanzees suggest that this isolated and nearly extinct ape may provide the best model for understanding the evolution of arboreal ape into primitive man

Wray Herbert

In 1928, Harvard University zoologist Harold J. Coolidge was examining a collection of chimpanzee skulls at the Congo Museum in Terveuren, Belgium, with a mind to revising the taxonomy of living apes. Having already examined similar collections in Stockholm, London, Berlin, Paris and Brussels, Coolidge felt quite comfortable with the existing evidence of African chimpanzees. He expected nothing untoward.

This past summer, while addressing the International Primatological Society in Atlanta, Coolidge recalled that day: "I shall never forget, late one afternoon, I casually picked up from a storage tray what looked like a clearly juvenile chimp's skull from south of the Congo [River], and, to my amazement, the [bones] were totally fused. It was clearly an adult! I picked up four similar skulls in adjoining trays and found the same condition, which I measured up for my future paper on revision of chimpanzees."

The "future paper," published in 1933, contained no minor revision of ape taxonomy. For what Coolidge had stumbled upon in Terveuren was the first evidence of a previously unknown species of living ape, a pygmy chimpanzee. The new species, which he names *Pan paniscus,* immediately attracted the attention of the scientific community, and pygmy chimpanzees were soon identified in several zoo populations. What struck observers most about these apes was how unlike common chimpanzees they were in demeanor and behavior. They were less robust in body build and facial features; more versatile in movement; and, by some reports, more communicative and sociable. Without knowing he was describing a pygmy chimpanzee, Yale zoologist Robert M. Yerkes had a few years before written of the extraordinary alertness, sociability and intelligence of a diminutive chimp called Prince Chim. He titled his book *Almost Human.*

If Coolidge was unprepared for his zoological coup, he must certainly have been unprepared for the revisions that his discovery would push upon the theory of human evolution. How would such an uncommon ape fit into the existing phylogenetic tree, which at the time had humans evolving on a separate branch from all the living apes? Raymond Dart had only a few years before discovered the first Australopithecine, or ape-man, in South Africa, and anthropologists were quickly converging on the idea that all living apes (including humans) must have shared a common ancestor—the so-called "missing link." But what would such an animal have looked like before it speciated into such different creatures as chimpanzees, gorillas and man?

For some, the newly discovered pygmy chimpanzee, graceful and human-like, provided the perfect answer: *Pan paniscus,* Coolidge declared in 1933, offered the best model for understanding the missing common ancestor. By observing an extant beast, Coolidge suggested, scientists could actually catch a glimpse of what the earliest humans must have looked like in action.

Despite the boldness of Coolidge's evolutionary model, it languished, neither accepted nor discredited, until quite recently. The reason the pygmy chimpanzee had gone undiscovered for so long is that it lives only in an inaccessible jungle region of equatorial Africa—part of what is now the Republic of Zaire. For the same reason the pygmy chimp (or "bonobo," as it is known in that region) continued relatively unobserved and unstudied for another generation; and the "bonobo model" of human evolution obscured itself in the scientific literature.

All of that changed in recent years, as a new generation of anthropologists dusted off the Coolidge model and began an intensive search for data to support or reject it. Beginning in the 1960s, young scientists turned increasingly to pygmy chimpanzees as the focus of their research: Vincent M. Sarich undertook a biochemical study of living apes; Donald C. Johanson concentrated on the teeth; Adrienne L. Zihlman studied the post-cranial skeleton; Douglas L. Cramer, the skull; and Randall L. Susman headed for Zaire to find out how pygmy chimpanzees actually behaved in the wild. A decade later, these scientists remain embroiled in an ongoing dispute about *Pan pan-*

iscus and its importance to an understanding of human origins.

Sarich, now at the University of California at Berkeley, was the first in the fray. Using new techniques to compare the proteins (and the genetic material) of the living apes, he and biochemist Allan C. Wilson (also of Berkeley) demonstrated in the 1960s that the structure of DNA of humans, chimpanzees and gorillas varied by less than 2 percent; humans, that is to say, were shown to be as biochemically intimate with gorillas and chimps as they are with each other. The implication of this work was that the three apes had split, or speciated, at the same time, and using the biochemical data the scientists devised a "molecular clock" to estimate the timing of that evolutionary split: contrary to the generally accepted estimate of 15 million years ago, they put the date at 4 to 5 million years. Echoing Coolidge's declaration of 1933, Sarich suggested again that the common ancestor (now not nearly so ancient as believed) must have looked something like a small chimpanzee.

Given this start, other scientists began to ask: what is there in the anatomy and behavior of living pygmy chimps, and in the fossil evidence of ancient hominids, to support such a view? Along with Sarich, Zihlman (of UC Santa Cruz) and Cramer (of New York University) have become the champions of the bonobo model, and they have based their claims primarily on studies of the anatomy of living apes and fossilized hominids. Sarich's biochemical data indicate that the two species of chimpanzee split about 2 to 3 million years ago, so that the pygmy chimp is fundamentally a chimp; but according to Zihlman, a comparative study of the limb bones reveals that the pygmy chimp is more "primitive" than its common cousin. In other words, it has gone through fewer specialized adaptations and therefore most closely resembles the ancestral condition.

To make her point, Zihlman compares the pygmy chimpanzee to "Lucy," one of the oldest hominid fossils known, and finds the similarities striking. They are almost identical in body size, in

stature and in brain size, she notes, and the major differences (the hip and the foot) represent the younger Lucy's adaptation to bipedal walking (Lucy, officially called *Australophithecus afarensis,* had been dated at 3.6 million years, although that date has recently been challenged [SN: 1/11/83, p. 5]). These commonalities, Zihlman argues, indicate that pygmy chimps use their limbs in much the same way that Lucy did—and that they inherited those habits from the same ancestor.

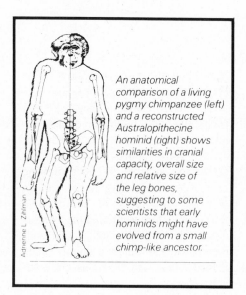

An anatomical comparison of a living pygmy chimpanzee (left) and a reconstructed Australopithecine hominid (right) shows similarities in cranial capacity, overall size and relative size of the leg bones, suggesting to some scientists that early hominids might have evolved from a small chimp-like ancestor.

Adrienne L Zihlman

In contrast to the shared traits of pygmy chimps and early hominids, Zihlman says, the common chimpanzee has legs that are shorter and arms that are longer, relative to its body size. Zihlman also made estimates of the muscle and tissue mass of an animal like Lucy and compared it to that of modern apes: only the pygmy chimpanzee, with its strong legs, smaller arms and slender chest, closely matches Lucy. What this suggests, according to Zihlman, is that the pygmy chimpanzee is more flexible than other modern apes; a common ancestor would have to be flexible—somewhere between a strict quadriped and a strict biped —in order to evolve simultaneously into man and ape.

The major critics of the pygmy chimpanzee model have been Johanson, discoverer of Lucy, and his co-workers—Tim D. White of Berkeley, C. Owen Lovejoy of Kent State Uni-

versity and Bruce Latimer of the Cleveland Museum of Natural History. They say that Zihlman has gone far beyond the fossil data in her interpretation. Johanson, who is director of the Berkeley-based Institute of Human Origins, argues that the pygmy chimpanzee may actually be a specialized, derived form of ape, whose anatomy is adapted specifically to the isolated jungle habitat that it now inhabits. Zihlman's anatomical comparisons Johanson says, reveal only a similarity in size and say nothing about common locomotive adaptations or taxonomic proximity; the same comparisons, he says, would show the pygmy chimp to be related to an American black bear.

Furthermore, Johanson and his colleagues say, the proponents of the pygmy chimpanzee have failed to explain some significant contrasts between bonobos and Lucy. Specifically, they note, the pygmy chimpanzee's teeth are much smaller and less rugged than those of the early hominids; and secondly, the male and female bonobos differ very little in anatomy, whereas the earliest hominids were extremely sexually dimorphic.

Zihlman and Sarich both concede that these differences exist. But in putting forth the bonobo model, they say, they were not trying to reconstruct the hominid *A. afarensis;* they were trying to reconstruct the common ancestor of chimpanzees, gorillas and *A. afarensis.* "That's one step further back," says Sarich. "We assume that *afarensis* is highly derived in certain features. Specifically it's an open country ape, which makes it much different. The common ancestor was almost certainly not an open country form." Lucy's rugged dentition, they say, could have evolved very rapidly as the species moved from the forests into the savannas and began dealing with heavy, rough food.

Similarly, Zihlman says, the sexual dimorphism of *A. afarensis* could have evolved very rapidly; as the ape-like race emerged from the jungle to take advantage of the resources of the savanna mosaic, she says, the male of the species probably became larger to provide the necessary protection against predation. Sexual dimorphism is one characteristic, Zihlman says, that can evolve rapidly in either direction, so that the extreme male-female differences of *A. afarensis* could easily appear in a brief period of evolutionary time—2 million years—and then disappear (as they have) in modern humans. Another possibility, however, is that *A. afarensis* is not as dimorphic as Johanson and his colleagues maintain; what they interpret as males and females of the same species, Zihlman says, may very well be two different species.

Susman rejects the extremism of both the Zihlman and the Johanson arguments, suggesting that, while the bonobo may not be a living replica of Lucy's predecessor, it nevertheless has a special role to play in illuminating that animal's nature. The idea of evolutionary modeling, he says, is to construct a mosaic of anatomical features, drawing on all the living apes to piece together a unique hypothetical ancestor; the pygmy chimpanzee might indeed be the best model for that ancestor's stature, but the common chimpanzee might be a more appropriate model for the sexual dimorphism of the species. (Susman agrees with Johanson that the small and large *A. afarensis* fossils are anatomically similar, most likely representing a single species.) In any case, he says, in order to make sense of the anatomical differences and similarities between living and long-dead apes, it is necessary to observe living apes in the forest—the ecological setting in which the common ancestor was most likely to have lived. The bonobo is the only true forest dweller among modern apes, and as a result it alone can model what the common forebear was doing 5 million years ago.

Only recently, with the completion of Susman's 18-month study of pygmy chimpanzees in the Lomako Forest of Zaire, has such evidence been available. Because almost all previous observation of pygmy chimpanzees had involved the dozen or so animals in captivity, it was unclear how much of the observed "human" behavior was a consequence of scientists' tendency to humanize their laboratory animals; much of it is, Susman concludes. But hours of observation along the Zaire River have confirmed that the bonobo is a unique ape—if not more human, then at least more flexible in its behavior than gorillas, humans or common chimpanzees.

Susman and his colleagues Noel and Alison Badrian have found, for example, that the pygmy chimpanzee is different from the other African apes in terms of sexual behavior; specifically, the females have extraordinarily long periods of sexual receptivity, like humans, and like humans they tend to mate front to front. From an evolutionary point of view, this evidence suggests one of two things: that humans and pygmy chimpanzees, once on their own evolutionary tracks, developed this behavior separately or that such sexual behavior was once an ancestral characteristic.

Susman also discovered that pygmy chimps have a unique style of locomotion. Like modern gorillas they tend to be knuckle-walkers on the ground, yet they seem to be natural bipeds, too, frequently walking upright both on the ground and in the trees. And even more important, Susman says, is that when they are in the trees, the pygmy chimps are by far the most acrobatic of the apes, capable of arm swinging, leaping and diving. This documented behavior is consistent with Susman's own anatomical studies, which have shown that the bonobo's shoulder blade, arm and hand are well adapted for arboreality—the primitive condition, according to Susman. Where it is difficult to conceive of a well-adapted terrestrial biped evolving into an agile arboreal animal, an animal with the locomotor flexibility of a pygmy chimpanzee could reasonably have speciated into both the arboreal African apes and the highly specialized human biped.

Susman's group has also gathered extensive data on social and feeding behaviors of living bonobos, and they are beginning to piece together a picture of what the hypothetical 5-million-year-old ancestor might have looked like. "What we have is a unique animal that didn't behave like any animal does today," Susman says. "It climbed trees and probably nested in trees. It weighed 60 pounds. It ate mostly fruit but perhaps some meat. It spent its nights and early mornings in trees, but it probably moved between patches of forest during the day by walking bipedally. It did not have tools or a tool-making hand, and it had a small brain."

So what adaptive advantage would such an animal have as the Pliocene age came to an end—a time when, most agree, the forests were disappearing? What was it that propelled humans on their special evolutionary track while keeping chimpanzees and gorillas—with 99 percent of the same DNA—in the woods? If the answer remains unclear, Susman thinks it is because scientists have been looking in the wrong place; because it is easier to observe animals in the open savannas, he says, anthropologists have tended to think of evolution exclusively in terms of a human adaptation to the open country life. But to the extent that the pygmy chimpanzee is a helpful model, he says, it indicates that Lucy's ancestors spent a lot of time in the trees—even while they were adapting to bipedalism. "We ought to be thinking about pygmy chimpanzee ecology as an interesting source of information about early human ecology," Susman concludes. "Perhaps early humans used their bipedalism to walk from one riverine region to another during an era when the forests were shrinking. If you're a novice biped, a novice hunter and a novice eater and you don't have real great tools, it seems to me you could best do your apprenticeship in a forest."

The Fossil Evidence

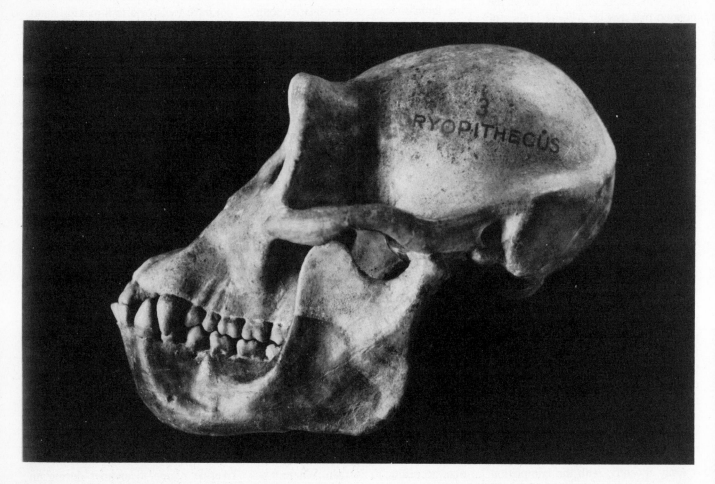

The central focus of this book as well as the whole of biological anthropology is the search for, and interpretation of, the fossil evidence for hominid (meaning human or human-like) evolution. Paleoanthropologists are those who carry out this task by conducting the painstaking excavations and detailed analyses that serve as a basis for understanding our past. Every fragment found is cherished like a ray of light that will help to illuminate the path taken by our ancestors in the process of becoming us. At least, this is what we would like to believe. In reality, each discovery leads to further mystery and for every fossil-hunting paleoanthropologist who thinks his or her find supports a particular theory, there are many others anxious to express their disagreement.

How wonderful it would be, we sometimes think in moments of frustration with inconclusive data, if the fossils would just speak for themselves and every primordial piece of humanity were to carry with it a self-evident explanation for its place in the evolutionary story. Paleoanthropology would then be more of a quantitative prob-

lem of amassing enough material to reconstruct our ancestral development rather than the qualitative problem of interpreting what it all means. It would certainly be a simpler process, but would it be as interesting? In "New Fossil Is Forcing Family Tree Revisions," for example, John Noble Wilford shows us how just one fossil find, and not even one of our direct ancestry, can throw the whole field of early hominid evolution into disarray, causing anthropologists to rethink treasured notions and shift away from established positions.

Most scientists tolerate, welcome, or even (dare it be said?) thrive on the resulting controversy, recognizing that diversity of opinion refreshes the mind, rouses students, and captures the imagination of the general public. As J. E. Ferrell describes the situation in "Bone Wars," science seems to have a need for obstacles to overcome, questions to be raised, and differences to be resolved, for without these storytelling elements of western culture, paleoanthropology would be as dry as the bones themselves. After all, adds Ferrell, where would paleoanthropology be without the gadflies, the near-mythic heroes and, least we forget, the research funds they generate?

None of this is to say that all the research and theoretical speculation taking place in the field of paleoanthropology is so highly volatile. Most scientists, in fact, go about their work quietly and methodically, generating hypotheses that are much less explosive and yet have the cumulative effect of enriching our understanding of the details of human evolution. The significance of the human brain size, for example, is not truly revealed without a comparison with body size of a whole range of mammals, particularly primates. (See Stephen J. Gould's article, "Sizing Up Human Intelligence.") The evolution of the human body is addressed in "The Scars of Human Evolution" by Wilton Krogman. Krogman discusses the imperfect adaptations the human race has made when we went from a four-legged to a two-legged mode of locomotion. Pat Shipman, furthermore, shows us in "Scavenger Hunt," how modern technology, in the form of the scanning electron microscope, combined with meticulous detailed analysis of cut marks on fossil animal bones, can help us better understand the locomotor and food-getting adaptations of our early hominid ancestors. In one stroke, she is able to challenge the traditional "Man the Hunter" theme that has pervaded most early hominid research and writing, and simultaneously sets forth an alternative hypothesis that will in turn inspire further research.

As we mull over the controversies outlined in this section, therefore, we should not take them to reflect upon an inherent weakness of the field of paleoanthropology, but rather accept them as symbolic of its strength: the ability and willingness to scrutinize, question, and reflect (seemingly endlessly) upon every bit of evidence. Even in the case of purposeful deception, as recounted in "Dawson's Dawn Man: the Hoax at Piltdown" by Kenneth L. Feder, it should be remembered that it was the skepticism of scientists themselves that finally led to the revelation of fraud.

Contrary to the way some would have it, the creationists coming to mind, an admission of doubt is not an expression of ignorance, but is simply a frank recognition of the imperfect state of our knowledge. If we are to improve upon our understanding of ourselves, we must maintain an atmosphere of free inquiry without preconceived notions and an unquestioning commitment to a particular point of view. To paraphrase Ashley-Montagu, whereas creationism proclaims certainty without proof, science proclaims proof without certainty.

Looking Ahead: Challenge Questions

For better or for worse, how have the "bone wars" affected the field of paleoanthropology?

What effect did the Piltdown hoax have upon paleoanthropology?

In what ways did the "black skull" shake up the family tree?

What evidence is there that human brain size is unprecedented in the natural world?

What is the "Man the Hunter" hypothesis and how might the "Scavenging Theory" better suit the early hominid data?

How would you draw the family tree?

Bone Wars

Take a 3.5-million-year-old woman, two big egos and the mystery of human origins and what do you get?

J. E. Ferrell

J. E. Ferrell is an Examiner *science and technology staff writer who walks upright, has a big brain and uses tools exhibiting a high degree of technical sophistication.*

Paleoanthropologists search for fossils of the earliest human ancestors—erect walking primates called hominids—in the vast, hot, quiet African wilderness. Like gamblers transfixed by bone dice, they walk, head down, looking for riches in the detritus of the ages. Bits and pieces of antelope, rhinoceros, elephant and other species litter the ground. Occasionally, among the scraps, they find a dull piece of what looks like rock to anyone else—a hominid fossil, usually an isolated fragment that belongs to a skull. They take it back to a lab, measure it, analyze it, write a paper about it and put it away.

Once or twice in a lifetime, a very few paleoanthropologists get lucky and find enough fragments to compose an unusually complete or different skull or skeleton, one that tells them a great deal about what our ancestors looked like and how they lived. Then come press conferences, elegant theories on how the bones fit into the puzzle of human origins—and fame.

And fighting. While the public sees only the headlines—"New Fossil Find Alters View of Human Evolution"— paleoanthropologists stave off vitriolic attacks by their colleagues. It may take

twenty years of arguing for everyone to agree on where a fossil should hang on the family tree. Behind the calm facade of science, even its practitioners admit, paleoanthropology is like comic opera—complete with shouting matches, venomous accusations of "sloppy science" and appellations such as "charlatan" and "bushwhacker."

The problems of ego obscure other, more serious issues facing this relatively young science. Increasingly, paleoanthropologists are facing a call to reassess the methods as well as the madness in the study of human origins.

Welcome to the top of the bone heap.

A few months before Richard Leakey and Alan Walker formally announced to the world their discovery last summer of the "black skull," a find that would again shift the lineages on the human family tree, Donald Johanson, dressed appropriately for a student audience in pressed tan slacks and a shirt with epaulets, strolled toward a building at Stanford University, where he teaches a course in the study of human origins. Johanson, who had come to fame by finding "Lucy," the oldest, most complete hominid ever discovered, had seen a slide of the black skull, he said. But he dared not comment on it publicly. He speculated that he had been shown the slide because his archrival, Leakey, was trying to set him up, to entice him into talking about the skull before the formal announcement—a paleoanthropological faux pas.

Last May, Johanson and his close friend and fellow researcher Tim White, a UC Berkeley professor of anthropology, announced a discovery of their own: They had found 302 fossil bones and teeth at Tanzania's Olduvai Gorge. It's impossible to talk about this area—part of Africa's desolate Rift Valley, which stretches through Kenya, Tanzania and Ethiopia and cradles the fossils of the earliest humans yet found—without thinking of Louis S. B. and Mary Leakey. The Leakeys come close to being legends in anthropological circles; they brought the focus of humankind's beginnings to Africa and spent more than 40 years finding enough fossils in the dry, scorched earth of Olduvai to kick the infant science of paleoanthropology into respectability. And now here was Johanson suggesting, in an aside at the press conference, that he and his team should go back to sites previously scrutinized—he didn't have to mention the Leakeys by name—for fossils that may have been missed.

Upon hearing of the comment, a friend of Mary Leakey's huffed, "Doesn't Johanson know the meaning of the word 'grace'?"

Of course he does. Johanson is the most graceful gadfly paleoanthropology has ever known. He is Luciano Pavarotti trying to grab history from Enrico Caruso. He is Ted Turner gleefully rankling the established New York Yacht Club. In the last ten years, he has skillfully maneuvered himself, the son of a Swedish immigrant cleaning woman, into the position of paleoanthropology's main antagonist—adamant about the place of "his" fossils in the human origins puzzle, relishing challenges to his judgments. And Richard Leakey, the son and heir to Louis and Mary Leakey's paleoanthropological aristocracy, has been a reluctant, but nevertheless pugnacious, protagonist.

Donald Johanson was, as Duke University anthropologist Matt Carmill has said, "a brash young Ph.D. with a nervous grin and promising Pliocene site," until 1974, when he and his eleven-member French and American team chanced upon the oldest and most complete hominid ever found.

Johanson is the most graceful gadfly paleoanthropology has ever known. He is Pavarotti trying to grab history from Caruso.

Paleoanthropologists had been looking for a common ancestor to the two major branches of hominids for years. One of the branches, which most paleoanthropologists call *Australopithecus,* appears to have become extinct somewhere between 1.5 million and 1 million years ago. *Homo,* the human branch, however, continued to evolve from a species that lived 2 million years ago (*Homo habilis*), to another (*Homo erectus*) at about 1.5 million years ago, to *Homo sapiens* at about 400,000 years ago, and *Homo sapiens sapiens*—us—at about 35,000 years ago.

Johanson danced a jig when he and graduate student Tom Gray discovered the 3.5-million-year-old partial skeleton fossil. He named it Lucy, after "Lucy in the Sky with Diamonds," a Beatles song he and his associates sang long into the African night. He eventually claimed that he had found the common ancestor to both branches of the hominid line. Many paleoanthropologists agree with this hypothesis; Leakey and others do not.

Lucy was the beginning of an astounding streak of luck for Johanson. She was found during the third of six years of field work organized by Johanson in the Afar region of Ethiopia. In the fourth year, Johanson and his team found fossils of at least thirteen hominids, which Johanson lumped together as the "First Family." In the fifth year, they found the earliest-known stone tools.

Johanson was only 31 when he found Lucy, and he wasted little time in capitalizing on his find. In the following years, he and his research associates gave Lucy a scientific name, *Australopithecus afarensis,* the "southern ape from the Afar region"; he co-authored a book, *Lucy,* with noted science writer Maitland Edey (who did all the writing); co-authored a description of Lucy in a scientific journal; and founded the Institute for Human Origins in Berkeley, one of the three major anthropological research organizations in the United States. Today, Johanson eagerly and without apology plays the role of celebrity, fund raiser and publicist—just as Richard Leakey does—for his field. It is part of the responsibility, he says, that come with such a discovery as Lucy.

Six feet tall, with refined features and a curiously delicate head of brown hair graying appropriately at the temples, Johanson has dark eyes that twinkle when he is being charming, a characteristic that he has honed to eliminate all touches of obsequiousness. His gestures, made with strong forearms and large, dexterous hands, are dramatic. Despite his meticulous attention to dress, he lectures before the public in stocking feet. He makes sublime scientific jokes. He slips "The Far Side" cartoons between slides of *Australopithecus* skulls. "I'm a pretty decent lecturer," he says. "I've worked on it and developed it."

Johanson delivers his public jabs at Leakey in cultured, dulcet tones, his face set as a network news anchor's: nonjudgmental, slightly superior, occasionally flashing a wry, boyish grin. Every field of science has its spokesperson, he says. "Deep-sea science has Cousteau. Astronomy has Sagan. Paleoanthropology has Leakey and Johanson."

Those in the Leakey camp would say, churlishly, that they are surprised that Johanson put Leakey's name first. But Leakey does have a certain advantage, notes University of Michigan anthropologist Milford Wolpoff, which is why he is the quieter of the two in the rivalry. "Why not?" says Wolpoff, who is on speaking terms with both men. "He is operating from a power base. He can afford to assume the more gentlemanly role. He doesn't have the same goals."

Leakey, heir to paleoanthropology's aristocracy, is "operating from a power base. He can afford to assume the more gentlemanly role."

Richard Leakey was not, at first, interested in pursuing a career similar to his parents'. For a time, he led wildlife expeditions in Africa. When he was 24, he organized a scientific expedition, more for amusement than serious scientific endeavor. But he discovered two skulls, Kenyan cousins of *Australopithecus* fossils his parents had found in Tanzania, and was hooked. Enticed by the fame afforded paleoanthropologists who discover fossils, he never pursued an academic degree. Instead, he led more expeditions and found more early hominid specimens. He announced the discoveries to the world in the highly respected scientific journal *Nature* and attached his name to the detailed scientific descriptions by his co-researchers in the *American Journal of Physical Anthropology.*

After his father died in 1972, Richard Leakey honed his already charismatic public-relations skills, became director of Kenya's National Museums in Nairobi, gave immensely popular lectures, founded his own fund-raising organization, the now-defunct Foundation for Research into the Origins of Man, and appeared on the cover of *Time* magazine in 1977. Leakey says the issue outsold the one with Cheryl Tiegs on the cover.

Science writer Roger Lewin, author of a fascinating and relatively unbiased book about paleoanthropology called *Bones of Contention[: Controversies in the Search for Human Origins* (1987)], says that the seeds of the public rift between Leakey and Johanson were planted when Johanson changed his mind about where Lucy stood in the family tree. At first, Johanson speculated that Lucy and the other hominids he found in Ethiopia were members of two previously described species. Later, against Mary Leakey's wishes, Johanson and Tim White lumped their fossils together with fossils Leakey found at a site 500 miles away and gave them all a single new species name, *Australopithecus afarensis*. Johanson dropped this bombshell in public, at a Nobel symposium at the Royal Swedish Academy of Sciences in 1978, attended by Mary Leakey.

"Mary Leakey had collaborated freely and congenially with Johanson over their fossils for some years, but the Nobel symposium marked a watershed in their relationship," writes Lewin in *Bones of Contention*. "Until that point . . . Mary Leakey apparently supported Johanson's position [that Lucy was possibly a new species], with some qualifications. But after the symposium she abruptly and dramatically began to dissociate herself from Johanson—an action that undoubtedly influenced the reception of *afarensis* [Lucy] by the paleoanthropological community." The split over Lucy's place in history—a scientific debate partly fueled by personal animosity—became public, and paleoanthropologists lined up on either side.

The feud with Richard Leakey, says Milford Wolpoff, began even earlier, after a disagreement between Leakey and then-graduate student Tim White over whether White could publish a paper that referred to a Leakey fossil find. Richard Leakey objected, and White then began working with Johanson. Others say the final break be-

tween the two men came when Johanson published his book *Lucy*, which contained some references to Leakey that he considered derogatory.

To this day, although Richard Leakey grants that the fossils Johanson found were extremely important—any fossils that can be reconstructed into 40 percent of a skeleton are significant in paleoanthropology—he refuses to acknowledge that Lucy is the common ancestry to the *Australopithecus* and the *Homo* lines.

The people who lead expeditions to find fossils become the superstars, whether they actually find the fossils or not, or are good scientists or not.

The last time Johanson and Leakey appeared in a public forum together was on Walter Cronkite's *Universe* in 1981. According to Lewin, Leakey had short notice before appearing on the program and was caught off-guard by Johanson, who came prepared with props: a cast of a hominid skull and a chart.

Although the program was supposed to focus on a general discussion of evolution theory and creationism, it turned to opposing views of the family tree. As Lewin described the confrontation, Johanson said, "It would be fun to show a portrayal of how I see the family tree," and pulled out a neatly drawn chart. He invited Leakey to draw his version on the chart's blank space.

"No, no, no . . . I haven't got crayons . . . I haven't got cutouts . . . I'm not an artist . . . I don't think I can do this," stammered Leakey. Johanson handed him a felt-tip pen. As Johanson began a discussion of the differences of opinion, Leakey finally took the bait. "I think I would probably do that," he said and placed a large X through the carefully drawn tree. Taken aback at Leakey's move, Johanson asked, "Well, what would you

draw in its place?" Leakey replied, "A question mark," and did so.

Johanson continued to outline their differences, and Leakey commented that he would like to see more fossils uncovered. "I would love to prove him right," he said, and paused. "But I might just prove him wrong."

Leakey, who has time and again expressed his reluctance to enter into public controversy, and yet has time and again responded to Johanson's nips, later told Roger Lewin that Cronkite's show was "unfortunate."

Johanson's response: "I won!"

"I'm sick of it," barks Harvard anthropologist David Pilbeam. "I made a decision not to talk about it. In ten years, it won't make any difference one way or another to the science."

"It's male posturing," says Adrienne Zihlman, a paleoanthropologist at UC Santa Cruz.

"It doesn't help the field. It doesn't help students. I've never been a part of it," intones UC Berkeley paleoanthropologist Clark Howell.

"I'll talk about anything else," says Mary Leakey in her soft, English voice, "but not that."

Anthropologists on all points of the pendulum's swing between Richard Leakey and Donald Johanson are exasperated and bored by the rivalry. But many admit that the feuding does some good.

"This affects funding directly," says UC Davis anthropologist Henry McHenry. "The publicity affects how open publishers will be for books. It affects whether there are speaking tours for paleoanthropologists, and it affects private funding."

Private funding is what keep the three major U.S. anthropology research organizations—Johanson's Institute of Human Origins in Berkeley, the L.S.B. Leakey Foundation in Pasadena, and the Wenner Gren Foundation in New York City, the oldest and largest—alive.

Researchers into other kinds of fossils also benefit. "I have a much better chance of getting funding," says paleontologist John Harris, head of the earth sciences division at the Los Angeles County Museum of Natural History, "since my particular animals [antelopes] are associated with fossil humans. If I were dealing with antelopes that lived well before human origins. I wouldn't get any money."

And the rivalry keeps the creationist argument against evolution at bay, says University of Michigan's Wolpoff. "It lets the public know that anthropologists are still out finding things."

But the fixation upon naming fossils and defending their position in the family tree is only one small part of paleo-anthropology. "It makes us look like clowns," says Wolpoff. "In the great scheme of things, it is a tweedly-dee, tweedly-dum issue. It is opera for the public, with chest-thumping and singing."

The debate over whether *Australopithecus afarensis* is the common ancestor also obscures work being done on the different ways hominids—different species of which lived side by side—functioned in their environment, says Adrienne Zihlman. For example, changes in types of teeth over time tell whether hominids ate grains and fruit or flesh, and might say something about whether one branch was more successful in the environment of the plains of Africa after the jungles receded. Changes in the length of limbs might give clues to when hominids spent more of their time on the ground rather than in trees.

But let's face it—the rivalry is an easy way for the media to cover paleoanthropology. The details that paleoanthropologists argue about, journalists and their editors think, are too esoteric for the lay public. When fossils are found, paleoanthropologists write 300-page descriptions that include intricate measurements—length, width, depth, angles—of all the parts. Then they write detailed papers comparing these measurements to previous finds. And then they write papers disagreeing with how others interpreted the finds. They discuss "mastoid processes" and write articles with titles such as "Basicranial Morphology of the Extant Hominoids and Pliocene Hominids: The New Material from the Hadar Formation, Ethiopia, and Its

Significance in Early Human Evolution and Taxonomy." Not sexy at all.

The theories of human origins, critics say, are like classic hero myths: A human struggles out of a lowly place, meets a challenge, overcomes it and rises to the top.

There are some traditional rules of etiquette in the science of paleoanthropology, but not everyone follows them religiously.

The people who lead expeditions to find the fossils become the superstars, whether they actually find the fossils or not, or are good scientists or not. "When you find new fossils, you become a member of the inner sanctum," says Todd Olson, associate professor in the department of anatomical sciences at the City of New York Medical School. "It's almost an unwritten rule that you don't offer a new theory unless you've discovered a fossil. So for people like me [the emerging generation of paleoanthropologists], the inner sanctum would portray us as contentious, but without the credentials to make a critique. They become the priests defending the temple."

There aren't more names associated with recent fossil finds because it is extremely difficult to arrange for the money, the scientists, the support staff and the equipment necessary for an expedition and transport all that to Africa. And then, you have no guarantee that you'll find anything.

To date, the people who have found many of the fossils are named Leakey, says Zihlman, because Louis and Mary lived, worked and raised their three children virtually on top of a cache of early human fossils.

Another unwritten rule is that those few fossil hunters control access to the fossils. Thus scientists wishing to study them have to come knocking at the fossil hunters' door.

The rivalry between Johanson and Leakey has, upon occasion, kept paleoanthropologists from being able to study the forms that make up the raw data of their life's work. Adrienne Zihlman says she was refused a look at Johanson's Ethiopian hominids. Another anthropologist—who prefers anonymity in case he wants to study Johanson's recent Tanzanian finds—says that Johanson is well known in anthropological circles for such behavior. "On the other hand, in Kenya, their attitude is, "Here's the key to the safe and do what you want—just don't break anything." However, Lewin quotes William Kimbel, president of Johanson's Institute for Human Origins in Berkeley, as saying, "In Kenya, Richard Leakey is the guy who determines who gets access to what sites."

It's hard to tell who is the worst offender. The rivalry certainly "makes it more difficult to share results in looking at specimens," as UC Davis anthropologist Henry McHenry says. Dean Falk, a paleoanthropologist at Purdue University, draws an obvious conclusion: "My hunch is that access to fossils breaks down along party lines, whether you agree or disagree with the person or group that has them."

Another unwritten rule is that the fossil hunters have the right of first publication of their finds. It usually takes a full year for the detailed description of a fossil to appear in a scientific journal, so the bones, or their casts, may circulate, as in the case of Leakey's black skull, among universities and research organizations. But it is only when the description has been published that other scientists, using that information as raw data, can publish their critiques or amplifications.

With Lucy and the other hominids, Johanson bent the rules. He published a short article in *Nature* in 1976, another article in *Science* in 1979 and wrote a popular book published in 1981. It wasn't until 1982, when the formal, detailed description of the fossils appeared in the *American Journal of Physical Anthropology*, that other paleoanthropologists, most of whom did not have direct access to Lucy, could begin using the data in their own research. By that time, Johanson was already a star.

Paleoanthropology is not like applied physics or chemistry. "It's an observational and inferential science," says John Harris. "You're not dealing with an entire body of evidence. You're dealing with fragments of fossil that you interpret the best you can. There are occasions where two interpretations are viable, if not equally valid, and so controversy raises it head."

Hominids were very scarce millions of years ago. As UC Berkeley's Clark Howell says, "You see hundreds of antelope crossing the plains. You don't see herds of people." In addition, says William Kimbel, of the Institute of Human Origins, "a carcass faces astronomically infinitesimal odds of becoming a fossil. Thus, the bias on our samples is beyond comprehension."

Paleoanthropologists make their best guess, and then "wait for a new discovery that will prove them wrong," says McHenry. And they often make too much of a little bit of information, says Carl Koch, a paleoanthrpologist at Old Dominion University in Norfolk, Virginia, who studies clam fossils and is breaking ground in statistical sampling to determine more accurately the variation in a single species. "When they find a new fossil, well, that changes the whole idea of what they saw in the past. And that's only because they draw too detailed a picture in the first place."

The sampling bias is complicated by another, more subtle problem. Most paleoanthropologists are westerners, and their hypotheses of human origins have a storytelling theme common to their culture—the classic hero myth: A human struggles out of a lowly place, meets a challenge, overcomes it and rises to the top.

This startling trend was described by Misia Landau in 1979, when she was an anthropology doctoral candidate at Yale, and reported by Lewin in *Bones of Contention*: "The effect in stories of human origins is to make authors view each step in a chain of events as . . . a preparation for the next—the end product, necessarily, to

be *Homo sapiens,*" Lewin writes. "A second element . . . is the idea of progress, that evolution is a program of constant improvement, whose crowing glory is us. And the third . . . is the belief that man is the inevitable outcome of evolution, that we are, in effect, the purpose of it all."

But time does move on. What if the future does not reveal humans as conquering the challenges of the world and managing its riches benevolently? What if the future determines that humans are merely the most complex (self-defined as intelligent) and destructive parasites to infect Earth? The fact that they make beautiful music while they ravage the organism may, in the long run, be incidental.

And in the meantime, the theorists keep juggling their bones in the air. As Lewin quotes David Pilbeam, "Virtually all our theories about human origins were relatively unconstrained by fossil data. The theories are . . . fossil-free or in some cases even fossil-proof. Our theories have often said far more about the theorists than they have about what actually happened."

An example, notes Lewin, is the shift in theory from the 1950s, when "Man the Hunter" and "Man the Killer Ape" dominated paleoanthropology, to the 1980s, when "Man the Social Animal" emerged. There was no change in the fossil record to reflect this, but there was an emphasis on peace and cooperation in our society.

Women in the discipline may bring their own biases to theorizing, but they are beginning to challenge male-authored hypotheses. One rather sexist theory was published in *Science* in 1981, said Dean Falk, a paleoanthropologist at Purdue University and one of the few women in the field. "It said that bipedalism [walking erect] originally developed in males to bring food to helpless females." Women who lug children around on their hips, shop for food and cook dinner while their husbands turn into helpless couch potatoes in front of a television set might offer a different explanation.

Early last year, Donald Johanson was preparing his expedition to Olduvai Gorge, the result of delicate nego-

tiations with the National Museums of Tanzania. Some people advised him to stay away from the area, because it was the place where Louis and Mary Leakey had worked.

In terms of the public rivalry, Johanson was doomed no matter what he did. Ethiopia had been closed to western anthropologists since 1982—a measure of the changes African nationalism holds for the practice of anthropology. If he waited until Ethiopia opened up, people could begin accusing him of resting on his laurels and not keeping up with his rival. And by going to Tanzania, he raised eyebrows among paleoanthropologists still locked into the idea that African land is white Europeans' and Americans' research territory.

That's not to say that Johanson didn't appreciate the irony of the public enemy of the Leakeys going to Tanzania, says McHenry. "He must have been delighted."

And so, the media was interested in his finds both because of where he was and who he was. They would have been less interested if he had announced his latest find in May as some interesting fossils that may or may not be a species of *Homo,* but could be *Australopithecus*. Instead, the headline in the *New York Times* announced: "New Fossil Find Alters View of Man's Evolution."

In fact, several anthropologists disagree wholeheartedly with Johanson's view that the very primitive fossils he found represent a three-foot-tall *Homo habilis,* which used rudimentary tools and was the first human species, and that he can make the conclusion that there was extremely fast evolution between 1.6 million and 1.8 million years to *Homo erectus,* which was six feet tall and had a bigger brain and a more erect stature. "Johanson is piling illogic upon illogic. I can't wait to see the response in *Nature,*" says Zihlman, referring to the journal in which Johanson published his findings, which also is a forum for scientists who disagree with a position to publish their opinions.

But, as it goes, the public usually hears little after the first press conference. No doubt, few are aware that some anthropologists say that Johanson's first find, the indomitable Lucy, was not unique. Although she was the most complete of *Australopithecus afarensis* ever discovered, two other fossils had been found in the 1930s. Ironically, Louis Leakey found a tooth, but he misidentified it as belonging to a monkey; a German named Hans Weinert recognized the pieces as a new species in 1950. It took Johanson's discovery to give the original finds perspective.

Nevertheless, says Olson, "Don and Tim haven't discovered a new species. They usurped a lot of glory."

On it goes at the top of the bone heap. But to Johanson, in some ways, none of it really matters. In his office at Stanford, Johanson leans over a desk to point to a page of *Humankind Emerging* by UCLA professor Bernard Campbell, a text used in human origins classes across the country. He leaned back, stood erect and said, "I'm in the book."

The Scars of Human Evolution

Although man stands on two legs, his skeleton was originally designed for four.
The result is some ingenious adaptations, not all of them successful.

Wilton M. Krogman

Wilton M. Krogman is Chairman of the Department of Physical Anthropology at the Graduate School of Medicine, University of Pennsylvania.

It has been said that man is "fearfully and wonderfully made." I am inclined to agree with that statement—especially the "fearfully" part of it. As a piece of machinery we humans are such a hodgepodge and makeshift that the real wonder resides in the fact that we get along as well as we do. Part for part our bodies, particularly our skeletons, show many scars of Nature's operations as she tried to perfect us.

I am not referring to our so-called vestiges—those tag-ends of structures which once were functional, such as the remnant of a tail at the base of the spine, the appendix, the pineal or "third eye," the misplaced heart openings of "blue babies," or the like. Nor do I mean the freak variations that crop up in individuals. I am discussing the imperfect adaptations the human race has made in getting up from all fours.

We have inherited our "basic patents," as W. K. Gregory of the American Museum of Natural History calls them, from a long line of vertebrate (backboned) ancestors; from fish to amphibian to reptile to mammal and finally from monkey to ape to anthropoid to *Homo sapiens*. In all this evolution the most profound skeletal changes occurred when we went from a four-legged to a two-legged mode of locomotion.

Gregory has very aptly called a four-legged animal "the bridge that walks." Its skeleton is built like a cantilever bridge: the backbone is the arched cantilever; the vertebrae of the forward part of the backbone are slanted backward and those of the rear forward, so that the "thrust" is all to the apex of the arch; the four limbs are the piers or supports; the trunk and abdomen are the load suspended from the weight-balanced arch; in front the main bridge has a draw-bridge or jointed crane (the neck) and with it a grappling device (the jaws). [See Figure 1.]

When all this was up-ended on the hind limbs in man, the result was a terrific mechanical imbalance. Most of the advantages of the cantilever system were lost, and the backbone had to accommodate itself somehow to the new vertical weight-bearing stresses. It did so by breaking up the single-curved arch into an S-curve. We are born, interestingly enough, with a backbone in the form of a simple ancestral arch, but during infancy it bends into the human shape. When we begin to hold our head erect, at about the age four months, we get a forward curve in the backbone's neck region; when we stand up, at about a year, we get a forward curve in the lower trunk; in the upper trunk and pelvic regions the backbone keeps its old backward curve.

But we achieve this at a price. To permit all this twisting and bending, Nature changed the shape of the vertebrae to that of a wedge, with the thicker edge in front and the thinner in back. This allows the vertebrae to pivot on their front ends as on hinges, like the segments of a toy snake. On the other hand, it also weakens the backbone, particularly in the lower back region, where the wedge shape is most pronounced. Heavy lifting or any other sudden stress may cause the lowermost lumbar vertebra to slip backward along the slope of the next vertebra. The phrase "Oh my aching back" has an evolutionary significance!

There are other ways in which the backbone may literally let us down. The human backbone usually has 32 to 34 vertebrae, each separated from its neighbor by a disk of cartilage which acts as a cushion. Of these vertebrae 7 are cervical (in the neck), 12 thoracic (upper trunk), 5 lumbar (lower trunk), 5 sacral (at the pelvis), and 3 to 5 caudal (the tail). Every once in a while the seventh cervical vertebra may have an unusually long lateral process; if long enough, the protruding piece of bone may so interfere with the big nerves going down the arm that it has to be sawed off by a surgeon. Most people have 12 pairs of ribs, borne by the 12 thoracic vertebrae, but occasionally the transverse processes of the next lower segment, the first lumbar vertebra, are so exaggerated that they form a 13th pair of ribs. In some people the lowest (fifth) lumbar vertebra is fused with the sacral vertebrae.

From *Scientific American*, December 1951, pp. 54-57. Copyright © 1951 by Scientific American, Inc. Reprinted by permission. All rights reserved.

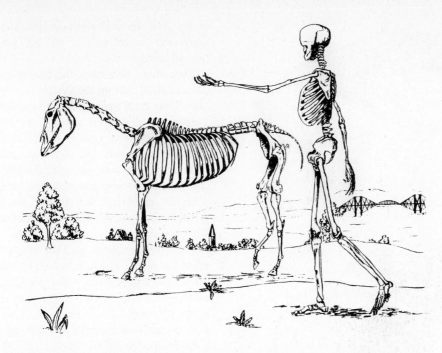

FIGURE 1: Backbones of the horse and man illustrate the principal problem of adapting the quadruped skeleton to biped purposes. The horizontal backbone of the horse is gently arched between two supports, rather like the cantilever bridge in the right background. The vertical backbone of man, in contrast, is curved like an S. (Adapted by Margaret Kowalczyk.)

The latter are usually united into one bone, called the sacrum, but sometimes the first sacral vertebra fails to join with its mates. All these idiosyncrasies can cause trouble.

The "Achilles' heel" of our backbone is the unstable lower end of the vertebral column. This is where we reap most of the evil consequences of standing up on our hind legs. It is a crucial zone of the body—the pathway for reproduction and the junction point where the backbone, the hind end of the trunk and the legs come together. The skeletal Grand Central Station where all this happens is a rather complicated structure consisting of the sacrum and the pelvis. The pelvis is not only a part of the general skeletal framework of the body but also a channel for the digestive and urogenital systems and the coupling to which the muscles of the hind legs are attached. When we stood up on our hind legs, we burdened the pelvis with still another function, namely, bearing the weight of the upper part of the body. How have we changed our pelvis to adapt it to its new position and burdens?

The pelvic structure is made up of three sets of paired bones, the ilium, the ischium, and the pubis. The three bones meet at each side in the hip socket, where the head of the thighbone articulates. In standing erect man tilted the whole structure upward, so that the pelvis is at an angle to the backbone instead of parallel to it. The relative position of the three pelvic bones changed, with the pubis now in front instead of below. The bones also were altered in shape. The iliac bones, formerly elongate and bladelike (in the anthropoids), are now shortened and broadened. They form the crests of our hips, and they help support the sagging viscera, especially the large intestine. The pubic bones help to form the subpubic arch—that "arch of triumph" beneath which we must all emerge to life and to the world. The ischial bones retreat to the rear; they are the bones that bear the brunt of sitting through a double feature or before a television screen. [See Figure 2.]

The greatest change is in the zone of contact between the iliac bones and the wedgelike sacrum—the so-called sacroiliac articulation. Here are focused the weight-bearing stresses set up by the erect posture. Two things have happened to adapt the pelvic structure for "thrusting" the weight of the trunk to the legs. The area of contact between the sacrum and the iliac bones has increased, strengthening the articulation. In the process the sacrum has been pushed down, so that its lower end is now well below the hip socket and also below the upper level of the pubic articulation. This has brought trouble, for the sacrum now encroaches upon the pelvic cavity and narrows the birth canal that must pass the fetus along to life. Furthermore, the changes have created an area of instability which far too often results in obscure "low back pain" and in "slipped sacroiliacs."

The shortening of the iliac bones has increased the distance between the 12th (lowest) rib and the top or crest of the ilium. This has given us our waist, but it has also materially weakened the abdominal wall, which now, for about a palm's breadth, has only muscle to support it. The greatest weakness of the upright posture is the lower abdominal wall. In four-legged animals, the gut is suspended by a broad ligament from the mechanically efficient convex vertebral arch. The burden of carrying the weight of the viscera is distributed evenly along the backbone. Up-end all this and what happens? First of all, the gut no longer hangs straight down from the backbone but sags parallel to it. Secondly, the supporting ligament has a smaller and less secure hold on the backbone. One result of the shift in weight-bearing thrust of the abdominal viscera is that we are prone to hernia.

Nature has made a valiant effort to protect our lower belly wall. She invented the first "plywood," and made it of muscle. Three sheets of muscle make up the wall, and their fibers criss-cross at right and oblique angles. This is all right as far as it goes, but it has not gone far enough: there is a triangular area in the wall which was left virtually without muscular support—a major scar of our imperfect evolution.

The upright posture required a major shift in the body's center of gravity, but here Nature seems to have done a pretty good job. The hip sockets have

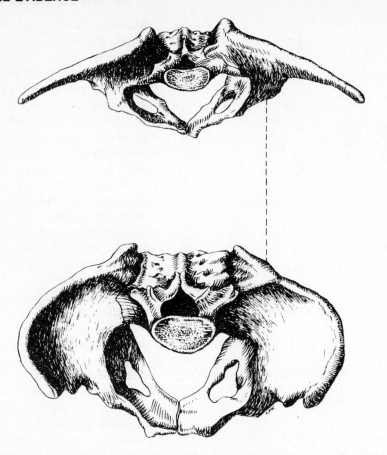

FIGURE 2: Top view of the pelvis of the gorilla (top) and man (bottom) shows how the latter has developed to support the weight of the abdominal organs. The dotted line indicates the width of the sacrum in man. (Adapted by Margaret Kowalczyk.)

ended in a vertical position, become congested more easily, so we get hemorrhoids.

Even more serious is the danger to the circulation along the vertebral column. Two great vessels, an artery and a vein, run down this column. At the level where these vessels divide into two branches, one for each leg, the right-sided artery crosses over the left-sided vein. In a quadruped this presents no problems, but in the erect position the two vessels must cross a sharp promontory of bone at the junction of two vertebrae, and the viscera piled up in the pelvis press down on them. During pregnancy the pressure may increase so much that the vein is nearly pressed shut, making for very poor venous drainage of the left leg. This is the so-called "milk leg" of pregnancy.

Going back to the skeleton, it is clear that the two-legged posture places a much bigger burden on our feet. They have adapted themselves to this by becoming less of a grasping tool (as in the monkeys) and more of a load-distributing mechanism. We have lost the opposability of the big toe, short-

turned to face slightly forward instead of straight to the sides; the sockets and the heads of the thighbones have increased in size, and the neck of the thighbone is angled a bit upward. As a result of this complex of adjustments the bodily center of gravity is just about on a level with a transverse line through the middle of the hip sockets, and the weight of the trunk upon the pelvis is efficiently distributed on the two legs. [See Figure 3.]

Though it does not directly involve the skeleton, I might mention here that the blood circulation is another factor that is not helped by our upright position. Since the heart is now about four feet above the ground, the blood returned to the heart from the veins of the legs must overcome about four feet of gravitational pull. Often our pumping system and veins find the job too much, and the result is varicose veins. The lower end of the large intestine also is affected, for its veins, when up-

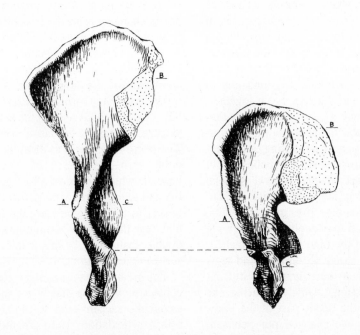

FIGURE 3: Inside view of the hipbone of the gorilla (left) and man (right) shows how the latter has become shorter. The dotted line and the letters A, B, and C indicate similar anatomical features in both structures. (Adapted by Margaret Kowalczyk.)

ened the other toes, and increased the length of the rest of the foot. The main tarsal bones, which form the heel, ankle joint, and most of the instep, now account for half the total length of the foot, instead of only a fifth as in the chimpanzee. We have also achieved a more solid footing by developing two crosswise axes, one through the tarsals and the other through the main bones of the toes. The little-toe side of our foot is relatively neglected—the toe is little because it is not so useful. Our fallen-arch troubles, our bunions, our calluses, and our foot miseries generally hark back to the fact that our feet are not yet healed by adaptation and evolutionary selection into really efficient units.

Now let us go to the other extreme—to the head. A lot has gone on there, too. We have expanded our brain case tremendously, and there can be no doubt that many of the obstetrical problems of Mrs. H. Sapiens are due to the combination of a narrower pelvis and a bigger head in the species. How long it will take to balance that ratio we

have no idea. It seems reasonable to assume that the human head will not materially shrink in size, so the adjustment will have to be in the pelvis: i.e., evolution should favor women with a broad, roomy pelvis.

If the head has increased in size, the reverse is true of the facial skeleton. Bone for bone the face has decreased in size as we proceed from anthropoid to man. To put it succinctly, we have a face instead of a snout.

What about the teeth, in that face of ours? All mammals have four kinds of teeth: incisors in front, canines at the corner, premolars and molars along the sides. With but few exceptions the mammals have both a milk set and a permanent set of teeth. About 100 million years ago, or maybe a bit more, the first mammals had 66 permanent teeth, of which 44 were molars or premolars. Most mammals today have 44 teeth, including 28 molars and premolars. But man, and the anthropoid, has only 32 teeth—8 incisors (upper and lower), 4 canines, 8 premolars, and 12 molars. The loss has been great-

est in molars, next in incisors, then in premolars, with the canine a veritable Rock Of Gibraltar.

While the face bones have decreased in size, our teeth have remained relatively large. Many orthodontists believe that this uneven evolutionary development may be partly responsible for the malocclusion of teeth in children. Certain it is that some human teeth are apparently on the way out: the third molars ("wisdom teeth") are likely to be impacted or come in at a bad angle, and many people never have them at all. Perhaps in another million years or so we shall be reduced to no more than 20 teeth.

It is mayhap a form of human conceit—the egotism born of a highly evolved brain—to worry about our bodily imperfections or inadequacies. As the philosopher said:

The world is old and thou art young;
  The world is large and thou art small;
Cease, atom of a moment's span
  To hold thyself an All-in-All.

Dawson's Dawn Man: The Hoax at Piltdown

Kenneth L. Feder

The Piltdown Man fossil is a literal skeleton in the closet of prehistoric archaeology and human paleontology. This single specimen seemed to turn our understanding of human evolution on its head and certainly did turn the heads of not just a few of the world's most talented scientists. The story of Piltdown has been presented in detail by Ronald Millar in his 1972 book *The Piltdown Men,* by J. S. Weiner in his 1955 work *The Piltdown Forgery,* and most recently in 1986 by Charles Blinderman in *The Piltdown Inquest.* The story is useful in its telling if only to show that even scientific observers can make mistakes. This is particularly the case when trained scientists are faced with that which they are not trained to detect—intellectual criminality. But let us begin before the beginning, before the discovery of the Piltdown fossil.

THE EVOLUTIONARY CONTEXT

We need to turn the clock back to Europe of the late nineteenth and early twentieth centuries. The concept of evolution—the notion that all animal and plant forms seen in the modern world had descended or evolved from earlier, ancestral forms—had been debated by scientists for quite some time (Greene 1959). It was not until Charles Darwin's *On the Origin of Species* was

published in 1859, however, that a viable mechanism for evolution was proposed and supported with an enormous body of data. Darwin had meticulously studied his subject, collecting evidence from all over the world for more than thirty years in support of his evolutionary mechanism called *natural selection.* Darwin's arguments were so well reasoned that most scientists soon became convinced of the explanatory power of his theory. Darwin went on to apply his general theory to humanity in *The Descent of Man,* published in 1871. This book was also enormously successful, and more thinkers came to accept the notion of human evolution.

Around the same time that Darwin was theorizing about the biological origin of humanity, discoveries were being made in Europe and Asia that seemed to support the concept of human evolution from ancestral forms. In 1856, workmen building a roadway in the Neander Valley of Germany came across some remarkable bones. The head was large but oddly shaped (Figure 1). The cranium (the skull minus the mandible or jaw) was much flatter than a modern human's, the bones heavier. The face jutted out, the forehead sloped back, and massive bone ridges appeared just above the eye sockets. Around the same time, other skeletons were found in Belgium and Spain that looked very similar. The postcranial bones (all the bones below the skull) of these fossils were quite similar to those of modern humans.

There was some initial confusion about how to label these specimens. Some scientists concluded that they simply represented pathological freaks. Rudolf Virchow, the world's preeminent anatomist, explained the curious bony ridges above the eyes as the result of blows to the foreheads of the creatures (Kennedy 1975). Eventually, however, scientists realized that these creatures, then and now called *Neandertals* after their most famous find-spot, represented a primitive and ancient form of humanity.

The growing acceptance of Darwin's theory of evolution and the discovery of primitive-looking, though humanlike, fossils combined to radically shift people's opinions about human origins. In fact, the initial abhorrence many felt concerning the entire notion of human evolution from lower, more primitive forms was remarkably changed in just a few decades (Greene 1959). By the turn of the twentieth century, not only were many people comfortable with the general concept of human evolution, but there actually was also a feeling of national pride concerning the discovery of a human ancestor within one's borders.

The Germans could point to their Neandertal skeletons and claim that the first primitive human being was a German. The French could counter that their own Cro-Magnon—ancient, though not as old as the German Neandertals—was a more humanlike and advanced ancestor; therefore, the first true human was a Frenchman. Fossils had also been found in Belgium and Spain, so Belgians and Spaniards could claim for themselves a place within the story of human origin and development. Even so small a nation as Holland could lay claim to a place in human evolutionary history since a Dutchman, Eugene Dubois, in 1891 had discovered the fossilized remains of a primitive human ancestor in Java, a Dutch-owned colony in the western Pacific.

However, one great European nation did not and could not participate fully in the debate over the ultimate origins of humanity. That nation was England. Very simply, by the beginning of the second decade of the twentieth century, no fossils of human evolutionary significance had been located in England. This lack of fossils led French scientists to label English human paleontology mere "pebble-collecting" (Blinderman 1986).

The English, justifiably proud of their cultural heritage and cultural evolution, simply could point to no evidence that humanity had initially developed within their borders. The conclusion reached by most was completely unpalatable to the proud English—no one had evolved in England. The English must have originally arrived from somewhere else.

At the same time that the English were feeling like a people with no evolutionary roots of their own, many other Europeans were still uncomfortable with the fossil record as it stood in the first decade of the twentieth century. While most were happy to have human fossils in their countries, they were generally not happy with what those fossils looked like and what their appearance implied about the course of human evolution.

Java Man (now placed in the category *Homo erectus* along with Peking Man), with its small cranium—its volume was about 900 cubic centimeters (cc), compared to a modern human average of about 1,450 cc—and large eyebrow ridges seemed quite apelike (see Figure 1). Neandertal Man, with his sloping forehead and thick, heavy brow ridges appeared to many to be

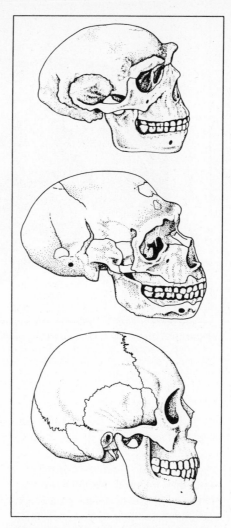

Figure 1 *Drawings showing the general differences in skull size and form between* Homo erectus *(Peking Man—500,000 years ago [top]), Neandertal Man (100,000 years ago [center]), and a modern human being [bottom]. Note the large brow ridges and forward-thrusting faces of* Homo erectus *and Neandertal, the rounded outline of the modern skull, and the absence of a chin in earlier forms. (Carolyn Whyte)*

quite ugly, stupid, and brutish. While the skulls of these fossil types were clearly not those of apes, they were equally clearly not fully human. On the other hand, the femur (thigh bone) of Java Man seemed identical to the modern form. While some emphasized what they perceived to be primitive characteristics of the postcranial skeleton of the Neandertals, this species clearly had walked on two feet; and apes do not.

All this evidence suggested that ancient human ancestors had primitive heads and, by implication, primitive

brains, seated atop rather modern-looking bodies. This further implied that it was the human body that evolved first, followed only later by the development of the brain and associated human intelligence.

Such a picture was precisely the opposite of what many people had expected and hoped for. After all, it was argued, it is intelligence that most clearly and absolutely differentiates humanity from the rest of the animal kingdom. It is in our ability to think, to communicate, and to invent that we are most distant from our animal cousins. This being the case, it was assumed that such abilities must have been evolving the longest; in other words, the human brain and the ability to think must have evolved first. Thus, the argument went, the fossil evidence for evolution should show that the brain had expanded first, followed by the modernization of the body.

Such a view is exemplified in the writings of anatomist Grafton Elliot Smith. Smith said that what most characterized human evolution must have been the "steady and uniform development of the brain along a well-defined course . . ." (as quoted in Blinderman 1986:36). Arthur Smith Woodward, ichthyologist and paleontologist at the British Museum of Natural History, later characterized the human brain as "the most complex mechanism in existence. The growth of the brain preceded the refinement of the features and of the somatic characters in general" (Dawson and Woodward 1913).

Put most simply, many researchers in evolution were looking for fossil evidence of a creature with the body of an ape and the brain of a human being. What was being discovered, however, was the reverse; both Java and Neandertal Man seemed more to represent creatures with apelike, or certainly not humanlike, brains but with humanlike bodies. Many were uncomfortable with such a picture.

A REMARKABLE DISCOVERY IN SUSSEX

Thus was the stage set for the initially rather innocuous announcement that appeared in the British science journal *Nature* on December 5, 1912, concerning a fossil find in the Piltdown section of Sussex in southern England. The notice read, in part:

> Remains of a human skull and mandible, considered to belong to the early Pleistocene period, have been discovered by Mr. Charles Dawson in a gravel-deposit in the basin of the River Ouse, north of Lewes, Sussex. Much interest has been aroused in the specimen owing to the exactitude with which its geological age is said to have been fixed. . . . (p. 390)

In the December 19 issue of *Nature,* further details were provided concerning the important find:

> The fossil human skull and mandible to be described by Mr. Charles Dawson and Dr. Arthur Smith Woodward at the Geological Society as we go to press is the most important discovery of its kind hitherto made in England. The specimen was found in circumstances which seem to leave no doubt of its geological age, and the characters it shows are themselves sufficient to denote its extreme antiquity. (p. 438)

According to the story later told by those principally involved, in February 1912 Arthur Smith Woodward at the British Museum received a letter from Charles Dawson—a Sussex lawyer and amateur scientist. Woodward had previously worked with Dawson and knew him to be an extremely intelligent man with a keen interest in natural history. Dawson informed Woodward in the letter that he had come upon several fragments of a fossil human skull. The first piece had been discovered in 1908 by workers near the Barcombe Mills manor in the Piltdown region of Sussex, England. In 1911, a number of other pieces of the skull came to light in the same pit, along with a fossil hippopotamus bone and tooth.

In the letter to Woodward, Dawson expressed some excitement over the discovery and claimed to Woodward that the find was quite important and might even surpass the significance of Heidelberg Man, an important specimen found in Germany just the previous year.

Due to bad weather, Woodward was not immediately able to visit Piltdown. Dawson, undaunted, continued to work

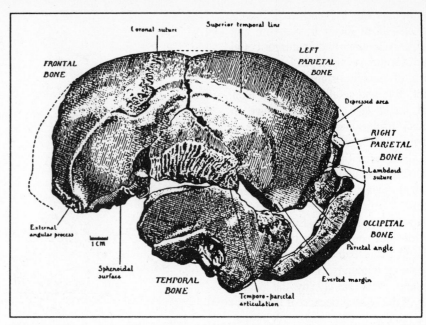

Figure 2 *This drawing with anatomical labels of the fragmentary remains of the Piltdown cranium appeared in a book written by one of the fossil's chief supporters. (From* The Evolution of Man, *by Grafton Elliot Smith, Oxford University Press)*

in the pit, finding fossil hippo and elephant teeth. Finally, in May 1912, he brought the fossil to Woodward at the museum. What Woodward saw was a skull that matched his own expectations and those of many others concerning what a human ancestor should look like. The skull, stained a dark brown from apparent age, seemed to be quite modern in many of its characteristics. The thickness of the bones of the skull, however, argued for a certain primitiveness. The association of the skull fragments with the bones of extinct animals implied that an ancient human ancestor indeed had inhabited England. By itself this was enormous news; at long last, England had a human fossil (Figure 2).

Things were to get even more exciting for English paleontologists. At the end of May 1912 Dawson, Woodward, and Pierre Teilhard de Chardin—a Jesuit priest with a great interest in geology, paleontology, and evolution whom Dawson had met in 1909—began a thorough archaeological excavation at the Piltdown site. . . . More extinct animal remains and flint tools were recovered. The apparent age of the fossils based upon comparisons to other sites indicated not only that Pilt-

down was the earliest human fossil in England, but also that, at an estimated age of 500,000 years, the Piltdown fossil represented potentially the oldest known human ancestor in the world.

Then, to add to the excitement, Dawson discovered one half of the mandible. Though two key areas—the chin, and the condyle where the jaw connects to the skull—were missing, the preserved part did not look anything like a human jaw. The upright portion or *ramus* was too wide, and the bone too thick. In fact, the jaw looked remarkably like that of an ape (Figure 3). Nonetheless, and quite significantly, the molar teeth exhibited humanlike wear. The human jaw, lacking the large canines of apes, is free to move from side to side while chewing. The molars can grind in a sideways motion in a manner impossible in monkeys or apes. The wear on human molars is, therefore, quite distinct from that of other primates. The Piltdown molars exhibited such humanlike wear in a jaw that was otherwise entirely apelike.

That the skull and the jaw had been found close together in the same geologically ancient deposit seemed to argue for the obvious conclusion that

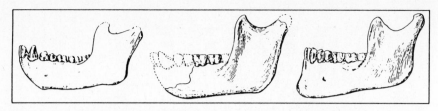

Figure 3 *Comparison of the mandibles (lower jaws) of a young chimpanzee [left], modern human [right], and Piltdown [center]. Note how much more similar the Piltdown mandible is to that of the chimp, particularly in the absence of a chin. The presence of a chin is a uniquely human trait. (From Dawson and Woodward, 1913, The Geological Society of London)*

they belonged to the same ancient creature. But what kind of creature could it have been? There were no large brow ridges like those of Java or Neandertal Man. The face was flat as in modern humans and not snoutlike as in the Neandertals. The profile of the cranium was round as it is in modern humans, not flattened as it appeared to be in the Java and Neandertal specimens (Figure 4). According to Woodward, the size of the skull indicated a cranial capacity or brain size of at least 1,100 cc (Dawson and Woodward 1913), much larger than Java and within the range of modern humanity. Anatomist Arthur Keith (1913) suggested that the capacity of the skull was actually much larger, as much as 1,500 cc, placing it close to the modern mean. But the jaw, as described above, was entirely apelike.

The conclusion drawn first by Dawson, the discoverer, and then by Woodward, the professional scientist, was that the Piltdown fossil—called *Eoanthropus dawsoni,* meaning Dawson's Dawn Man—was the single most important fossil find yet made anywhere in the world. Concerning the Piltdown discovery, the *New York Times* headline of December 19, 1912, proclaimed "Paleolithic Skull Is a Missing Link." Three days later the *Times* headline read "Darwin Theory Is Proved True."

The implications were clear. Piltdown Man, with its modern skull, primitive jaw, and great age, was the evidence many human paleontologists had been searching for: an ancient man with a large brain, a modern-looking head, and primitive characteristics below the important brain. As anatomist G. E. Smith summarized it:

The brain attained what may be termed the human rank when the jaws and face, and no doubt the body also, still retained much of the uncouthness of Man's simian ancestors. In other words, Man at first, so far as his general appearance and "build" are concerned, was merely an Ape with an overgrown brain. The importance of the Piltdown skull lies in the fact that it affords tangible confirmation of these inferences. (Smith 1927:105–6)

If Piltdown were the evolutionary "missing link" between apes and people, then neither Neandertal nor Java Man could be. Since Piltdown and Java Man lived at approximately the same time, Java might have been a more primitive offshoot of humanity that had

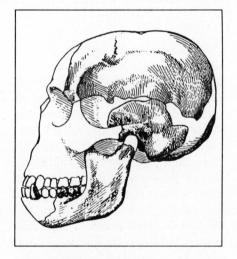

Figure 4 *Drawn reconstruction of the Piltdown skull. The portion of the skull actually recovered is shaded. As reconstructed, the cranium shows hominid (human) traits and the mandible shows pongid (ape) traits. Compare this drawing to those in Figure 1. With its humanlike head and apelike jaw, the overall appearance of the Piltdown fossil is far different from* Homo erectus, *Neandertal, or modern humans. (From* The Evolution of Man, *Grafton Elliot Smith, Oxford University Press)*

become extinct. Since Neandertal was much more recent than Piltdown, yet looked more primitive where it really counted (that is, the head), Neandertal must have represented some sort of primitive throwback, an evolutionary anachronism (Figure 5).

By paleontological standards the implications were breathtaking. In one sweeping blow Piltdown had presented England with its first ancestral human fossil, it had shown that human fossils found elsewhere in the world were either primitive evolutionary offshoots or later throwbacks to a more primitive type, and it had forced the rewriting of the entire story of human evolution. Needless to say, many paleontologists, especially those in England, were enthralled by the discovery in Sussex.

In March 1913, Dawson and Woodward published the first detailed account of the characteristics and evolutionary implications of the Piltdown fossil. Again and again in their discussion, they pointed out the modern characteristics of the skull and the simian appearance of the mandible. Their comments regarding the modernity of the skull and the apelike characteristics of the jaw, as you will see, turned out to be accurate in a way that few suspected at the time.

Additional discoveries were made at Piltdown. In 1913 a right canine tooth apparently belonging to the jaw was discovered by Teilhard de Chardin. It matched almost exactly the canine that had previously been proposed for the Piltdown skull in the reconstruction produced at the British Museum of Natural History. Its apelike form and wear were precisely what had been expected: "If a comparative anatomist were fitting out *Eoanthropus* with a set of canines, he could not ask for anything more suitable than the tooth in question," stated Yale University professor George Grant MacCurdy (1914: 159).

Additional artifacts, including a large bone implement, were found in 1914. Then, in 1915, Dawson wrote Woodward announcing spectacular evidence confirming the first discovery; fragments of another fossil human skull were found (possibly at a site just two miles from the first—Dawson never revealed the location). This skull, dubbed Piltdown II, looked just like the first with a rounded profile and thick cranial bones. Though no jaw was discovered, a molar recovered at the site bore the same pattern of wear as that seen in the first specimen.

Dawson died in 1916 and, for reasons not entirely clear, Woodward held back announcement of the second discovery until the following year. When the existence of a second specimen became known, many of those skeptical after the discovery of the first Piltdown fossil became supporters. One of those converted skeptics, Henry Fairfield Osborn, president of the American Museum of Natural History, suggested:

If there is a Providence hanging over the affairs of prehistoric man, it certainly manifested itself in this case, because the three minute fragments of this second Piltdown man found by Dawson are exactly those which we should have selected to confirm the comparison with the original type. (1921:581)

THE PILTDOWN ENIGMA

There certainly was no unanimity of opinion, however, concerning the significance of the Piltdown discoveries. The cranium was so humanlike and the jaw so apelike that some scientists maintained that they simply were the fossils of two different creatures; the skeptics suggested that the association of the human cranium and ape jaw was entirely coincidental. Gerrit S. Miller, Jr. (1915) of the Smithsonian Institution conducted a detailed analysis of casts of Piltdown I and concluded that the jaw was certainly that of an ape (See Figure 3). Many other scientists in the United States and Europe agreed. Anatomy professor David Waterson (1913) at the University of London, King's College, thought the mandible was that of a chimpanzee. The very well-known German scientist Franz Weidenreich concluded that Piltdown I was " . . . the artificial combination of fragments of a modern-human braincase with an orangutan-like mandible and teeth" (1943:273).

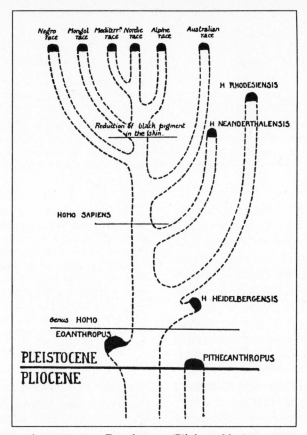

Figure 5 *Among its supporters,* Eoanthropus *(Piltdown Man) was seen as more directly ancestral to modern humanity than either* Homo erectus—*here labeled* Pithecanthropus *and depicted as an entirely separate evolutionary pathway—or Neandertal—shown here as a short-lived diversion off the main branch of human evolution. (From* The Evolution of Man, *Grafton Elliot Smith, Oxford University Press)*

Coincidentally or not, after Dawson's death no further discoveries were made in either the Piltdown I or II localities, though Woodward continued excavating at Piltdown through the 1920s. Elsewhere in the world, however, human paleontology became an increasingly exciting and fruitful endeavor. Beginning in the late 1920s as many as forty individuals of a species now called *Homo erectus* were unearthed at Zhoukoudian, a cave near Beijing in China (see Figure 1). Ironically, Davidson Black, anatomist at the Peking Union Medical College, who was instrumental in obtaining financial support for the excavation, had visited Grafton Elliot Smith's laboratory in 1914 and had become fascinated by the Piltdown find (Shapiro 1974). Further, Teilhard de Chardin participated in the excavation at the cave. The Zhoukoudian fossils were estimated to be one-half million years old. Also on Java,

another large group of fossils (close to twenty) were found at Sangiran; these were similar to those from Zhoukoudian.

Also in the 1920s, in Africa, the discovery was made of a fossil given the name *Australopithecus africanus*. It was initially estimated to be more than one million years old. In the 1930s and 1940s additional finds of this and other varieties of *Australopithecus* were made. In Europe the number of Neandertal specimens kept increasing; and even in England, in 1935, a fossil human ancestor was discovered at a place called Swanscombe.

Unfortunately for *Eoanthropus,* all of these discoveries seemed to contradict its validity. The Chinese and Sangiran *Homo erectus* evidence pointed to a fossil ancestor with a humanlike body and primitive head; these specimens were quite similar to Java Man in appearance (Java Man is also now considered to belong to the species *Homo erectus*), possessing large brow ridges, a flat skull, and a thrust-forward face while being quite modern from the neck down. Even the much older australopithecines showed clear evidence of walking on two feet; their skeletons were remarkably humanlike from the neck down, though their heads were quite apelike. Together, both of these species seemed to confirm the notion that human beings began their evolutionary history as upright apes, not as apelike people. *Eoanthropus* seemed more and more to be the evolutionary "odd man out."

How could Piltdown be explained in light of the new fossil evidence from China, Java, Europe, and Africa? Either Piltdown was a human ancestor, rendering all the manifold other discoveries members of extinct offshoots of the main line of human evolution, or else Piltdown was the remarkable coincidental find of the only known ape fossil in England within a few feet of a rather modern human skull that seemed to date back 500,000 years. Neither explanation sat well with many people.

UNMASKING THE HOAX

This sort of confusion characterized the status of Piltdown until 1949, when a new dating procedure was applied to the fossil. A measurement was made of the amount of the element fluorine in the bones. This was known to be a relative measure of the amount of time bone had been in the ground. Bones pick up fluorine in groundwater; the longer they have been buried, the more fluorine they have. Kenneth Oakley of the British Museum of Natural History conducted the test. While the fossil animal bones from the site showed varying amounts of fluorine, they exhibited as much as ten times more than did either the cranium or jaw of the fossil human. Piltdown Man, Oakley concluded, based on comparison to fluorine concentrations in bones at other sites in England, was no more than 50,000 years old (Oakley and Weiner 1955).

While this certainly cast Piltdown in a new light, the implications were just as mysterious; what was a fossil human doing with an entirely apelike jaw at a date as recent as 50,000 years ago? Then, in 1953 a more precise test was applied to larger samples of the cranium and jaw. The results were quite conclusive; the skull and jaw were of entirely different ages. The cranium possessed .10 percent fluorine, the mandible less than .03 percent (Oakley 1976). The inevitable conclusion was reached that the skull and jaw must have belonged to two different creatures.

As a result of this determination, a detailed reexamination of the fossil was conducted and the sad truth was finally revealed. The entire thing had been a hoax. The skull was that of a modern human being. Its appearance of age was due, at least in part, to its having been artificially chemically stained. The thickness of the bone may have been due to a pathological condition (Spencer 1984) or the result of a chemical treatment that had been applied, perhaps to make it appear older than it was (Montague 1960).

Those scientific supporters of *Eoanthropus* who previously had pointed out the apelike character of the jaw were more right than they could have imagined; it was, indeed, a doctored ape jaw, probably that of an orangutan. When Gerrit Miller of the Smithsonian Institution had commented on the broken condyle of the mandible by saying, "Deliberate malice could hardly have been more successful than the hazards of deposition in so breaking the fossils as to give free scope to individual judgement in fitting the parts together" (1915:1), he was using a literary device and not suggesting that anyone had purposely broken the jaw. But that is likely precisely what happened. An ape's jaw could never articulate with the base of a human skull, and so the area of connection had to be removed to give "free scope" to researchers to hypothesize how the cranium and jaw went together. Otherwise the hoax would never have succeeded. Beyond this, the molars had been filed down to artificially create the humanlike wear pattern. The canine tooth had been

stained with an artist's pigment and filed down to simulate human wear; the pulp cavity had been filled with a substance not unlike chewing gum.

It was further determined that at least one of the fragments of the Piltdown II skull was simply another piece of the first one. Oakley further concluded that all the other paleontological specimens had been planted at the site; some were probably found in England, but others had likely originated as far away as Malta and Tunisia. Some of the ostensible bone artifacts had been carved with a metal knife.

The verdict was clear; as Franz Weidenreich (1943) put it, Piltdown was like the chimera of Greek mythology—a monstrous combination of different creatures. The question of Piltdown's place in human evolution had been answered: it had no place. That left still open two important questions: who did it and why?

WHODUNNIT?

The most succinct answer that can be provided for the question "Whodunnit?" is "No one knows." It seems, however, that every writer on the subject has had a different opinion.

Each of the men who excavated at Piltdown has been accused at one time or another. . . . Charles Dawson is an obvious suspect. He is the only person who was present at every discovery. He certainly gained notoriety; even the species name is *dawsoni*. Blinderman (1986) points out, however, that much of the evidence against Dawson is circumstantial and exaggerated. Dawson did indeed stain the fossil with potassium bichromate and iron ammonium sulfate. These gave the bones a more antique appearance, but such staining was fairly common. It was felt that these chemicals helped preserve fossil bone, and Dawson was quite open about having stained the Piltdown specimens. In an unrelated attack on his character, some have even accused Dawson of plagiarism in a book he wrote on Hastings Castle (Weiner 1955), but this seems to be unfair; as Blinderman points out, the book was explicitly a compilation of previous sources and Dawson did not attempt to take credit for the work of others.

Dawson's motive might have been the fame and notoriety that accrued to this amateur scientist who could command the attention of the world's most famous scholars. But there is no direct evidence concerning Dawson's guilt, and questions remain concerning his ability to fashion the fraud. And where would Dawson have obtained the orangutan jaw?

Arthur Smith Woodward certainly possessed the opportunity and expertise to pull off the fraud. His motive might have been to prove his particular view of human evolution. That makes little sense though, since he could not have expected the kind of confirming evidence he knew his colleagues would demand. Furthermore, his behavior after Dawson's death seems to rule out Woodward as the hoaxer. His fruitlessly working the original Piltdown pit in his retirement renders this scenario nonsensical.

Even the priest Teilhard de Chardin has been accused, most recently by Harvard paleontologist and chronicler of the history of science Stephen Jay Gould (1980). The evidence marshalled against the Jesuit is entirely circumstantial, the argument strained. The mere facts that Teilhard mentioned Piltdown but little in his later writings on evolution and was confused about the precise chronology of discoveries in the pit do not add up to a convincing case.

Others have had fingers pointed at them. W. J. Sollas, a geology professor at Oxford and a strong supporter of Piltdown, has been accused from beyond the grave. In 1978, a tape-recorded statement made before his death by J. A. Douglass, who had worked in Sollas's lab for some thirty years, was made public. The only evidence provided is Douglass's testimony that on one occasion he came across a package containing the fossil-staining agent potassium bichromate in the lab—certainly not the kind of stuff to convince a jury to convict.

Even Sir Arthur Conan Doyle has come under the scrutiny of would-be Piltdown detectives. Doyle lived near Piltdown and is known to have visited the site at least once. He may have held a grudge against professional scientists who belittled his interest in and credulity concerning the paranormal. Doyle, the creator of the most logical, rational mind in literature, Sherlock Holmes, found it quite reasonable that two young English girls could take photographs of real fairies in their garden. But why would Doyle strike out at paleontologists, who had nothing to do with criticizing his acceptance of the occult? Again, there is no direct evidence to implicate Doyle in the hoax.

The most recent name added to the roster of potential Piltdown hoaxers is that of Lewis Abbott, another amateur scientist and artifact collector. Blinderman (1986) argues that Abbott is the most likely perpetrator. He had an enormous ego and felt slighted by professional scientists. He claimed to have been the one who directed Dawson to the pit at Piltdown and may even have been with Dawson when Piltdown II was discovered (Dawson said only that he had been with a friend when the bones were found). Abbott knew how to make stone tools and so was capable of forging those found at Piltdown. Again, however, the evidence, though tantalizing, includes no smoking gun.

A definitive answer to the question "whodunnit" may never be forthcoming. The lesson in Piltdown, though, is clear. Unlike the case for the Cardiff Giant where scientists were not fooled, here many were convinced by what appears to be, in hindsight, an inelegant fake. It shows quite clearly that scientists, though striving to be objective observers and explainers of the world around them, are, in the end, human. Many accepted the Piltdown evidence because they wished to—it supported a more comfortable view of human evolution. Furthermore, perhaps out of naïveté, they could not even conceive that a fellow thinker about human origins would wish to trick them; the possibility that Piltdown was a fraud probably occurred to few, if any, of them.

Nevertheless, the Piltdown story, rather than being a black mark against science, instead shows how well it ultimately works. Even before its unmasking, Piltdown had been consigned by most to a netherworld of doubt. There was simply too much evidence supporting a different human pedigree than that implied by Piltdown. Proving it a hoax was just the final nail in the coffin lid for this fallacious fossil. As a result, though we may never know the hoaxer's name, at least we know this: if the goal was to forever confuse our understanding of the human evolutionary story, the hoax ultimately was a failure.

CURRENT PERSPECTIVES HUMAN EVOLUTION

With little more than a handful of cranial fragments, human paleontologists defined an entire species, *Eoanthropus,* and recast the story of human evolution. Later, in 1922, on the basis of a single fossil tooth found in Nebraska, an ancient species of man, *Hesperopithecus,* was defined. It was presumed to be as old as any hominid species found in the Old World and convinced some that thencurrent evolutionary models needed to be overhauled. The tooth turned out to belong to an ancient pig. Even in the case of Peking Man, the species was defined and initially named *Sinanthropus pekinensis* on the basis of only two teeth.

Today, the situation in human paleontology is quite different. The tapestry of our human evolutionary history is no longer woven with the filaments of a small handful of gauzy threads. We can now base our evolutionary scenarios (Figure 6) on enormous quantities of data supplied by several fields of science (see Feder and Park 1989 for a detailed summary of current thinking on human evolution).

Australopithecus afarensis, for example, the oldest known hominid, dating to more than 3.5 million years ago, is represented by more than a dozen fossil individuals. The most famous specimen, known as "Lucy," is more than 40 percent complete. Its pelvis is remarkably modern and provides clear evidence of its upright, and therefore

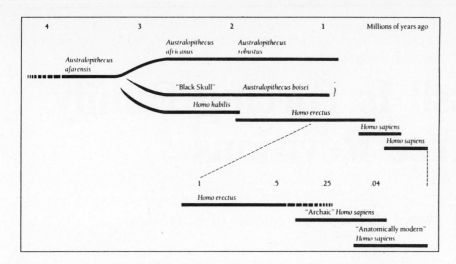

Figure 6 *Current human evolutionary chronologies are based on a large body of paleontological, archaeological, and genetic data. There is no room for—and no need for—a precociously large-brained human ancestor like* Eoanthropus *in the human pedigree. (From* Human Antiquity, *Feder and Park, Mayfield Publishing)*

humanlike, posture. Its skull, on the other hand, is quite apelike and contained a brain the size of a chimpanzee's. We even have a preserved pathway of footprints dating to the time when Lucy and her cohorts walked the earth, showing as dramatically as possible that they did so in a bipedal, humanlike fashion.

Homo erectus is known from dozens of individuals—forty from Zhoukoudian alone, nearly twenty from Java, and more than a dozen from Africa. In Kenya, the 80 percent complete skeleton of a twelve-year-old *Homo erectus* boy has been dated to more than 1.5 million years ago.

Archaic forms of *Homo sapiens,* especially the famous Neandertals, number in the hundreds. The fossil human record is rich and growing. Our evolu-

tionary scenarios are based, not on a handful of fragmentary bones, but on the remains of hundreds of individuals. Grafton Elliot Smith, Arthur Smith Woodward, and the others were quite wrong. The abundant evidence shows very clearly that human evolutionary history is characterized by the precedence of upright posture and the tardy development of the brain. It now appears that while our ancestors developed upright posture and humanlike bodies more than 3.5 million years ago, the modern human brain did not develop until as recently as 100,000 years ago.

Beyond this, human paleontologists are no longer restricted solely to the paleontological record. Exciting techniques of genetic analysis have allowed scientists to develop measures of dif-

ference between living species, including humans and our nearest extant relatives, the apes. Genetic "clocks" have been created from the results of such techniques.

For example, through DNA hybridization, scientists can quantify the difference between the genetic codes of people and chimpanzees. Here, an attempt is made to bond human and chimp DNA, much in the way the separate strands of the DNA double helix bond to produce the genetic code for a single organism. It turns out that the DNA of our two species is so similar that we can form a nearly complete bond. The opinion of most is that our two species could have split evolutionarily no more than five or six million years ago.

New dating techniques based on radioactive half-lives, biomechanical analysis of bones, scanning electron microscopy in bone and artifact examination, and many other new forms of analysis all make our evolutionary scenarios more concrete. It is to be expected that ideas will change as new data are collected and new analytical techniques are developed. Certainly our current views will be fine-tuned, and perhaps even drastic changes of opinion will take place. This is the nature of science. It is fair to suggest, however, that no longer could a handful of enigmatic bones that contradicted our mutually supportive paleontological, cultural, and genetic data bases cause us to unravel and reweave our evolutionary tapestry. Today, the discovery of a Piltdown Man likely would fool few.

New Fossil Is Forcing Family Tree Revisions

'Black Skull' should shed light on cousins of early man.

John Noble Wilford

When the discovery of the provocative "black skull" was announced last summer, the small, contentious fraternity of paleoanthropology was stunned into a rare state of unanimity. Everyone agreed that the skull was the most significant early humanlike fossil to be found in more than a decade. Everyone agreed it would necessitate a major rethinking of the human family tree.

Today, however, it is scholarly business as usual. Nearly everyone in the field has a different notion of how to redraw the family tree to accommodate the surprising and confounding attributes of the 2.5-million-year-old skull.

Although the skull has no bearing on the recent ancestry of modern humans, some proposed changes in the family tree include grafting another intermediate ancestor onto the branch leading to Homo sapiens.

Until now, scientists widely accepted a straightforward two-branch model of the human family tree. About 3 million years ago, according to this model, two distinct branches of hominids began to evolve—probably in competition—from the species Australopithecus afarensis, the first known upright hominid, whose best known member was Lucy. Her skeleton was discovered in Ethiopia in the early 1970's.

One branch, generally called the "robust" line, produced Australopithecus africanus, robustus and boisei before

it turned into an evolutionary dead end. These species were developing many humanlike characteristics before they mysteriously disappeared about 1.2 million years ago. The other branch produced hominids whose evolution culminated in Homo sapiens sapiens—the human race.

Much of the debate, which was aired at recent scientific conferences, centers on the question of whether the skull represents a new fossil species that had heretofore gone unobserved. Its features are a puzzling mosaic of the primitive and the more highly evolved: an apelike jaw and small braincase characteristic of much earlier creatures combined with the huge molars, long concave face and bony crest running along the top that are associated with much later creatures.

Alan Walker, a paleontologist and professor of anatomy at the Johns Hopkins University School of Medicine, found the fossils—a partial lower jaw and a skull lacking most of its teeth—in the summer of 1985. They were in a gully west of Lake Turkana in northern Kenya. The skull is known formally by its museum number, WT-17000. But since the manganese-rich sediments had given it a blue-black patina, the fossil is better known as the black skull.

The skull's features, particularly its protruding jaw, wide palate and enormous cheekbones, showed clearly that it belonged to an early hominid, a member of the primate family of hu-

manlike creatures that includes human beings. But where did it fit in the evolution of other hominids?

In their initial report of the discovery, published last August in the journal Nature, Dr. Walker and his expedition colleague, Richard E. Leakey, executive director of the National Museums of Kenya, chose to identify the skull as belonging to an early member of the "hyper-robust" species Australopithecus boisei. They said it resembled boisei more than any other known fossil hominid.

Dr. Walker and Mr. Leakey recognized that this finding would overturn most current versions of the hominid family tree. Analysis of volcanic ash in the sediments put the age of the skull at 2.5 million years, about 300,000 years earlier than the oldest known boisei fossils.

This meant, for one thing, that Australopithecus robustus could not be the ancestor of boisei, as had been supposed. Instead, the discovery indicated that robustus was a related, smaller species that evolved in parallel with boisei from a common ancestor. The only robustus fossils are found in southern Africa, and the only known boisei fossils come from eastern Africa.

The finding of such an old and massive skull also seemed to contradict the prevalent view that, in robustness and tooth size, the australopithecines grew larger as they evolved. Dr. Walker and Mr. Leakey said that at least some members of the early populations were as large as any later ones.

But as more paleoanthropologists pondered the skull, noting especially its intriguing mix of primitive and advanced features, the feeling grew that this surely was the most important fossil to come out of Africa since Lucy. The cranium, said Donald C. Johanson, director of the Institute of Human Origins in Berkeley, Calif., "provides an intermediate form and therefore represents a classic example of evolutionary change through time."

Dr. Johanson discovered the Lucy skeleton, along with William H. Kimbel of the Institute of Human Origins and Timothy D. White of the University of California at Berkeley. Lucy and similar fossils unearthed in Tanzania that were 3.7 million years old were recognized as belonging to a new species, afarensis.

Dr. Johanson set off a storm of controversy by proclaiming afarensis to be the common ancestor for the two main hominid branches. But most scientists now accept this view.

Scientists had, until the black skull discovery, also generally accepted the two-pronged-fork model of the hominid family tree, which Dr. Johanson and Dr. White proposed in 1979.

Anthropologists who met at the State University of New York at Stony Brook two weeks ago to review thinking about the black skull agreed that nothing about it appeared to displace afarensis from its status as common ancestor.

But the black skull has forced anthropologists to abandon their straightforward model of hominid evolution and consider a variety of new models. The minimum change in the family tree implied by the new fossil produces a three-pronged fork after afarensis.

In this model, favored by Dr. Johanson, the Homo line remains unchanged and a second line leads from afarensis to africanus to robustus. The species that the black skull belonged to is placed in the third line, serving as the intermediate step between afarensis and boisei.

Although Dr. Walker stands by his original contention that the skull repre-

sents an early boisei, the consensus at Stony Brook was that the skull was something new and deserved to be designated as a distinct australopithecine species, according to Frederick E. Grine, a Stony Brook anthropologist who directed the conference. But a few scientists, among them Dr. Johanson and Dr. White, said the skull could belong to a species called Australopithecus aethiopicus.

A consensus emerges that the skull represents a new species.

This species, proposed in 1967 by French scientists, Camille Arambourg and Yves Coppens, is not generally recognized because it is based on a single lower jaw found in Ethiopia. But the age of the jaw, at 2.6 to 2.8 million years, puts it in the same general time as the black skull. Dr. Walker and Mr. Leakey, in their announcement of the discovery, suggested that the new skull might be a specimen of aethiopicus, but concluded that it more likely was an early boisei.

Like many specialists in early human evolution, Eric Delson, an anthropologist at the City University of New York and the American Museum of Natural History, said: "Just because it's big and in east Africa is not enough to say the skull is an early boisei. But it could well be close to the common ancestor of both robustus and boisei."

Dr. Delson's proposed revisions in the family tree contain elements key to much of the new thinking. That is, he assigns the black-skull species, whatever it is finally named, to a place as the common ancestor to robustus and boisei, which then follow separate but parallel lines to eventual extinction.

In such revisions, africanus becomes a kind of wild card. Scientists were already growing uncomfortable about africanus's assigned place in the robust line. Its more delicate facial features seemed to set africanus apart. And now it seemed to be contemporary with the boisei-like black skull, which

presumably ruled it out as an ancestor to boisei.

Perhaps, as some scientists suggested even before the black-skull discovery, africanus belonged on the Homo side of the family tree. The idea appeals to anthropologists like Dr. Delson, Dr. Grine and Todd R. Olson of the City University of New York. Africanus could be the transitional species leading from afarensis to humans, as the black-skull species is the link to the robust australopithecines.

This would help account for what was happening in the million-year interval between afarensis and the first fossil evidence of the Homo line 2 million years ago. Anthropologists said they may not be able to reach consensus on the place of either the black skull or africanus on the family tree without further discoveries in this critical gap in the fossil record.

The discovery of the black skull and ensuing debate have focused new attention on the australopithecines, who evolved in parallel with the human line.

"We're looking at another kind of human being," said Milford Wolpoff, professor of anthropology at the University of Michigan. "Here's a completely different line that started out as primitive as we did and developed these humanlike features independently. It shows it has happened twice in this world."

Previously, Dr. Wolpoff noted, it was usually thought that most of the humanlike features of the australopithecines, such as a larger brain, had evolved before the branch split away from the line leading to modern humans. This idea is apparently contradicted by the evidence of the black skull. It held a brain no bigger than that of a chimpanzee, but the later boisei species had a brain 50 percent larger, and with advanced features indicating the capacity for some humanlike thinking.

In one sense, the australopithecines seem to evolve more rapidly than the Homo line, developing earlier and more striking differences from the common afarensis ancestor, according to Dr. Olson of the City University of

New York. This is most apparent, he said, in the larger teeth and skull musculature for chewing that gave the australopithecines their distinctively robust appearance.

To compensate for their slower evolution of chewing mechanisms, Dr. Wolpoff suggested, "Our people became more proficient at processing foods outside the mouth, learning to use grinding and chopping tools." This could have been the critical step giving the Homo line an evolutionary advantage.

Anthropologists are only beginning to conceive of life in early Africa with two emerging humanlike species. Dr. Wolpoff said there is no evidence for violence between the species. But they must have roamed the same savannas, eyed each other warily and perhaps competed for the same resources. This competition could have contributed to the extinction of the one group and shaped the evolution of the modern human line.

"This is a new realization," said Dr. Olson. "To me, this is one of the most exciting things to happen in the field in the past 30 years."

Sizing Up Human Intelligence

Stephen Jay Gould

HUMAN BODIES

"Size," Julian Huxley once remarked, "has a fascination of its own." We stock our zoos with elephants, hippopotamuses, giraffes, and gorillas; who among you was not rooting for King Kong in his various battles atop tall buildings? This focus on the few creatures larger than ourselves has distorted our conception of our own size. Most people think that *Homo sapiens* is a creature of only modest dimensions. In fact, humans are among the largest animals on earth; more than 99 percent of animal species are smaller than we are. Of 190 species in our own order of primate mammals, only the gorilla regularly exceeds us in size.

In our self-appointed role as planetary ruler, we have taken great interest in cataloging the features that permitted us to attain this lofty estate. Our brain, upright posture, development of speech, and group hunting (to name just a few) are often cited, but I have been struck by how rarely our large size has been recognized as a controlling factor of our evolutionary progress.

Despite its low reputation in certain circles, self-conscious intelligence is surely the *sine qua non* of our current status. Could we have evolved it at much smaller body sizes? One day, at the New York World's Fair in 1964, I entered the hall of Free Enterprise to escape the rain. Inside, prominently displayed, was an ant colony bearing the sign: "Twenty million years of evolutionary stagnation. Why? Because the ant colony is a socialist, totalitarian system." The statement scarcely requires serious attention; nonetheless, I should point out that ants are doing very well for themselves, and that it is their size rather than their social structure that precludes high mental capacity.

In this age of the transistor, we can put radios in watchcases and bug telephones with minute electronic packages. Such miniaturization might lead us to the false belief that absolute size is irrelevant to the operation of complex machinery. But nature does not miniaturize neurons (or other cells for that matter). The range of cell size among organisms is incomparably smaller than the range in body size. Small animals simply have far fewer cells than large animals. The human brain contains several billion neurons; an ant is constrained by its small size to have many hundreds of times fewer neurons.

There is, to be sure, no established relationship between brain size and intelligence among humans (the tale of Anatole France with a brain of less than 1,000 cubic centimeters vs. Oliver Cromwell with well above 2,000 is often cited). But this observation cannot be extended to differences between species and certainly not to ranges of sizes separating ants and humans. An efficient computer needs billions of circuits and an ant simply cannot contain enough of them because the relative constancy of cell size requires that small brains contain few neurons. Thus, our large body size served as a prerequisite for self-conscious intelligence.

We can make a stronger argument and claim that humans have to be just about the size they are in order to function as they do. In an amusing and provocative article (*American Scientist,* 1968), F. W. Went explored the impossibility of human life, as we know it, at ant dimensions (assuming for the moment that we could circumvent—which we cannot—the problem of intelligence and small brain size). Since weight increases so much faster than surface area as an object gets larger, small animals have very high ratios of surface to volume: they live in a world dominated by surface forces that affect us scarcely at all. . . .

An ant-sized man might don some clothing, but forces of surface adhesion would preclude its removal. The lower limit of drop size would make showering impossible; each drop would hit with the force of a large boulder. If our homunculus managed to get wet and tried to dry off with a towel, he would be stuck to it for life. He could pour no liquid, light no fire (since a stable flame must be several millimeters in length). He might pound gold leaf thin enough to construct a book for his size, but surface adhesion would prevent the turning of pages.

Our skills and behavior are finely attuned to our size. We could not be twice as tall as we are, for the kinetic energy of a fall would then be 16 to 32 times as great, and our sheer weight (increased eightfold) would be more than our legs could support. Human giants of eight to nine feet have either died young or been crippled early by failure of joints and bones. At half our size, we could not wield a club with sufficient force to hunt large animals (for kinetic energy would decrease 16 to 32-fold); we could not impart sufficient momentum to spears and arrows; we could not cut or split wood with primitive tools or mine minerals with picks and chisels. Since these all were essential activities in our historical development, we must conclude that the path of our evolution could only have been followed by a creature very close to our size. I do not argue that we inhabit the best of all possible worlds, only that our size has limited our activities and, to a great extent, shaped our evolution.

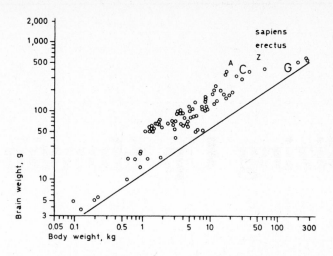

The correct criterion for assessing the superiority in size of our brains. The solid line represents the average relationship between brain weight and body weight for all body weights among mammals in general. Superiority in size is measured by upward deviation from this curve (i.e., "more" brain than an average mammal of the same body weight). Open circles represent primates (all have larger brains than average mammals). C is the chimpanzee, G the gorilla, and A the fossil hominid Australopithecus: erectus *covers the range of* Homo erectus *(Java and Peking Man); sapiens covers the field for modern humans. Our brains have the highest positive deviations of any mammal. (F. S. Szalay,* Approaches to Primate Paleobiology, *Contrib. Primat. Vol. 5, 1975, p. 267. Reproduced with the permission of S. Karger AG, Basel)*

HUMAN BRAINS

An average human brain weights about 1,300 grams (45.5 ounces); to accommodate such a large brain, we have bulbous, balloon-shaped heads unlike those of any other large mammal. Can we measure superiority by the size of our brains?

Elephants and whales have larger brains than ours. But this fact does not confer superior mental ability upon the largest mammals. Larger bodies need larger brains to coordinate their actions. We must find a way to remove the confusing influence of body size from our calculation. The computation of a simple ratio between brain weight and body weight will not work. Very small mammals generally have higher ratios than humans; that is, they have more brain per unit of body weight. Brain size does increase with body size, but it increases at a *much slower rate.*

If we plot brain weight against body weight for all species of adult mammals, we find that the brain increases at about two-thirds the rate of the body. Since surface areas also increase about two-thirds as fast as body weight, we

conjecture that brain weight is not regulated by body weight, but primarily by the body surfaces that serve as end points for so many innervations. This means that large animals may have absolutely larger brains than humans (because their bodies are bigger), and that small animals often have relatively larger brains than humans (because body size decreases more rapidly than brain size).

A plot of brain weight vs. body weight for adult mammals points the way out of our paradox. The correct criterion is neither absolute nor relative brain size—it is the difference between actual brain size and expected brain size at that body weight. To judge the size of our brain, we must compare it with the expected brain size for an average mammal of our body weight. On this criterion we are, as we had every right to expect, the brainiest mammal by far. No other species lies as far above the expected brain size for average mammals as we do.

This relationship between body weight and brain size provides important insights into the evolution of our brain. Our African ancestor (or at least close cousin), *Australopithecus afri-*

canus, had an average adult cranial capacity of only 450 cubic centimeters. Gorillas often have larger brains, and many authorities have used this fact to infer a distinctly prehuman mentality for *Australopithecus.* A recent textbook states: "The original bipedal apeman of South Africa had a brain scarcely larger than that of other apes and presumably possessed behavioral capacities to match." But *A. africanus* weighed only 50 to 90 pounds (female and male respectively—as estimated by Yale anthropologist David Pilbeam), while large male gorillas may weigh more than 600 pounds. We may safely state that *Australopithecus* had a much larger brain than other nonhuman primates, using the correct criterion of comparison with expected values for actual body weights.

The human brain is now about three times larger than that of *Australopithecus.* This increase has often been called the most rapid and most important event in the history of evolution. But our bodies have also increased greatly in size. Is this enlargement of the brain a simple consequence of bigger bodies or does it mark new levels of intelligence?

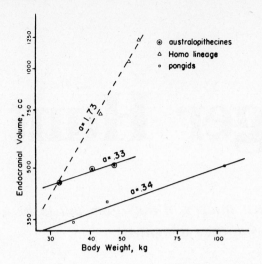

Evolutionary increase in human brain size (dotted line). The four triangles represent a rough evolutionary sequence: Australopithecus africanus, ER-1470 (Richard Leakey's new find with a cranial capacity just slightly less than 800 cc), Homo erectus *(Peking Man), and* Homo sapiens. *The slope is the highest ever calculated for an evolutionary sequence. The two solid lines represent more conventional scaling of brain size in australopithecines (above) and great apes (below).* ("Size and Scaling in Human Evolution," Pilbeam, David, and Gould, Stephen Jay, *Science* Vol. 186, pp. 892–901, Fig. 2, 6 December 1974. Copyright 1974 by the American Association for the Advancement of Science)

To answer this question, I have plotted cranial capacity against inferred body weight for the following fossil homids (representing, perhaps, our lineage): *Australopithecus africanus;* Richard Leakey's remarkable find with a cranial capacity of nearly 800 cubic centimeters and an antiquity of more than two million years (weight estimated by David Pillbeam from dimensions of the femur); *Homo erectus* from Choukoutien (Peking Man); and modern *Homo sapiens.* The graph indicates that our brain has increased much more rapidly than any prediction based on compensations for body size would allow.

My conclusion is not unconventional, and it does reinforce an ego that we would do well to deflate. Nonetheless, our brain has undergone a true increase in size not related to the demands of our larger body. We are, indeed, smarter than we were.

Scavenger Hunt

As paleoanthropologists close in on their quarry, it may turn out to be a different beast from what they imagined

Pat Shipman

Pat Shipman is an assistant professor in the Department of Cell Biology and Anatomy at The Johns Hopkins University School of Medicine.

In both textbooks and films, ancestral humans (hominids) have been portrayed as hunters. Small-brained, big-browed, upright, and usually mildly furry, early hominid males gaze with keen eyes across the gold savanna, searching for prey. Skillfully wielding a few crude stone tools, they kill and dismember everything from small gazelles to elephants, while females care for young and gather roots, tubers, and berries. The food is shared by group members at temporary camps. This familiar image of Man the Hunter has been bolstered by the finding of stone tools in association with fossil animal bones. But the role of hunting in early hominid life cannot be determined in the absence of more direct evidence.

I discovered one means of testing the hunting hypothesis almost by accident. In 1978, I began documenting the microscopic damage produced on bones by different events. I hoped to develop a diagnostic key for identifying the post-mortem history of specific fossil bones, useful for understanding how fossil assemblages were formed. Using a scanning electron microscope (SEM) because of its excellent resolution and superb depth of field, I inspected high-fidelity replicas of modern bones that had been subjected to known events or conditions. (I had to use replicas, rather than real bones, because specimens must fit into the SEM's small vacuum chamber.) I soon established that such common events as weathering, root etching, sedimentary abrasion, and carnivore chewing produced microscopically distinctive features.

In 1980, my SEM study took an unexpected turn. Richard Potts (now of Yale University), Henry Bunn (now of the University of Wisconsin at Madison), and I almost simultaneously found what appeared to be stone-tool cut marks on fossils from Olduvai Gorge, Tanzania, and Koobi Fora, Kenya. We were working almost side by side at the National Museums of Kenya, in Nairobi, where the fossils are stored. The possibility of cut marks was exciting, since both sites preserve some of the oldest known archaeological materials. Potts and I returned to the United States, manufactured some stone tools, and started "butchering" bones and joints begged from our local butchers. Under the SEM, replicas of these cut marks looked very different from replicas of carnivore tooth scratches, regardless of the species of carnivore or the type of tool involved. By comparing the marks on the fossils with our hundreds of modern bones of known history, we were able to demonstrate convincingly that hominids using stone tools had processed carcasses of many different animals nearly two million years ago. For the first time, there was a firm link between stone tools and at least some of the early fossil animal bones.

This initial discovery persuaded some paleoanthropologists that the hominid hunter scenario was correct. Potts and I were not so sure. Our study had shown that many of the cut-marked fossils also bore carnivore tooth marks and that some of the cut marks were in places we hadn't expected—on bones that bore little meat in life. More work was needed.

In addition to more data about the Olduvai cut marks and tooth marks, I needed specific information about the patterns of cut marks left by known hunters performing typical activities associated with hunting. If similar patterns occurred on the fossils, then the early hominids probably behaved similarly to more modern hunters; if the patterns were different, then the behavior was probably also different. Three activities related to hunting occur often enough in peoples around the world and leave consistent enough traces to be used for such a test.

First, human hunters systematically disarticulate their kills, unless the animals are small enough to be eaten on the spot. Disarticulation leaves cut marks in a predictable pattern on the skeleton. Such marks cluster near the major joints of the limbs: shoulder, elbow, carpal joint (wrist), hip, knee, and hock (ankle). Taking a carcass apart at the joints is much easier than breaking or cutting through bones. Disarticulation enables hunters to carry food back to a central place or camp, so that they can share it with others or cook it or even store it by placing portions in trees, away from the reach of carnivores. If early hominids were hunters who transported and shared their kills, disarticulation marks would occur near joints in frequencies comparable to those produced by modern human hunters.

Second, human hunters often butcher carcasses, in the sense of removing meat from the bones. Butchery marks are usually found on the shafts of bones from the upper part of the front or hind limb, since this is where the big muscle masses lie. Butchery may be carried out at the kill site—especially if the animal is very large and its bones very heavy—or it may take place at the base camp, during the process of sharing food with others. Compared with disarticulation, butchery leaves relatively few marks. It is hard for a hunter to locate an animal's joints without leaving cut marks on the bone. In contrast, it is easier to cut the meat away from the midshaft of the bone without making such marks. If early hominids shared their food, however, there ought to be a number of cut marks located on the midshaft of some fossil bones.

Finally, human hunters often remove skin or tendons from carcasses, to be used for clothing, bags, thongs, and so on. Hide or tendon must be separated from the bones in many areas where there is little flesh, such as the lower limb bones of pigs, giraffes, antelopes, and zebras. In such cases, it is difficult to cut the skin without leaving a cut mark on the bone. Therefore, one expects to find many more cut marks on such bones than on the flesh-covered bones of the upper part of the limbs.

Unfortunately, although accounts of butchery and disarticulation by modern human hunters are remarkably consistent, quantitative studies are rare. Further, virtually all modern hunter-gatherers use metal tools, which leave more cut marks than stone tools. For these reasons I hesitated to compare the fossil evidence with data on modern hunters. Fortunately, Diane Gifford of the University of California,

Santa Cruz, and her colleagues had recently completed a quantitative study of marks and damage on thousands of antelope bones processed by Neolithic (Stone Age) hunters in Kenya some 2,300 years ago. The data from Prolonged Drift, as the site is called, were perfect for comparison with the Olduvai material.

Assisted by my technician, Jennie Rose, I carefully inspected more than 2,500 antelope bones from Bed I at Olduvai Gorge, which is dated to between 1.9 and 1.7 million years ago. We made high-fidelity replicas of every mark that we thought might be either a cut mark or a carnivore tooth mark. Back in the United States, we used the SEM to make positive identifications of the marks. (The replication and SEM inspection was time consuming, but necessary: only about half of the marks were correctly identified by eye or by light microscope.) I then compared the patterns of cut mark and tooth mark distributions on Olduvai fossils with those made by Stone Age hunters at Prolonged Drift.

By their location, I identified marks caused either by disarticulation or meat removal and then compared their frequencies with those from Prolonged Drift. More than 90 percent of the Neolithic marks in these two categories were from disarticulation, but to my surprise, only about 45 percent of the corresponding Olduvai cut marks were from disarticulation. This difference is too great to have occurred by chance; the Olduvai bones did not show the predicted pattern. In fact, the Olduvai cut marks attributable to meat removal and disarticulation showed essentially the same pattern of distribution as the carnivore tooth marks. Apparently, the early hominids were not regularly disarticulating carcasses. This finding casts serious doubt on the idea that early hominids carried their kills back to camp to share with others, since both transport and sharing are difficult unless carcasses are cut up.

When I looked for cut marks attributable to skinning or tendon removal, a more modern pattern emerged. On both the Neolithic and Olduvai bones, nearly 75 percent of all cut marks

occurred on bones that bore little meat; these cut marks probably came from skinning. Carnivore tooth marks were much less common on such bones. Hominids were using carcasses as a source of skin and tendon. This made it seem more surprising that they disarticulated carcasses so rarely.

A third line of evidence provided the most tantalizing clue. Occasionally, sets of overlapping marks occur on the Olduvai fossils. Sometimes, these sets include both cut marks and carnivore tooth marks. Still more rarely, I could see under the SEM which mark had been made first, because its features were overlaid by those of the later mark, in much the same way as old tire tracks on a dirt road are obscured by fresh ones. Although only thirteen such sets of marks were found, in eight cases the hominids made the cut marks *after* the carnivores made their tooth marks. This finding suggested a new hypothesis. Instead of hunting for prey and leaving the remains behind for carnivores to scavenge, perhaps hominids were scavenging from the carnivores. This might explain the hominids' apparently unsystematic use of carcasses: they took what they could get, be it skin, tendon, or meat.

Man the Scavenger is not nearly as attractive an image as Man the Hunter, but it is worth examining. Actually, although hunting and scavenging are different ecological strategies, many mammals do both. The only pure scavengers alive in Africa today are vultures; not one of the modern African mammalian carnivores is a pure scavenger. Even spotted hyenas, which have massive, bone-crushing teeth well adapted for eating the bones left behind by others, only scavenge about 33 percent of their food. Other carnivores that scavenge when there are enough carcasses around include lions, leopards, striped hyenas, and jackals. Long-term behavioral studies suggest that these carnivores scavenge when they can and kill when they must. There are only two nearly pure predators, or hunters—the cheetah and the wild dog—that rarely, if ever, scavenge.

What are the costs and benefits of scavenging compared with those of predation? First of all, the scavenger avoids the task of making sure its meal is dead: a predator has already endured the energetically costly business of chasing or stalking animal after animal until one is killed. But while scavenging may be cheap, it's risky. Predators rarely give up their prey to scavengers without defending it. In such disputes, the larger animal, whether a scavenger or a predator, usually wins, although smaller animals in a pack may defeat a lone, larger animal. Both predators and scavengers suffer the dangers inherent in fighting for possession of a carcass. Smaller scavengers such as jackals or striped hyenas avoid disputes to some extent by specializing in darting in and removing a piece of a carcass without trying to take possession of the whole thing. These two strategies can be characterized as that of the bully or that of the sneak: bullies need to be large to be successful, sneaks need to be small and quick.

Because carcasses are almost always much rarer than live prey, the major cost peculiar to scavenging is that scavengers must survey much larger areas than predators to find food. They can travel slowly, since their "prey" is already dead, but endurance is important. Many predators specialize in speed at the expense of endurance, while scavengers do the opposite.

The more committed predators among the East African carnivores (wild dogs and cheetahs) can achieve great top speeds when running, although not for long. Perhaps as a consequence, these "pure" hunters enjoy a much higher success rate in hunting (about three-fourths of their chases end in kills) than any of the scavenger-hunters do (less than half of their chases are successful). Wild dogs and cheetahs are efficient hunters, but they are neither big enough nor efficient enough in their locomotion to make good scavengers. In fact, the cheetah's teeth are so specialized for meat slicing that they probably cannot withstand the stresses of bone crunching and carcass dismembering carried out by scavengers. Other carnivores are less successful at hunting, but have specializations of size, endurance, or

(in the case of the hyenas) dentition that make successful scavenging possible. The small carnivores seem to have a somewhat higher hunting success rate than the large ones, which balances out their difficulties in asserting possession of carcasses.

In addition to endurance, scavengers need an efficient means of locating carcasses, which, unlike live animals, don't move or make noises. Vultures, for example, solve both problems by flying. The soaring, gliding flight of vultures expends much less energy than walking or cantering as performed by the part-time mammalian scavengers. Flight enables vultures to maintain a foraging radius two to three times larger than that of spotted hyenas, while providing a better vantage point. This explains why vultures can scavenge all of their food in the same habitat in which it is impossible for any mammal to be a pure scavenger. (In fact, many mammals learn where carcasses are located from the presence of vultures.)

Since mammals can't succeed as fulltime scavengers, they must have another source of food to provide the bulk of their diet. The large carnivores rely on hunting large animals to obtain food when scavenging doesn't work. Their size enables them to defend a carcass against others. Since the small carnivores—jackals and striped hyenas— often can't defend carcasses successfully, most of their diet is composed of fruit and insects. When they do hunt, they usually prey on very small animals, such as rats or hares, that can be consumed in their entirety before the larger competitors arrive.

The ancient habitat associated with the fossils of Olduvai and Koobi Fora would have supported many herbivores and carnivores. Among the latter were two species of large saber-toothed cats, whose teeth show extreme adaptations for meat slicing. These were predators with primary access to carcasses. Since their teeth were unsuitable for bone crushing, the saber-toothed cats must have left behind many bones covered with scraps of meat, skin, and tendon. Were early hominids among the scavengers that exploited such carcasses?

All three hominid species that were present in Bed I times (*Homo habilis, Australopithecus africanus, A. robustus*) were adapted for habitual, upright bipedalism. Many anatomists see evidence that these hominids were agile tree climbers as well. Although upright bipedalism is a notoriously peculiar mode of locomotion, the adaptive value of which has been argued for years (see Matt Cartmill's article, "Four Legs Good, Two Legs Bad," *Natural History,* November 1983), there are three general points of agreement.

First, bipedal running is neither fast nor efficient compared to quadrupedal gaits. However, at moderate speeds of 2.5 to 3.5 miles per hour, bipedal *walking* is more energetically efficient than quadrupedal walking. Thus, bipedal walking is an excellent means of covering large areas slowly, making it an unlikely adaptation for a hunter but an appropriate and useful adaptation for a scavenger. Second, bipedalism elevates the head, thus improving the hominid's ability to spot items on the ground—an advantage both to scavengers and to those trying to avoid becoming a carcass. Combining bipedalism with agile tree climbing improves the vantage point still further. Third, bipedalism frees the hands from locomotive duties, making it possible to carry items. What would early hominids have carried? Meat makes a nutritious, easy-to-carry package; the problem is that carrying meat attracts scavengers. Richard Potts suggests that carrying stone tools or unworked stones for toolmaking to caches would be a more efficient and less dangerous activity under many circumstances.

In short, bipedalism is compatible with a scavenging strategy. I am tempted to argue that bipedalism evolved because it provided a substantial advantage to scavenging hominids. But I doubt hominids could scavenge effectively without tools, and bipedalism predates the oldest known stone tools by more than a million years.

Is there evidence that, like modern mammalian scavengers, early hominids had an alternative food source, such as either hunting or eating fruits and insects? My husband, Alan Walker, has shown that the microscopic wear on an animal's teeth reflects its diet. Early hominid teeth wear more like that of chimpanzees and other modern fruit eaters than that of carnivores. Apparently, early hominids ate mostly fruit, as the smaller, modern scavengers do. This accords with the estimated body weight of early hominids, which was only about forty to eighty pounds—less than that of any of the modern carnivores that combine scavenging and hunting but comparable to the striped hyena, which eats fruits and insects as well as meat.

Would early hominids have been able to compete for carcasses with other carnivores? They were too small to use a bully strategy, but if they scavenged in groups, a combined bully-sneak strategy might have been possible. Perhaps they were able to drive off a primary predator long enough to grab some meat, skin, or marrow-filled bone before relinquishing the carcass. The effectiveness of this strategy would have been vastly improved by using tools to remove meat or parts of limbs, a task at which hominid teeth are poor. As agile climbers, early hominids may have retreated into the trees to eat their scavenged trophies, thus avoiding competition from large terrestrial carnivores.

In sum, the evidence on cut marks, tooth wear, and bipedalism, together with our knowledge of scavenger adaptation in general, is consistent with the hypothesis that two million years ago hominids were scavengers rather than accomplished hunters. Animal carcasses, which contributed relatively little to the hominid diet, were not systematically cut up and transported for sharing at base camps. Man the Hunter may not have appeared until 1.5 to 0.7 million years ago, when we do see a shift toward omnivory, with a greater proportion of meat in the diet. This more heroic ancestor may have been *Homo erectus,* equipped with Acheulean-style stone tools and, increasingly, fire. If we wish to look further back, we may have to become accustomed to a less flattering image of our heritage.

Late Hominid Evolution

The most important aspect of human evolution is also the most difficult to decipher from the fossil evidence: our development as sentient, social beings capable of communicating by means of language. Although we may detect hints of incipient humanity in the form of crudely chipped tools, the telltale signs of a home base or even the changing anatomy at the base of the skull (reflecting developing linguistic abilities), none of these indicators of a distinctly hominid way of life can provide us with the nuances of the everyday lives of these creatures, their social relations, or their supernatural beliefs, if any. All that seems to remain is the rubble of the bones and stones from which we interpret what we can of their lifestyle and thought processes. Our ability to glean from the fossil record is not completely without hope, however. In fact, informed speculation is what makes possible such articles as "What Was the Acheulian Hand Ax?" by Eileen O'Brien, "Bamboo and Human Evolution" by Geoffrey G. Pope, and "Hard Times Among the Neanderthals" by Erik Trinkaus. Each is a fine example of the kind of careful, systematic, and thought-provoking work that is based upon an increased understanding of hominid fossil sites as well as the more general environmental circumstances in which our predecessors lived.

Beyond the technological and anatomical adaptations, questions have arisen as to how our hominid forebears organized themselves socially and whether or not modern-day human behavior is inherited as a legacy of our evolutionary past or is a learned product of contemporary circumstances. Attempts to address this issue have given rise to the technique referred to as the "ethnographic analogy." This is a method whereby anthropologists use "enthnographies" or field studies of modern-day hunters and gatherers whom we take to be the best approximations we have to what life might have been like for our ancient ancestors. While it is granted that these contemporary foragers have been living under conditions of environmental and social change just as industrial peoples have, it nevertheless seems that, at least in some aspects of their lives, they have not changed as much as we have, and if we are to make any kind of enlightened assessments of prehistoric behavior patterns, we are better off looking at them than looking at ourselves. This technique of interpreting the past by observing contemporary peoples is the basis for the article "Life as a Hunter-Gatherer" by Richard Leakey. Using a similar method in relation to a somewhat broader issue, Richard Leakey and Roger Lewin call into question the popular view of innate human violence in "Is It Our Culture, Not Our Genes, That Makes Us Killers?"

As if to show that controversy over lineages is not limited to the earlier hominid period (see section 3), in this section we have the raging debate surrounding the "Eve hypothesis," as recounted in "The Search for Adam and Eve" by John Tierney et al. In this case, the issue of when and where the family tree of modern humans actually began has pitted the bone experts on the one hand against a new type of anthropologist specializing in molecular biology on the other. Granted, for some scientists such as Stephen J. Gould ("A Novel Notion of Neanderthal"), the new evidence fits in quite comfortably with previously held positions, while for others it seems that reputations, as well as theories, are at stake.

Looking Ahead: Challenge Questions

What is an Acheulian hand ax and how might it have been used?

Where and why might bamboo have been important to hominid survival?

What evidence is there for hard times among the Neanderthals?

What are the strengths and weaknesses of the "Eve hypothesis?"

What happened to the Neanderthals?

How would you draw the late hominid family tree?

What can contemporary hunter-gatherers tell us about the lives of our ancestors over the past million years?

Are human beings innately aggressive?

Unit 4

What Was the Acheulean Hand Ax?

Contrary to its name, this prehistoric stone tool may have been a projectile weapon

Eileen M. O'Brien

Eileen M. O'Brien is a research associate in the Department of Anthropology at the University of Georgia.

About one and one-half million years ago, a new type of large, symmetrically shaped stone implement entered the prehistoric tool kit, signaling both an advance in early craftsmanship and the advent of *Homo erectus,* a small-brained but otherwise fairly recognizable form of human being. The tool was the hand ax, which these ancestral humans faithfully made for well over one million years. Named for archeological finds at Saint Acheul, France, examples of the Acheulean hand ax are found from the Vaal River of South Africa to the lakes, bogs, and rivers of Europe, from the shores of the Mediterranean to India and Indonesia. Such continuity over time and space speaks to us of use, success, and reuse—a design integral to some task, a task appropriate or essential to diverse environments. *Homo erectus* needed tools: tools to cut, slice, and chop; to dig, pound, and grind; tools to defend against predators and competitors, to procure and process food or other materials, even tools to make tools. But which task (or tasks) the hand ax performed is still being debated.

The average hand ax looks like a giant stone almond, although some are more ovate and others are triangular. Crafted from a stone core or flake, it can range in size from only a few inches to a foot or more, but most are six or seven inches long. Whether roughly finished or as refined as a work of art, the hand ax always has an eccentric center of gravity and a sharp edge around all or most of its perimeter. Thus in cross section lengthwise, it resembles a stretched-out teardrop.

Some have speculated that the hand ax's design was not functional but purely aesthetic or that it was a by-product of the manufacture of the sharp flakes used in butchering. Most anthropologists, however, assume it was a practical implement. Initially, prehistorians thought it was a hafted, multipurpose tool and weapon like the stone hatchet, or ax, of the aboriginal Americans and Australians. But there is no evidence that it was hafted until much later in time, not until after the evolution of *Homo sapiens.* Another proposal, advanced to explain why excavators find some hand axes standing on edge, *in situ,* is that the hand ax acted as a stationary tool, one edge embedded in the earth while the exposed edge cut or scraped an object passed over it. But the common and traditional interpretation is that it was a hand-held tool for butchering, cutting, scraping, digging, or as its name implies, chopping.

Experiments show that these important tasks can be accomplished with a hand ax. But *Homo erectus* possessed other tools suitable for these purposes—tools that precede and continue alongside the hand ax in the archeological record. Compared with these, the hand ax was costly to produce in terms of time, labor, and skill, and required larger blocks of fine-grained, faultless stone such as flint or basalt. The hand ax also presented a hazard. Since a heavy object requires effort to wield and carry, we may assume the mass of the hand ax was important to its function. Force in the form of increased momentum would be useful for chopping, for example, as compared with a task like scraping, where the user exerts all the energy in the form of pressure. But without a safe handhold, the sharp edge of the hand ax, when used with force, was (and is) capable of inflicting as much damage on the user as on the material being worked.

Whatever its function, the hand ax represented to its users not only an investment of energy but also a source of raw material. They would have saved and reused a hand ax for as long as possible and retouched it when necessary. With time and repeated repair, it would have become smaller; once irreparably damaged, what remained could then have served as a core in the production of still smaller stone tools. Accordingly, except for those hand axes that were misplaced or lost, the hand ax should not be in the archeological record. Excavators, however, recover hand axes in abundance, mostly at sites that are within or alongside what were once (and may still be) watercourses or wetland environments. For example, at the Acheulean site of Olorgesailie (one of the East African sites southwest of Nairobi, Kenya, in the Eastern Rift Valley), hundreds of large hand axes were deposited about four hundred thousand years ago in what appears to have been a shallow stream bed. Elsewhere across the landscape, hand axes are rare, although they are occasionally found in some numbers in prehistoric cave sites. This suggests that during some activity that took place near water, hand axes were used and lost with astonishing frequency.

If we let the evidence speak for itself, the appropriate question is: What task would require force, call for a tool with a sharp edge around all (or most) of its perimeter but without a safe handhold, occur in or near water, and often result in the loss of a potentially reusable and valuable artifact? The possibility that occurred to me is that the hand ax was a projectile weapon. The idea, I have since discovered, has been thought of before, but not pursued. Use of the hand ax as a weapon has been suggested since at least the sixteenth century, and small hand axes have been proposed as projectiles since the nineteenth century, most enjoyably by H.G. Wells in his *Tales of Time and Space* (1899). More recently, M.D.W. Jeffreys, a South African anthropologist, wrote that the small- to medium-sized Vaal River hand axes would make good bird-hunting weapons if thrown overhand, like a knife ("The Handbolt." *Man*, 1965). But the idea that hand axes were in general used as projectiles has not taken hold, probably because it is not obvious how the larger hand axes could have been thrown.

By analogy with modern forms, we understand how prehistoric stone arrowheads and spearpoints were propelled and used as weapons or how a stone ball ("spheroid," to archeologists) could be thrown or used in a bola (a weighted thong or cord thrown to entangle prey). But what about the hand ax? One way might be overhand, as Jeffreys suggested. Other methods of throwing a small- to medium-sized

hand ax might be the side/overhand throw used in baseball and perhaps the backhand throw used in both knife and frisbee throwing. To throw a large, heavy hand ax, however, a sidearm or underhand throw might be preferable. A few years ago, I decided that a practical experiment was what was needed. From my limited knowledge of track and field, I thought that for sidearm throwing, an analogy might be made between a hand ax and the Olympic discus.

Like a hand ax, the early discus of the ancient Greeks was unhafted, edged all around, and made of stone. It also varied in size from about half a foot to more than one foot in diameter, and in weight from about two and one-quarter pounds to more than fourteen and one-half pounds. (Actually, the word *discus* means "a thing for throwing" or "a thing thrown"; the discus thrown by Odysseus in Homer's *Odyssey*, for example, is thought by some scholars to refer to a beach cobble.) Unlike a hand ax, the classic Greek discus was perfectly round. (The modern regulation discus, which weighs 2 kilograms, or 4.4 pounds, is made of wood and weighted with metal around the edge to accelerate its spinning motion. The longer and faster it spins, the more stable the flight pattern and the longer the flight, all else being equal.)

The hand ax I chose for the throwing experiment was the largest I could find in the Olorgesailie collection at the National Museums of Kenya, Nairobi (I was in Africa at the time doing fieldwork unrelated to this topic). Because the original could not be used—and raw material for making a "real" hand ax of such size was difficult to obtain—a fiberglass replica was made. The original hand ax is a little more than a foot long, ovate shaped, and edged all around. It is made of basalt and weighs about four pounds, three ounces. J.D. Ambrosse Esa (then head of the museum's casting department) supervised the casting and the accurate weighting of the facsimile to within one and one-half ounces of the original.

The experiment took place in 1978, in the discus practice area at the Uni-

versity of Massachusetts, where I was then a student. Two student athletes participated: Karl Nyholm, a discus thrower, and George Peredy, a javelin thrower. One day in late April, and again two weeks later, both threw the hand ax discus-style. Peredy also threw it overhand. To maximize potential accuracy in the discus throw, the thrower did not whirl.

The first to throw the hand ax discus-style was Karl Nyholm. He took the unfamiliar object in his right hand, grasping it every which way before settling on the butt. He tossed it up and down for balance and "feel," then crouched and practiced his swing. Ready, he paced off from the release line. With his back to the field, he spread his legs apart, bent at the knees, and twisted his right arm far behind him. Then he began the throw: his outstretched left hand grasping at air, weight shifting from right foot to left, he rotated to face the field. The burdened right hand swung wide and low and then raced upward. With a great exhalation of breath, he hurled himself out straight and let go. Silently, gracefully spinning, the hand ax soared.

Like a discus, the hand ax spun horizontally as it rose, but changed its orientation in midair. On reaching its maximum altitude, it rolled onto its edge and descended in a perpendicular position, its spinning motion appearing to decline. Then, with a thud, it landed point first, slicing deeply into the thawing earth. In both throwing bouts, regardless of thrower, the hand ax repeated this flight pattern when thrown discus-style. It landed on edge forty-two out of forty-five throws, thirty-one of which were point first. The average throw was about one-third the length of a football field (almost 102 feet), and usually accurate to within two yards right or left of the line of trajectory.

The propensity of the hand ax to pivot onto its edge in mid-flight was unexpected and curious. But, as suggested to me by several track coaches, it may be related to the same factors that can produce the "peel-off" pattern in a thrown discus, some function of the manner of release and the thrower's expertise. A full explanation of the physical principles involved must await an interpretation by someone with the relevant expertise. What is important is that it does happen. By so doing, it makes on-edge impact of a thrown hand ax predictable. The further tendency of the hand ax to land point first does not appear accidental and adds to the implement's potential to inflict damage. If the hand ax can also be thrown so that it behaves exactly like the discus in both ascent and descent (more recent demonstrations support this possibility), then by simply changing the angle and manner of release it should be possible to strike a target with either a horizontally or vertically directed edge.

Modern discus throwing is not known for its accuracy. But in terms of how far a hand ax might ideally be thrown, it is worth noting that the 1980 Olympic record in discus was 218.8 feet. Since the experimental hand ax weighs only two and a half ounces less than the modern Olympic discus, this suggests that as the thrower's skill and/or strength increase, the potential flight distance of the hand ax increases.

When grasped and thrown overhand, like a knife, the experimental hand ax performed like one, rotating symmetrically on edge in both ascent and descent. The average throw was just short of discus-style, but more accurate, about half a yard right or left of the line of trajectory. It always landed on edge, but less often point first. Unfortunately, these results are the product of only six throws; owing to its weight and the ovate, broad point, the experimental hand ax was difficult to grasp and throw overhand. George Peredy, who was the thrower, also appeared to tire more quickly using this method and probably could not have used it at all if he had not had large hands, in proportion to his six-foot six-inch frame. This overhand style would probably be more suitable for lighter, more triangular hand axes. In contrast, weight and shape were of no real concern when throwing the

hand ax discus-style. Even a significant increase in weight might not have impeded the throwing motion, although it would have affected the distance of the throw.

Further testing is needed (and is currently under way), but these first trials showed that a hand ax could perform appropriately as a projectile. The hand ax demonstrated a propensity to land on edge when thrown overhand or discus-style, a tendency to land point first, and a potential for distant and accurate impact. Its overall shape minimizes the effects of resistance while in flight, as well as at impact. This is not true of an unshaped stone or a spheroid, for example. And despite its sharp edge, the hand ax could be launched without a safe handhold. The only apparent limitations to the hand ax's use as a projectile weapon are the strength, coordination, and skill of the thrower.

Homo erectus was bipedal, probably dexterous enough to manipulate a hand ax in either of the tested throwing styles, and very much stronger than most modern humans. With their technique perfected over years of practice and use, our ancestors probably surpassed the accuracy shown in the experimental throws. I suspect the hand ax simply reflects a refinement in missile design, one that allowed for successful long-distance offense and defense against larger animals. This is consistent with evidence that big-game hunting appears for the first time in the archeological record along with *Homo erectus.*

Perfected through trial and error, the hand ax would not necessarily have replaced preexisting projectile or handheld weapons, because weapons and strategies probably varied with the predator being deterred or the game being hunted. Hand axes would have been especially effective in a collective strategy, such as a group of hunters bombarding a herd. To overcome any difficulty in transporting hand axes, *Homo erectus* could have used carrying slings made from hide, stockpiled

hand axes near hunting areas, or cached them (in caves, for example) prior to seasonal migrations.

Hunting near water, where game is relatively predictable and often concentrated, offers a simple explanation of why hand axes are recovered there in abundance—as well as the phenomenon of hand axes embedded on edge *in situ.* Hand axes that missed their mark, landing in water or dense vegetation on the banks of a river, might have been difficult or impossible to retrieve. Over time, with continued exploitation of an area, projectiles would accumulate like golf balls in a water trap. Elsewhere across the landscape, retrieval is more likely and the hand ax should be rare. This distribution pattern, as noted by English archeologist L.H. Keeley, resembles that of the Indian projectile points across the American Southwest. (Keeley, however, does not believe that the hand ax was a projectile.)

Homo erectus, like later *Homo sapiens,* was physically defenseless compared with the rest of the animal kingdom. Relatively slow, without canines, claws, tusks, or other natural means of defense, these early humans were easy prey when out of a tree. With handheld weapons they could defend themselves, once attacked. With projectile weapons they could wound, maim, or kill without making physical contact, avoiding assault or retaliation. Modern humans are notoriously expert at killing from a distance. The hand ax may be proof that this behavioral strategy was refined long ago, at a time when truly "giants strode the earth"— when by dint of size the megamammals of the Pleistocene asserted their dominance, when migrating game might pass in a continuous parade for days without a break in their ranks, and humankind struggled to survive, both consumer and consumed. At the other end of time, at the dawn of history, is it possible that the ancient Greeks preserved as a sport a tradition handed down from that distant yesterday?

Bamboo and Human Evolution

In Asia, a giant grass may have shaped the course of prehistoric technology for more than one million years.

Geoffrey G. Pope

Today the seven-mile journey from the highway to our field camp in the Wang Valley seems almost too easy. In the ten years since I began paleoanthroplogical work in northern Thailand, roads have replaced bullock paths, and sugar cane fields lie where dense teak stands once towered. Taking only minutes to pass through the local village, our *song-tao,* or "two-bench" pickup truck, is well on the way to Kao Pah Nam (Wild Thorn Hill), a craggy spine of limestone clothed in treacherous thorn scrub. Everybody in the *song-tao* knows enough to lean into the center of the vehicle to avoid the razor-sharp thorns that rake the open sides.

Reaching our destination, we file out, impatient to flex cramped limbs, shake off the layers of cold dust, and rub new bruises. We are standing at the base of a karst ridge. Karst (first named for the Karst region of Yugoslavia) is an irregular terrain that develops when ground water saturated with carbonic acid erodes limestone. In tropical forests the effects are particularly striking because the dense root systems and thick layers of decaying organic matter give off a great deal of carbon dioxide, which in combination with water forms carbonic acid. All around us are imposing pinnacles with intriguing fissures and caves. For the paleoanthropologist, karst is especially inviting since caves attract animals seeking shelter, and early hominids—

human ancestors and their relatives—would have been no exception. The caves trap bones and cement them in a limestone breccia, preserving fossils that would otherwise disintegrate on the tropical forest floor, with its acid soil and its active insect and micro-organic life.

In prehistoric times the karst environment would have provided attractive resources for early humans. Today people still seek out caves during the hot dry season for their shaded, cool, subterranean waters. Bats, birds, snakes, and small mammals that live there are routinely collected for food. Karst towers also provide convenient points from which to survey the surrounding countryside and are important in the rainy season, when most rivers flood and the lowland country becomes inundated for months at a time. The limestone is also mined for phosphates, quicklime, and building stone.

From the forest around us comes the complacent, comforting cooing of "forest chickens." Suddenly, a series of explosions silences the birds. Some of the reports are as loud as dynamite blasts, but local inhabitants take no notice. For them the explosions are as natural as the sounds of the forest animals. They emanate from an unseen grove of bamboo that some villagers have set alight; the crackling sound of a brush fire accompanies them. The air in the sealed bases of the hollowed bamboo trunks expands until they blow apart, felling the giant stalks (the word

bamboo is Malay in origin and thought to be onomatopoeic for these explosions). This is the first step in the harvesting of a versatile raw material. For me, the explosions are fascinating, because I suspect that these same sounds have echoed in this valley for a million years, and that bamboo has shaped the course of human evolution in this part of the world.

Bamboo provides, I believe, the solution to a puzzle first raised in 1943, when the late archeologist Hallam Movius of Harvard began to publish his observations on paleolithic (Old Stone Age) cultures of the Far East. In 1937 and 1938 Movius had investigated a number of archeological localities in India, Southeast Asia, and China. Although most of the archeological "cultures" that he recognized are no longer accepted by modern workers, he made another, more lasting contribution. This was the identification of the "Movius line" (which his colleague Carleton Coon named in his honor): a geographical boundary, extending through northern India, that separates two long-lasting paleolithic cultures. West of the line are found collections of tools with a high percentage of symmetrical and consistently proportioned hand axes (these are called Acheulean tools, after the French site of Saint Acheul). More or less similar tool kits also occur in Mongolia and Siberia, but with few exceptions (which are generally relatively late in time), not in eastern China or Southeast Asia, where more crudely made tools known as choppers and chopping tools prevail.

Although both types of tools are attributed to our hominid ancestor *Homo erectus* and are of similar age (Acheulean tools are from 1.5 million to 200,000 years old; chopper-chopping tools from 1 million to 200,000 years old), Acheulean tools have long been regarded as more advanced than the more crudely made and less standardized tools of the Far East, which some have called a smash-and-grab technology. Movius was among the first to ponder the significance of this geographical division. In 1948 he published his conclusion that the Far East was a region of "cultural retardation," which he believed could never have

played a vital and dynamic role in early human evolution, although very primitive forms of Early Man apparently persisted there long after types at a comparable stage of physical evolution had become extinct elsewhere.

For years this explanation was accepted and even, in the interpretations of Carleton Coon and others, taken as evidence of racial isolation and backwardness.

With the flowering of the civil rights movement in the 1960s, most anthropologists rejected the notion of cultural retardation, especially if it had racial overtones. Now some suggest that *all* early human ancestors (not just the Asian hominids) had minimal capacities for culture, that is, for toolmaking and other types of socially learned behavior. Lewis Binford, of the University of New Mexico, has been influential in this view. He has spent the last few years reexamining evidence from a number of archeological localities and has concluded that many characterizations of past cultural behavior are based on very little solid data. At any rate, Binford and others would attribute the crudeness of the artifacts from China to the general inability of early hominids to manufacture standardized stone tools.

The problem with this is that it doesn't really solve the mystery of the Movius line. Over the years, however, a few archeologists have put forward a very different line of reasoning, which

I have found to be more fruitful. Their idea is that the early Asians may have relied heavily on tools that they made from raw materials other than stone, and since these are seldom preserved at archeological sites, we simply lack a balanced appreciation of their accomplishments. This suggestion has not generally been pursued, primarily because it is hard to confirm—after all, there is not much use in going out to dig for what probably has not been preserved.

One promising method of detecting nonlithic technology is to study the cut marks on fossil bones. Jolee West, a graduate student at the University of Illinois, has been experimenting with using the electron microscope to differentiate between the kinds of damage left by stone and other cutting implements. Continued development of this approach should eventually offer a direct means to test for the prehistoric use of nonlithic tools.

My own research on the Movius line and related questions evolved almost by accident. During the course of my work in Southeast Asia, I excavated many sites, studied a variety of fossil faunal collections, and reviewed the scientific literature dealing with Asia. As part of this research I compared fossil mammals from Asia with those recovered from other parts of the world. In the beginning, my purpose was biostratigraphic—to use the animals to estimate the most likely dates of various sites used by early hominids. On the basis of the associated fauna, for example, I estimate that Kao Pah Nam may be as old as 700,000 years.

After years of looking at fossil collections and faunal lists, I realized that something was very strange about the collections from Southeast Asia: there were no fossil horses of Pleistocene age (1.6 million to 12,000 years ago) or for a considerable time before that. The only exceptions were a few horse fossils from one place in southern China, the Yuanmou Basin, which was and is a special grassland habitat in a low, dry valley within the Shan-Yunnan Massif.

To mammalian biostratigraphers this is unusual, since members of the horse

family are so common in both the Old and New World that they are a primary means of dating various fossil localities. Fossil horses have been reported from western Burma, but the last one probably lived there some twenty million years ago. Not a single fossil horse turns up later than that in Southeast Asia, although they are known from India to the west and China to the north and every other part of Europe and Asia.

I then began to wonder what other normally common animals might be missing. The answer soon became apparent: camels—even though they too were once widespread throughout the world—and members and relatives of the giraffe family. Pleistocene Southeast Asia was shaping up as a kind of "black hole" for certain fossil mammals! These animals—horses, camels, and giraffids—all dwell in open country. Their absence on the Southeast Asian mainland and islands (all once connected, along with the now inundated Sunda Shelf) is indicative of a forested environment. The mammals that are present—orangutans, tapirs, and gibbons—confirm this conclusion.

The significance of this is that most reconstructions of our evolutionary past have emphasized the influence of savanna grassland habitats, so important in Africa, the cradle of hominid evolution. Many anthropologists theorize that shrinking forests and spreading grasslands encouraged our primarily tree-dwelling ancestors to adapt to ground-dwelling conditions, giving rise to the unique bipedal gait that is the hallmark of hominids. Bipedalism, in turn, freed the hands for tool use and ultimately led to the evolution of a large-brained, cultural animal. Tropical Asia, instead, apparently was where early hominids had to readapt to tropical forest.

In studying the record, I noticed that the forested zone—the zone that lacked open-dwelling mammals—coincided generally with the distribution of the chopper-chopping tools. The latter appeared to be the products of a forest adaptation that, for one reason or another, deemphasized the utilization of standardized stone tools. At least this held for Southeast Asia; what at first I could not explain was the existence of similar tools in northern China, where fossil horses, camels, and giraffids were present. Finally, I came upon the arresting fact that the distribution of naturally occurring bamboo coincided almost perfectly with the distribution of chopper-chopping tools. The only exceptions that may possibly be of real antiquity—certain hand ax collections from Kehe and Dingcun, in China, and Chonggok-Ni, in Korea—fall on the northernmost periphery of the distribution of bamboo and probably can be attributed to fluctuation of the boundary.

Today there are, by various estimates some 1,000 to 1,200 species of bamboo. This giant grass is distributed worldwide, but more than 60 percent of the species are from Asia. Only 16 percent occur in Africa, and those on the Indian subcontinent—to an unknown extent the product of human importation and cultivation—are discontinuous in distribution and low in diversity. By far, the greatest diversity occurs in East and Southeast Asia.

Based on these observations, I hypothesized that the early Asians relied on bamboo for much of their technology. At first I envisioned bamboo simply as a kind of icon representing all nonlithic technology. I now think bamboo specifically must have been an extremely important resource. This was not, in my opinion, because appropriate rock was scarce but because bamboo tools would have been efficient, durable, and highly portable.

There are few useful tools that cannot be constructed from bamboo. Cooking and storage containers, knives, spears, heavy and light projectile points, elaborate traps, rope, fasteners, clothing, and even entire villages can be manufactured from bamboo. In addition to the stalks, which are a source of raw material for the manufacture of a variety of artifacts, the seeds and shoots of many species can be eaten. In historical times, bamboo has been to Asian civilization what the olive tree was to the Greeks. In the great cities of the Far East, bamboo is still the preferred choice for the scaffolding used in the construction of skyscrapers. This in-

comparable resource is also highly renewable. One can actually hear some varieties growing, at more than one foot per day.

Some may question how bamboo tools would have been sufficient for killing and processing large and medium-size animals. Lethal projectile and stabbing implements can in fact be fashioned from bamboo, but their importance may be exaggerated. Large game accounts for a relatively small proportion of the diet of many modern hunters and gatherers. Furthermore, animals are frequently trapped, collected, killed, and then thrown on a fire and cooked whole prior to using bare hands to dismember the roasted carcass. There are many ethnographic examples among forest peoples of this practice.

The only implements that cannot be manufactured from bamboo are axes or choppers suitable for the working of hard woods. More than a few archeologists have suggested that the stone choppers and resultant "waste" flakes of Asia were created with the objective of using them to manufacture and maintain nonlithic tools. Bamboo can be easily worked with stone flakes resulting from the manufacture of choppers (many choppers may have been a throwaway component in the manufacture of flakes).

In addition to bamboo, other highly versatile resources such as liana, rattan, and various reeds are also found in Asian forests. To really appreciate the wealth of resources one has to visit Southeast Asia today. Even though many forested areas have been disturbed or even destroyed by humans, those that remain offer an accurate picture of the variety of habitats that early hominids encountered when they first reached the Far East. Southeast Asia is dominated by tropical forest, but this is not necessarily rain forest. While evergreen rain forest exists in Indonesia, the monsoon forest in northern Thailand is deciduous. In northern China there is boreal woodland forest.

Most of my work has been in northern Thailand where the forests are burned every year, frequently not for agricultural reasons but to permit the

passage of human foot traffic. Despite burning during the dry season (January-April), the forests are once again impenetrable at the end of the wet season (September-December). Many of the hardwood trees, such as the various kinds of teak, are fire resistant and seem little affected by these seasonal conflagrations, indicating that fire played an important role in their evolution. This may be evidence that fire, first used by our ancestors in tropical Africa, aided the colonization of the Asian forests by *Homo erectus.* Fire would also have been instrumental in the working and utilization of nonlithic resources such as bamboo. This relationship between humans, fire, and the forest is probably more than one million years old in Asia.

Our thorn-bedecked site of Kao Pah Nam, where we have been excavating a rock-shelter (shallow cave), itself preserves evidence of fire. Here we have discovered a roughly circular arrangement of fire-cracked basalt cobbles, in association with other artifacts and animal bones. These hearth stones had to have been brought in by early hominids, as very few nonlimestone rocks lie in the rock-shelter. At first I wondered why our early ancestors would have bothered to lug these heavy rocks into their shelter when limestone was abundant at the site.

The answer emerged as the result of a sort of accident in our field camp. For a number of days we had been cooking our meals on a hearth made of local limestone. A few days into the field season we began to notice that people were complaining of itchy and burning skin rashes. The symptoms were very unpleasant. At first we assumed the cause to be some sort of malevolent plant or fungus. By this time camp life had become uncomfortable and there were further complaints of shortness of breath and burning lungs. Finally, one of our Thai workers pointed out that the rocks of our cooking hearth, after numerous heatings and coolings from our fires, had begun to turn to quicklime. The heat, in conjunction with water from numerous spilled pots of soup and boiling kettles of coffee, had caused this caustic sub-

Prehistoric tools made in eastern and south-eastern Asia are less standardized than those—such as the Acheulean hand ax—fashioned elsewhere in the Old World during the same period. A distinct boundary between the two types was delineated more than forty years ago by archeologist Hallam Movius. Since then, new finds have begun to fill in our knowledge of toolmaking in northern Asia. The distribution of the Asian tools corresponds closely to the natural range of bamboo.

Jia Lanpo, *Early Man in China*

stance to become distributed throughout the dusty camp. We quickly replaced the limestone rocks with ones made of basalt. Only months later did it dawn on me that the early hominids that lived at Kao Pah Nam also must have known about the dangers of cooking on limestone. This explained why they bothered to bring in non-native rocks.

On the basis of our ongoing excavations we have concluded that Kao Pah Nam was occupied intermittently by both carnivores and hominids. Bones of extinct hyenas, tigers, and other carnivores are confined primarily to the deeper recesses of the rock-shelter, likely to have been preferred by denning animals. The hearth and other artifacts, on the other hand, are located near what was the entrance. Many of the prey animals that have been recovered are large by modern standards and include hippo and giant forms of ox, deer, bamboo rat, and porcupine. Nothing about the animals suggests anything but a forested environment.

Artificial cut marks (as well as gnaw

marks of large porcupines) are present on the bones associated with the hearth and artifacts. Bones that apparently had been burned have also been recovered. Other evidence that bears on the diet of early hominids consists of extinct freshwater oyster shells piled on top of one another against the rock-shelter wall. This area remains to be fully excavated.

As the result of our work at Kao Pah Nam and other early Pleistocene sites in Thailand, we are beginning to put together a picture of regional artifact types, frequency, and age. There appears to be a simple but systematic pattern of manufacturing choppers and other artifacts by removing a few flakes from one side of a lump of stone.

A similar pattern is turning up in karst caves in southern China. In all these sites, small flakes are absent or rare. One interpretation is that the flakes were carried off into the forest for use in processing raw materials.

Of particular concern to paleoanthropologists is establishing the age of early Asian artifacts. In China, a number of sites are now reliably dated (by paleomagnetic evidence) to approximately one million years ago, and a variety of dating techniques suggest the earliest fossils and artifacts of *Homo erectus* on Java (so-called Java man) are somewhere between 800,000 and 1.3 million years old. In mainland Southeast Asia, however, artifacts demonstrably older than 100,000 years have long been elusive. Paleomagnetic studies

have not yet been carried out to check our estimated biostratigraphic age of 700,000 years for Kao Pah Nam, but both radiometric and paleomagnetic studies were conducted at another site, Ban Don Mun. Artifacts beneath a basalt flow at that site can be assigned an early Pleistocene age of at least 700,000 years. For stratigraphic reasons, artifacts from a nearby site, Mae Tha, can also be accorded that antiquity.

One thing that still eludes us in mainland Southeast Asia are the fossils of the hominids that made the artifacts we have found. As we learn more about their environment, technology, and diet, however, we can see how capably they adapted to a land of bamboo and karst.

Hard Times Among the Neanderthals

Although life was difficult, these prehistoric people may not have been as exclusively brutish as usually supposed

Erik Trinkaus

Throughout the century that followed the discovery in 1856 of the first recognized human fossil remains in the Neander Valley (*Neanderthal* in German) near Düsseldorf, Germany, the field of human paleontology has been beset with controversies. This has been especially true of interpretations of the Neanderthals, those frequently maligned people who occupied Europe and the Near East from about 100,000 years ago until the appearance of anatomically modern humans about 35,000 years ago.

During the last two decades, however, a number of fossil discoveries, new analyses of previously known remains, and more sophisticated models for interpreting subtle anatomical differences have led to a reevaluation of the Neanderthals and their place in human evolution.

This recent work has shown that the often quoted reconstruction of the Neanderthals as semierect, lumbering caricatures of humanity is inaccurate. It was based on faulty anatomical interpretations that were reinforced by the intellectual biases of the turn of the century. Detailed comparisons of Neanderthal skeletal remains with those of modern humans have shown that there is nothing in Neanderthal anatomy that conclusively indicates locomotor, manipulative, intellectual, or linguistic abilities inferior to those of modern humans. Neanderthals have therefore been added to the same spe-

cies as ourselves—*Homo sapiens*—although they are usually placed in their own subspecies, *Homo sapiens neanderthalensis.*

Despite these revisions, it is apparent that there are significant anatomical differences between the Neanderthals and present-day humans. If we are to understand the Neanderthals, we must formulate hypotheses as to why they evolved from earlier humans about 100,000 years ago in Europe and the Near East, and why they were suddenly replaced about 35,000 years ago by peoples largely indistinguishable from ourselves. We must determine, therefore, the behavioral significance of the anatomical differences between the Neanderthals and other human groups, since it is patterns of successful behavior that dictate the direction of natural selection for a species.

In the past, behavioral reconstructions of the Neanderthals and other prehistoric humans have been based largely on archeological data. Research has now reached the stage at which behavioral interpretations from the archeological record can be significantly supplemented by analyses of the fossils themselves. These analyses promise to tell us a considerable amount about the ways of the Neanderthals and may eventually help us to determine their evolutionary fate.

One of the most characteristic features of the Neanderthals is the exaggerated massiveness of their trunk and limb bones. All of the preserved bones

suggest a strength seldom attained by modern humans. Furthermore, not only is this robustness present among the adult males, as one might expect, but it is also evident in the adult females, adolescents, and even children. The bones themselves reflect this hardiness in several ways.

First, the muscle and ligament attachment areas are consistently enlarged and strongly marked. This implies large, highly developed muscles and ligaments capable of generating and sustaining great mechanical stress. Secondly, since the skeleton must be capable of supporting these levels of stress, which are frequently several times as great as body weight, the enlarged attachments for muscles and ligaments are associated with arm and leg bone shafts that have been reinforced. The shafts of all of the arm and leg bones are modified tubular structures that have to absorb stress from bending and twisting without fracturing. When the habitual load on a bone increases, the bone responds by laying down more bone in those areas under the greatest stress.

In addition, musculature and body momentum generate large forces across the joints. The cartilage, which covers joint surfaces, can be relatively easily overworked to the point where it degenerates, as is indicated by the prevalence of arthritis in joints subjected to significant wear and tear over the years. When the surface area of a joint is increased, the force per unit

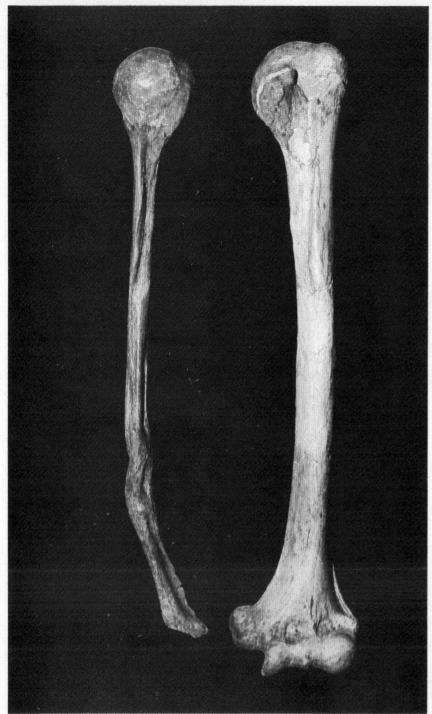

Diagonal lines on these two arm bones from Shanidar 1 are healed fractures. The bone on the right is normal. That on the left is atrophied and has a pathological tip, caused by either amputation or an improperly healed elbow fracture.

area or a crest, especially the muscles used in grasping objects. In fact, Neanderthal hand bones frequently have clear bony crests, where on modern human ones it is barely possible to discern the attachment of the muscle on the dried bone.

In addition, the flattened areas on the ends of the fingers, which provide support for the nail and the pulp of the finger tip, are enormous among the Neanderthals. These areas on the thumb and the index and middle fingers are usually two to three times as large as those of similarly sized modern human hands. The overall impression is one of arms to rival those of the mightiest blacksmith.

Neanderthal legs are equally massive; their strength is best illustrated in the development of the shafts of the leg bones. Modern human thigh and shin bones possess characteristic shaft shapes adapted to the habitual levels and directions of the stresses acting upon them. The shaft shapes of the Neanderthals are similar to those in modern humans, but the cross-sectional areas of the shafts are much greater. This implies significantly higher levels of stress.

Further evidence of the massiveness of Neanderthal lower limbs is provided by the dimensions of their knee and ankle joints. All of these are larger than in modern humans, especially with respect to the overall lengths of the bones.

The development of their limb bones suggests that the Neanderthals frequently generated high levels of mechanical stress in their limbs. Since most mechanical stress in the body is produced by body momentum and muscular contraction, it appears that the Neanderthals led extremely active lives. It is hard to conceive of what could have required such exertion, especially since the maintenance of vigorous muscular activity would have required considerable expenditure of energy. That level of energy expenditure would undoubtedly have been maladaptive had it not been necessary for survival.

The available evidence from the archeological material associated with

area of cartilage is reduced, decreasing the pressure on the cartilage.

Most of the robustness of Neanderthal arm bones is seen in muscle and ligament attachments. All of the muscles that go from the trunk or the shoulder blade to the upper end of the arm show massive development. This applies in particular to the muscles responsible for powerful downward movements of the arm and, to a lesser extent, to muscles that stabilize the shoulder during vigorous movements.

Virtually every major muscle or ligament attachment on the hand bones is clearly marked by a large roughened the Neanderthals is equivocal on this matter. Most of the archeological evidence at Middle Paleolithic sites concerns stone tool technology and hunting activities. After relatively little change in technology during the Middle Paleolithic (from about 100,000 years to 35,000 years before the present), the advent of the Upper Paleolithic appears to have brought significant technological advances. This transition about 35,000 years ago is approximately coincident with the replacement of the Neanderthals by the earliest anatomically modern humans. However, the evidence for a significant

change in hunting patterns is not evident in the animal remains left behind. Yet even if a correlation between the robustness of body build and the level of hunting efficiency could be demonstrated, it would only explain the ruggedness of the Neanderthal males. Since hunting is exclusively or at least predominantly a male activity among humans, and since Neanderthal females were in all respects as strongly built as the males, an alternative explanation is required for the females.

Some insight into why the Neanderthals consistently possessed such massiveness is provided by a series of

partial skeletons of Neanderthals from the Shanidar Cave in northern Iraq. These fossils were excavated between 1953 and 1960 by anthropologist Ralph Solecki of Columbia University and have been studied principally by T. Dale Stewart, an anthropologist at the Smithsonian Institution, and myself. The most remarkable aspect of these skeletons is the number of healed injuries they contain. Four of the six reasonably complete adult skeletons show evidence of trauma during life.

The identification of traumatic injury in human fossil remains has plagued paleontologists for years. There has been a tendency to consider any form of damage to a fossil as conclusive evidence of prehistoric violence between humans if it resembles the breakage patterns caused by a direct blow with a heavy object. Hence a jaw with the teeth pushed in or a skull with a depressed fracture of the vault would be construed to indicate blows to the head.

The central problem with these interpretations is that they ignore the possibility of damage after death. Bone is relatively fragile, especially as compared with the rock and other sediment in which it is buried during fossilization. Therefore when several feet of sediment caused compression around fossil remains, the fossils will almost always break. In fact, among the innumerable cases of suggested violence between humans cited over the years, there are only a few exceptional examples that cannot be readily explained as the result of natural geologic forces acting after the death and burial of the individual.

One of these examples is the trauma of the left ninth rib of the skeleton of Shanidar 3, a partially healed wound inflicted by a sharp object. The implement cut obliquely across the top of the ninth rib and probably pierced the underlying lung. Shanidar 3 almost certainly suffered a collapsed left lung and died several days or weeks later, probably as a result of secondary complications. This is deduced from the presence of bony spurs and increased density of the bone around the cut.

The position of the wound on the

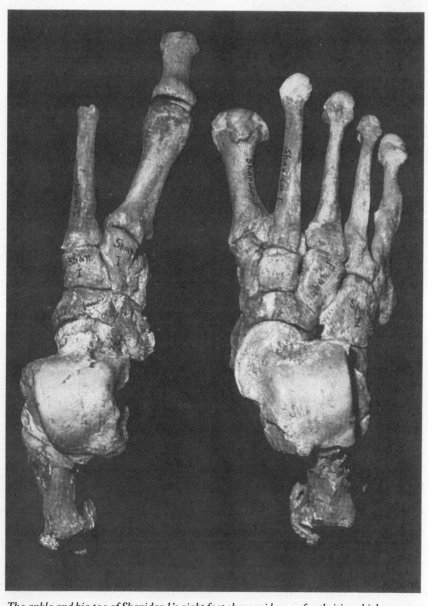

The ankle and big toe of Shanidar 1's right foot show evidence of arthritis, which suggests an injury to those parts. The left foot is normal although incomplete.

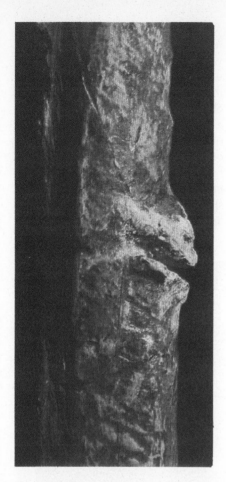

The scar on the left ninth rib of Shanidar 3 is a partially healed wound inflicted by a sharp object. This wound is one of the few examples of trauma caused by violence.

rib, the angle of the incision, and the cleanness of the cut make it highly unlikely that the injury was accidentally inflicted. In fact, the incision is almost exactly what would have resulted if Shanidar 3 had been stabbed in the side by a right-handed adversary in face-to-face conflict. This would therefore provide conclusive evidence of violence between humans, the *only* evidence so far found of such violence among the Neanderthals.

In most cases, however, it is impossible to determine from fossilized remains the cause of an individual's death. The instances that can be positively identified as prehistoric traumatic injury are those in which the injury was inflicted prior to death and some healing took place. Shortly after an injury to bone, whether a cut or a fracture, the damaged bone tissue is resorbed by the body and new bone

tissue is laid down around the injured area. As long as irritation persists, new bone is deposited, creating a bulge or spurs of irregular bone extending into the soft tissue. If the irritation ceases, the bone will slowly re-form so as to approximate its previous, normal condition. However, except for superficial injuries or those sustained during early childhood, some trace of damage persists for the life of the individual.

In terms of trauma, the most impressive of the Shanidar Neanderthals is the first adult discovered, known as Shanidar 1. This individual suffered a number of injuries, some of which may be related. On the right forehead there are scars from minor surface injuries, probably superficial scalp cuts. The outside of the left eye socket sustained a major blow that partially collapsed that part of the bony cavity, giving it a flat rather than a rounded contour. This injury possibly caused loss of sight in the left eye and pathological alterations of the right side of the body.

Shanidar 1's left arm is largely preserved and fully normal. The right arm, however, consists of a highly atrophied but otherwise normal collarbone and shoulder blade and a highly abnormal upper arm bone shaft. That shaft is atrophied to a fraction of the diameter of the left one but retains most of its original length. Furthermore, the lower end of the right arm bone has a healed fracture of the atrophied shaft and an irregular, pathological tip. The arm was apparently either intentionally amputated just above the elbow or fractured at the elbow and never healed.

This abnormal condition of the right arm does not appear to be a congenital malformation, since the length of the bone is close to the estimated length of the normal left upper arm bone. If, however, the injury to the left eye socket also affected the left side of the brain, directly or indirectly, by disrupting the blood supply to part of the brain, the result could have been partial paralysis of the right side. Motor and sensory control areas for the right side are located on the left side of the brain, slightly behind the left eye socket. This would explain the atrophy

of the whole right arm since loss of nervous stimulation will rapidly lead to atrophy of the affected muscles and bone.

The abnormality of the right arm of Shanidar 1 is paralleled to a lesser extent in the right foot. The right ankle joint shows extensive arthritic degeneration, and one of the major joints of the inner arch of the right foot has been completely reworked by arthritis. The left foot, however, is totally free of pathology. Arthritis from normal stress usually affects both lower limbs equally; this degeneration therefore suggests that the arthritis in the right foot is a secondary result of an injury, perhaps a sprain, that would not otherwise be evident on skeletal remains. This conclusion is supported by a healed fracture of the right fifth instep bone, which makes up a major portion of the outer arch of the foot. These foot pathologies may be tied into the damage to the left side of the skull; partial paralysis of the right side would certainly weaken the leg and make it more susceptible to injury.

The trauma evident on the other Shanidar Neanderthals is relatively minor by comparison. Shanidar 3, the individual who died of the rib wound, suffered debilitating arthritis of the right ankle and neighboring foot joints, but lacks any evidence of pathology on the left foot; this suggests a superficial injury similar to the one sustained by Shanidar 1. Shanidar 4 had a healed broken rib. Shanidar 5 received a transverse blow across the left forehead that left a large scar on the bone but does not appear to have affected the brain.

None of these injuries necessarily provides evidence of deliberate violence among the Neanderthals; all of them could have been accidentally self-inflicted or accidentally caused by another individual. In either case, the impression gained of the Shanidar Neanderthals is of a group of invalids. The crucial variable, however, appears to be age. All four of these individuals died at relatively advanced ages, probably between 40 and 60 years (estimating the age at death for Neanderthals beyond the age of 25 is extremely difficult); they therefore had considerable time to accumulate the scars of past injuries. Shanidar 2 and 6, the other reasonably complete Shanidar adults, lack evidence of trauma, but they both died young, probably before reaching 30.

Other Neanderthal remains, all from Europe, exhibit the same pattern. Every fairly complete skeleton of an elderly adult shows evidence of traumatic injuries. The original male skeleton from the Neander Valley had a fracture just below the elbow of the left arm, which probably limited movement of that arm for life. The "old man" from La Chapelle-aux-Saints, France, on whom most traditional reconstructions of the Neanderthals have been based, suffered a broken rib. La Ferrassi 1, the old adult male from La Ferrassie, France, sustained a severe injury to the right hip, which may have impaired his mobility.

In addition, several younger specimens and ones of uncertain age show traces of trauma. La Quina 5, the young adult female from La Quina, France, was wounded on her right upper arm. A young adult from Sala, Czechoslovakia, was superficially wounded on the right forehead just above the brow. And an individual of unknown age and sex from the site of Krapina, Yugoslavia, suffered a broken forearm, in which the bones never reunited after the fracture.

This evidence suggests several things. First, life for the Neanderthals was rigorous. If they lived through childhood and early adulthood, they did so bearing the scars of a harsh and dangerous life. Furthermore, this incidence of trauma correlates with the massiveness of the Neanderthals; a life style that so consistently involved injury would have required considerable strength and fortitude for survival.

There is, however, another, more optimistic side to this. The presence of so many injuries in a prehistoric human group, many of which were debilitating and sustained years before death, shows that individuals were taken care of long after their economic usefulness to the social group had ceased. It is perhaps no accident that among the Neanderthals, for the first time in human history, people lived to a comparatively old age. We also find among the Neanderthals the first intentional burials of the dead, some of which involved offerings. Despite the hardships of their life style, the Neanderthals apparently had a deep-seated respect and concern for each other.

Taken together, these different pieces of information paint a picture of life among the Neanderthals that, while harsh and dangerous, was not without personal security. Certainly the hardships the Neanderthals endured were beyond those commonly experienced in the prehistoric record of human caring and respect as well as of violence between individuals. Perhaps for these reasons, despite their physical appearance, the Neanderthals should be considered the first modern humans.

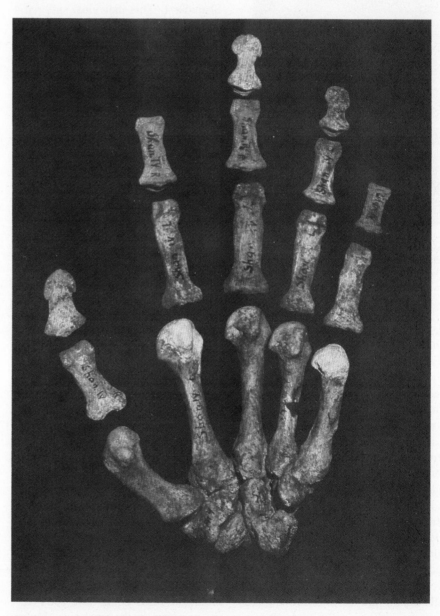

The right hand of Shanidar 4 demonstrates the enlarged finger tips and strong muscle markings characteristic of Neanderthal hands.

The Search for Adam and Eve

Scientists claim to have found our common ancestor—a woman who lived 200,000 years ago and left resilient genes that are carried by all of mankind

Scientists are calling her Eve, but reluctantly. The name evokes too many wrong images—the weak-willed figure in Genesis, the milk-skinned beauty in Renaissance art, the voluptuary gardener in "Paradise Lost" who was all "softness" and "meek surrender" and waist-length "gold tresses." The scientists' Eve—subject of one of the most provocative anthropological theories in a decade—was more likely a dark-haired, black-skinned woman, roaming a hot savanna in search of food. She was as muscular as Martina Navratilova, maybe stronger; she might have torn animals apart with her hands, although she probably preferred to use stone tools. She was not the only woman on earth, nor necessarily the most attractive or maternal. She was simply the most fruitful, if that is measured by success in propagating a certain set of genes. Hers seem to be in all humans living today: 5 billion blood relatives. She was, by one rough estimate, your 10,000th-great-grandmother.

When scientists announced their "discovery" of Eve last year, they rekindled perhaps the oldest human debate: where did we come from? They also, in some sense, confirmed a belief that existed long before the Bible. Versions of the Adam-and-Eve story date back at least 5,000 years and have been told in cultures from the Mediterranean to the South Pacific to the Americas. The mythmakers spun their tales on the same basic assump-tion as the scientists: that at some point we all share an ancestor. The scientists don't claim to have found the *first* woman, merely a common ancestor—possibly one from the time when modern humans arose. What's startling about this Eve is that she lived 200,000 years ago. This date not only upsets fundamentalists (the Bible's Eve was calculated to have lived 5,992 years ago), it challenges many evolutionists' conviction that the human family tree began much earlier.

Sturdy and fruitful, Eve probably lived in a small group that scoured the plains for food. But where? 'We can't yet decide whether it was Asia or Africa.'

Douglas Wallace

Eve has provoked a scientific controversy bitter even by the standards of anthropologists, who have few rivals at scholarly sniping. Their feuds normally begin when someone's grand theory of our lineage is contradicted by the unearthing of a few stones or bones. This time, however, the argument involves a new breed of anthropologists who work in air-conditioned American laboratories instead of dessicated African rift valleys. Trained in molecular biology, they looked at an international assortment of genes and picked up a trail of DNA that led them to a single woman from whom we are all descended. Most evidence so far indicates that Eve lived in sub-Saharan Africa, although a few researchers think her home might have been southern China. Meanwhile, other geneticists are trying to trace our genes back to a scientifically derived Adam, a putative "great father" of us all. As is often the case, paternity is proving harder to establish: the molecular trail to Adam involves a different, more elusive sort of DNA.

The most controversial implication of the geneticists' work is that modern humans didn't slowly and inexorably evolve in different parts of the world, as many anthropologists believed. The evolution from archaic to modern *Homo sapiens* seems to have occurred in only one place, Eve's family. Then, sometime between 90,000 and 180,000 years ago, a group of her progeny left their homeland endowed apparently with some special advantage over every tribe of early humans they encountered. As they fanned out, Eve's descendants replaced the locals, eventually settling the entire world. Some "stones-and-bones" anthropologists accept this view of evolution, but others refuse to accept this interpretation of the genetic evidence. They think our common ancestor must have lived much farther in the past, at least a million years ago, because that was when humans first left Africa and began spreading out over the world, presumably evolving separately into the modern races. As the veteran excavator Richard Leakey declared in 1977: "There is no single center where modern man was born."

But now geneticists are inclined to believe otherwise, even if they can't agree where the center was. "If it's correct, and I'd put money on it, this idea is tremendously important," says Stephen Jay Gould, the Harvard paleontologist and essayist. "It makes us realize that all human beings, despite differences in external appearance, are really members of a single entity that's had a very recent origin in one place. There is a kind of biological brotherhood that's much more profound than we ever realized."

This brotherhood was not always obvious in Chicago two months ago, when the Eve hypothesis was debated by the American Anthropological Association. Geneticists flashed diagrams of DNA, paleoanthropologists showed slides of skulls and everyone argued with everyone else. "What bothers many of us paleontologists," said Fred Smith of the University of Tennessee, "is the perception that this new data from DNA is so precise and scientific and that we paleontologists are just a bunch of bumbling old fools. But if you listen to the geneticists, you realize they're as divided about their genetic data as we are about the bones. We may be bumbling fools, but we're not any more bumbling than they are." For all their quarrels, though, the two groups left Chicago convinced they're closer than ever to establishing the origin of modern humanity. To make sense of their bumbling toward Eden, it may be best to go back to one ancient relative accepted by all scientists. That would be the chimpanzee.

Until the molecular biologists came along, the role of the chimpanzee in evolution rested on the usual evidence: skeletons. Scientists have relied on bones ever since the 1850s, when Darwin published his theory of evolution and some quarriers unearthed a strange skeleton in Germany's Neander Valley. Was the stooped apelike

figure a remnant of an ancient race? Leading scientists thought not. One declared it a Mongolian soldier from the Napoleonic Wars. A prominent anatomist concluded it was a recent "pathological idiot."

But more skeletons kept turning up across Europe and Asia. Anthropologists realized that Neanderthal man was one of many brawny, beetle-browed humans who mysteriously disappeared about 34,000 years ago. These early Homo sapiens, incidentally, were not stooped (that first skeleton was hunched with arthritis). Nor did they fit the stereotype of the savage cave man. Their skulls were thicker than ours, but their brains were as large. Their fossils show that they cared for the infirm elderly and buried the dead. It seemed they might be our ancestors after all.

Meanwhile, fossil hunters in Asia more than a half century ago found the still older bones of Java man and Peking man, who had smaller brains and even more muscular bodies. These skeletons dated back as far as 800,000 years. Perhaps they represented evolutionary dead ends. Or perhaps they, too, were human ancestors, with their descendants evolving into modern Asians while the Neanderthals were becoming modern Europeans—a process of racial differentiation that lasted a million years. Either way, it appeared that all these ancient humans traced their lineage back to Africa, because that was the only place with evidence of humans living more than a million years ago. Stone tools were invented there about 2 million years ago by an ancestor named Homo habilis ("Handy Man"). Before him was Lucy, whose 3 million-year-old skeleton was unearthed in the Ethiopian desert in 1974. (Her discoverers celebrated by staying up all night drinking beer, and they named her after the Beatles' song that kept blaring on the camp's tape player, "Lucy in the Sky with Diamonds.") Lucy was three and a half feet tall and walked erect—not ape, not quite human. At some point her hominid ancestors had begun evolving away from the forebears of our closest relative, the chimpanzee.

But when? Most anthropologists thought it was at least 15 million years ago, because they had found bones from that era of an apelike creature who seemed to be ancestral to humans but not apes. Then, for the first time, geneticists intruded with contradictory evidence, led in 1967 by Vincent Sarich and Allan Wilson of the University of California, Berkeley. They drew blood from baboons, chimps and humans, then looked at the molecular structure of a blood protein that was thought to change at a slow, steady rate as a species evolved. There were major

---

To find Eve, she first had to persuade 147 pregnant women to donate their babies' placentas to science.

Rebecca Cann

---

differences between the molecules of chimps and baboons, as expected, since the two species have been evolving separately for 30 million years. But the difference between humans and chimps was surprisingly small—so small, the geneticists concluded, that they must have parted company just 5 million years ago. Other genetics used different techniques and came up with a figure of 7 million years.

Traditional anthropologists did not appreciate being told their estimates were off by 8 million or 10 million years. The geneticists' calculation was dismissed and ignored for more than a decade, much to Wilson's displeasure. "He was called a lunatic for 10 years. He's still sensitive," recalls Rebecca Cann, a former colleague at Berkeley who is now at the University of Hawaii. But eventually the geneticists were vindicated by the bones themselves. As more fossils turned up, anthropologists realized that the 15 million-year-old bones didn't belong to a human ancestor and that chimps and humans did indeed diverge much more recently.

Now Wilson, who won a Mac-

Arthur "genius grant" in 1986, is once again trying to speed up evolution. The Eve hypothesis, being advanced both by his laboratory and by a group at Emory University, is moving up the date when the races of humanity diverged—and once again Wilson faces resistance. Some anthropologists aren't happy to see Neanderthal and Peking man removed from our lineage, consigned to dead branches of the family tree. Wilson likes to remind the critics of the last fight. "They're being dragged slowly along," he says. "They'll eventually come around."

To find Eve, Cann first had to persuade 147 pregnant women to donate their babies' placentas to science. The placentas were the easiest way to get large samples of body tissue. Working with Wilson and a Berkeley biologist, Mark Stoneking, Cann selected women in America with ancestors from Africa, Europe, the Middle East and Asia. Her collaborators in New Guinea and Australia found Aboriginal women there. The babies were born, the placentas were gathered and frozen, and the tissue analysis began at Wilson's lab in Berkeley. The tissues were ground in a souped-up Waring blender, spun in a centrifuge, mixed with a cell-breaking detergent, dyed fluorescent and spun in a centrifuge again. The result was a clear liquid containing pure DNA.

'I believe we have a long history of people constantly mixing with one another and cooperating with one another and evolving into one great family.'

Milford Wolpoff

This was not the DNA in the nucleus of the babies' cells—the genes that determine most physical traits. This DNA came from outside the nucleus, in a compartment of the cell called the mitochondrion, which produces nearly all the energy to keep the cell alive. Scientists didn't learn that the mito-

chondrion contained any genes until the 1960s. Then in the late 1970s they discovered that mitochondrial DNA was useful for tracing family trees because it's inherited only from the mother. It's not a mixture of both parents' genes, like nuclear DNA, so it preserves a family record that isn't scrambled every generation. It's altered only by mutations—random, isolated mistakes in copying the genetic code, which are then passed on to the next generation. Each random mutation produces a new type of DNA as distinctive as a fingerprint. (The odds against two identical mitochondrial DNA's appearing by chance are astronomical because there are so many ways to rearrange the units of the genetic code.)

To study these mutations, the Berkeley researchers cut each sample of DNA into segments that could be compared with the DNA of other babies. The differences were clear but surprisingly small. There weren't even telltale distinctions between races. "We're a young species, and there are really very few genetic differences among cultures," Stoneking says. "In terms of our mitochondrial DNA, we're much more closely related than almost any other vertebrate or mammalian species. You find New Guineans whose DNA is closer to other Asians' than to other New Guineans'." This may seem odd, given obvious racial differences. In fact, though, many differences represent trivial changes. Skin color, for instance, is a minor adaptation to climate—black in Africa for protection from the sun, white in Europe to absorb ultraviolet radiation that helps produce vitamin D. It takes only a few thousand years of evolution for skin color to change. The important changes—in brain size, for instance—can take hundreds of thousands of years.

The babies' DNA seemed to form a family tree rooted in Africa. The DNA fell into two general categories, one found only in some babies of recent African descent, and a second found in everyone else and the other Africans. There was more diversity among the exclusively African group's DNA,

suggesting that it had accumulated more mutations because it had been around longer—and thus was the longest branch of the family tree. Apparently the DNA tree began in Africa, and then at some point a group of Africans emigrated, splitting off to form a second branch of DNA and carrying it to the rest of the world.

All the babies' DNA could be traced back, ultimately, to one woman. In itself that wasn't surprising, at least not to statisticians familiar with the quirks of genetic inheritance. "There *must* be one lucky mother," Wilson says. "I worry about the term 'Eve' a little bit because of the implication that in her generation there were only two people. We are not saying that. We're saying that in her generation there was some unknown number of men and women, probably a fairly large number, maybe a few thousand." Many of these other women presumably are also our ancestors, because their nuclear genes would have been passed along to sons and daughters and eventually would have reached us. But at some point these other women's mitochondrial genes disappeared because their descendants failed to have daughters, and so the mitochondrial DNA wasn't passed along. At first glance it may seem inconceivable that the source of all mitochondrial DNA was a single woman, but it's a well-established outcome of the laws of probability.

You can get a feel for the mathematics by considering a similar phenomenon: the disappearance of family names. Like mitochondrial DNA, these are generally passed along by only one sex—in this case, male. If a son marries and has two children, there's a one-in-four chance that he'll have two daughters. There's also a chance that he won't have any children. Eventually the odds catch up and a generation passes without a male heir, and the name disappears. "It's an inevitable consequence of reproduction," says John Avise, a geneticist at the University of Georgia. "Lineages will be going extinct all the time." After 20 generations, for instance, it's statistically likely that only 90 out of 100 original surnames will disappear. Avise cites the history of Pitcairn Island in the Pacific, which was settled in 1790 by 13 Tahitian women and six British sailors who had mutinied on the Bounty. After just seven generations, half of the original names have disappeared. If the island remained isolated, eventually everyone would have the same last name. At that point a visitor could conclude that every inhabitant descended from one man—call him the Pitcairn Adam.

So thus there must be a mitochondrial Eve, and even traditional anthropologists can't really argue against her existence. What shocked them about Mitochondrial Mom was her birthday, which the Berkeley researchers calculated by counting the mutations that have occurred to her DNA. They looked at the most distant branches of the family tree—the DNA types most different from one another—and worked backward to figure out how many steps it would have taken for Eve's original DNA to mutate into these different types. They assumed that these mutations occurred at a regular rate—a controversial assumption that might be wrong, but which has been supported by some studies of humans and animals. Over the course of a million years, it appears that 2 to 4 percent of the mitochondrial DNA components will mutate. By this mo-

lecular calculus, Eve must have lived about 200,000 years ago (the range is between 140,000 and 290,000 years). This date, published this past January by the Berkeley group, agrees with the estimate of a team of geneticists led by Douglas Wallace of Emory University.

But the Emory researchers think Eve might have lived in Asia. They base their conclusion also on mitochondrial DNA, which they gathered from the blood of about 700 people on four continents. They used different methods in chopping up the DNA and arranging the types in a family tree. Their tree also goes back to one woman, who lived 150,000 to 200,000 years ago, they estimate. Unlike the Berkeley researchers, however, they found that the races have distinctive types of DNA. They also found that the human DNA type most similar to that of apes occurred at the highest frequency in Asia, making that the likely root of the family tree. Wallace's data suggests that Eve can be traced to southeast China, but he cautions that this is only one possible interpretation of the data. "If we make other assumptions, we can run our data through a computer and come up with a family tree starting in Africa," he says. "So I'm not ruling out Africa. I'm just saying that we can't yet decide whether it's Asia or Africa."

The rival geneticists are quick to criticize one another. Wallace faults the Berkeley researchers for getting most of their African DNA samples from American blacks, whose ancestors could have mixed with Europeans and American Indians. The Berkeley researchers insist that their study is better because they chopped the DNA into smaller pieces, enabling them to analyze differences more carefully. Both groups acknowledge that there's room for improvement, and they're planning to gather more samples and look more closely at the DNA's structure.

Genes, like family names, die out. 'It's an inevitable consequence of reproduction. Lineages will be going extinct all the time.'

John Avise

At the moment, the evidence seems to favor an African Eve, because other genetic studies (of nuclear DNA) also point to an origin there and because that's where the earliest fossils of modern humans have been found. But wherever Eve's home was, the rival

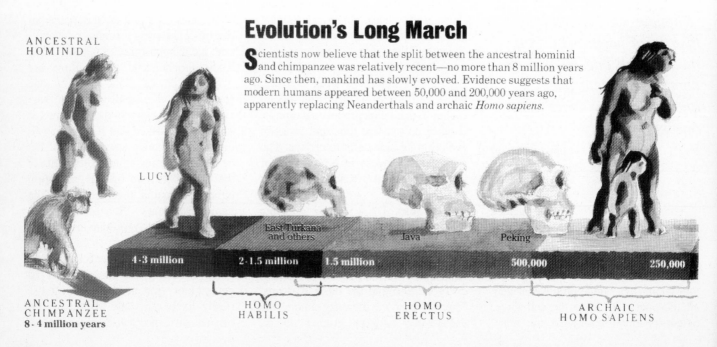

Evolution's Long March

Scientists now believe that the split between the ancestral hominid and chimpanzee was relatively recent—no more than 8 million years ago. Since then, mankind has slowly evolved. Evidence suggests that modern humans appeared between 50,000 and 200,000 years ago, apparently replacing Neanderthals and archaic *Homo sapiens*.

ANCESTRAL HOMINID

LUCY

East Turkana and others

Java

Peking

4 · 3 million   2 · 1.5 million   1.5 million   500,000   250,000

ANCESTRAL CHIMPANZEE
8 · 4 million years

HOMO HABILIS

HOMO ERECTUS

ARCHAIC HOMO SAPIENS

geneticists agree that she lived relatively recently, and this is what provokes anthroplogists to start arguing—often with biblical metaphors of their own.

If Eve lived within the past 200,000 years, she may have been a modern human, perhaps one of the first to appear. In that case she might have looked like a more muscular version of today's Africans. Or maybe it was her descendants who evolved into modern humans. Even herself might have been our immediate ancestor, an archaic Homo sapiens, and therefore brawnier, with a large protruding face and a forehead receding behind prominent brow ridges. She was certainly a hunter-gatherer, probably much like today's Bushmen in southern Africa, living in a group of maybe 25, carrying a nursing child across the plains in search of food. Humans around the world—Java man, Peking man—were living like this for hundreds of thousands of years before our mitochondrial Eve.

The question is: what happened to all the other populations around the world? For their women's mitochondrial genes apparently all vanished.

The Berkeley biologists conclude that everyone outside Africa stems from a group of Eve's descendants who left their homeland between 90,000 and 180,000 years ago. As they moved across Asia and Europe, they would have encountered Neanderthals and populations of archaic Homo sapiens. They were probably outnumbered in many places. But wherever the daughters of Eve went, only their mitochondrial DNA survived.

Did the immigrants kill the natives? Possibly, but the conquests may have been peaceful. Because they were modern humans, Eve's descendants were less muscular than the archaic natives, but they were more organized, more able to plan ahead. They could make better stone tools. As they prospered and multiplied, consuming more of the local fruit and game, the natives would have suffered; a slight increase in their mortality rate could have led to their extinction in just a thousand years.

The immigrants may have been able to interbreed with the locals. Some anthropologists see physical vestiges of the Neanderthals in modern Europeans, and the Eve hypothesis doesn't

rule out the possibility that the Neanderthals' nuclear genes were passed along to us. But the fact remains that the Neanderthals' mitochondrial genes all disappeared after Eve's descendants arrived, so both the Berkeley and Emory biologists suspect there was little or no mixing. Maybe the immigrants were so different that they couldn't interbreed. Or maybe they simply shunned the natives as being too "primitive." The Neanderthals' attempts at courtship presumably suffered if, as some scientists speculate, they lacked modern humans' power of speech.

This question of interbreeding is the crux of the bones-molecules debate. The geneticists' most vehement critic is Milford Wolpoff, a University of Michigan paleoanthropologist who believes our common ancestor lived closer to a million years ago. "The most obvious conclusion from the genetic evidence," he says, "is that Eve's descendants spread out of Africa and weren't incorporated at all into the local populations. I find that incredible. In recorded history, there always has been intermixing as populations moved or villages exchanged wives. I

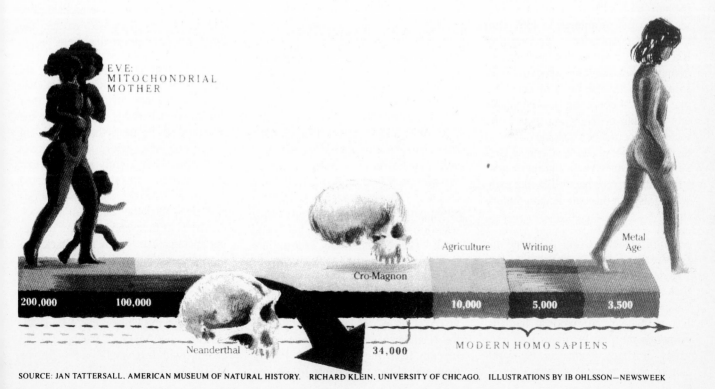

EVE:
MITOCHONDRIAL
MOTHER

Agriculture   Writing   Metal Age

200,000   100,000   10,000   5,000   3,500

Cro-Magnon

Neanderthal   34,000   MODERN HOMO SAPIENS

SOURCE: JAN TATTERSALL, AMERICAN MUSEUM OF NATURAL HISTORY.   RICHARD KLEIN, UNIVERSITY OF CHICAGO.   ILLUSTRATIONS BY IB OHLSSON—NEWSWEEK

believe we have a long history of people constantly mixing with one another and evolving into one great family." Wolpoff finds his version of evolution more satisfying than "this business about Eve showing the common nature of everything." If Eve's descendants wiped out all rivals, Wolpoff suggests, maybe the theory should be named after her murderous son, Cain.

Actually, the more common term for this idea is Noah's Ark, coined by Harvard's W. W. Howells in describing the two classic schools of anthropological thought on the origin of modern humans. One school believes that a small group of modern humans appeared in one place recently—perhaps 100,000 to 200,000 years ago—and colonized the entire world, like the survivors of Noah's ark. The other populations were not inexorably climbing the ladder or the tree of evolution—they were more like twigs on a bush or the arms of a hatrack, branching off to an inglorious end. The idea of a recent common origin for humanity was held by many anthropologists long before DNA provided supporting evidence.

The opposing school believes in what Howells called the "candelabra hypothesis": the different races diverged long ago and evolved independently into modern humans, progressing like the parallel candles of candelabra. This view became prominent in 1962 with Carleton Coon's book "The Origin of Races." He insisted that modern humans did not suddenly appear, "fully formed as from the brow of Zeus," in one place. "I could see that the visible and invisible differences between living races could be explained only in terms of history," wrote Coon, a University of Pennsylvania anthropologist. "Each major race had followed a pathway of its own through the labyrinth of time."

Unfortunately, Coon published his theory along with a speculation that was denounced as racist. He suggested that African civilization was less advanced because black people were the last to evolve into modern humans. Although the first hominids may have arisen in Africa, Coon said, the evolution of modern humans seemed to occur first in Europe and Asia. "If Africa was the cradle of mankind, it was only an indifferent kindergarten." He couldn't have been more wrong. Bones subsequently discovered in Africa are believed to be from modern humans living there about 100,000 years ago. These bones (as well as some from Israel that might be as old) represent the earliest known modern humans. Before their discovery it was assumed that modern humans didn't evolve until 35,000 years ago, which is when they first appear in the European fossil records. So blacks were hardly the last to reach modernity.

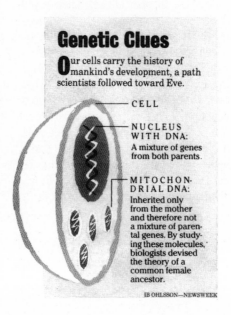

Genetic Clues

Our cells carry the history of mankind's development, a path scientists followed toward Eve.

CELL

NUCLEUS WITH DNA: A mixture of genes from both parents.

MITOCHONDRIAL DNA: Inherited only from the mother and therefore not a mixture of parental genes. By studying these molecules, biologists devised the theory of a common female ancestor.

IB OHLSSON—NEWSWEEK

Coon's mistake didn't invalidate the basic candelabra hypothesis, which is still popular in a modified version. Wolpoff prefers to think of a trellis: the separate races gradually evolving along parallel lines but connected by a network of genes flowing back and forth. The Neanderthals turned into modern Europeans while Peking man's descendants were becoming modern Chinese. Immigrants brought in new genes, but the natives' basic traits survived. This would explain why both the Neanderthals and the modern Europeans have big noses, why Peking man and current residents of Beijing have flat faces, why today's Aboriginal Australians have flat foreheads like Java man. These similarities presumably wouldn't persist if the ancient natives had disappeared when Eve's descendants arrived.

Other anthropologists, however, find these similarities unconvincing. It might just be a coincidence that modern Europeans have big noses like the Neanderthals. To the Noah's-ark school, what's striking are the *differences* between ancients and moderns. Modern Europeans, for instance, are much less stocky than Neanderthals—their arms and legs are proportioned more like those of humans from the tropics, as Eve's presumably were. And there's no clear sign in the fossil records of a transition from Neanderthal to modern. Some anthropologists cite bones that might belong to hybrids of immigrants and natives, but these interpretations are disputed.

"I don't rule out the possibility that there was interbreeding, but I don't see it in the fossils," says The British Museum's Christopher Stringer. "In the two areas [where] we have the best fossil evidence, Europe and Southwest Asia, the gap between archaic and modern people is very large. The entire skeleton and brain case changed. I think the fossil evidence is clearly signaling replacement of the archaic population. I was delighted to see the DNA results support this view."

Most anthropologists, though, are still skeptical. They don't reject outright the genetic evidence, but they don't accept it flatly, either. After the mistakes of the past, they're leery of any grand new theory about human evolution. They rightly point out that the geneticists' molecular clock could be way off—change a few assumptions and Eve's birthday could move back hundreds of thousands of years, bringing ancients like Peking man back into our lineage. Above all, anthropologists would like to see the corroborating bones.

"We don't know what's going on here," says the University of Pennsylvania's Alan Mann. "Maybe we are dealing with a dramatic jump. Maybe the origin of creatures like us occurred very recently. Certainly the mitochondrial data is a significant advance. But there really isn't any good fossil evidence from that period to back it up. If you look at the fossils, the good evidence on Africa can be placed on the palm of your hand. In this field, a person kicks over a stone in Africa, and we have to rewrite the textbooks."

So the fossil hunters will keep digging—now they have something specific to look for in the sediments of 200,000 years ago. Maybe they'll vindicate the geneticists once again, but the geneticists aren't waiting to find out. They're already trying to expand the Eve theory by finding Adam. Researchers in England, France and the United States have begun looking at the Y chromosome, which is passed along only on the male side. Tracing it is difficult because it's part of the DNA in the cell's nucleus, where there are many more genes than in the mitochondrion. This Adam will be the one lucky father whose descendants always had at least one son every generation.

'This idea is tremendously important. . . . There is a kind of biological brotherhood that's much more profound than we ever realized.'

Stephen Jay Gould

He may have been hunting and gathering while Eve was, or he may have lived at another time (though it would cast doubt on the Eve hypothesis if the time and place of his birth were too distant). The researchers hope to get an answer within several years.

In the meantime, there is one temporary candidate for an Adam—not the one scientists are looking for but one defined simply as a man from whom we are all descended. Since we are all descended from Eve's daughters, any common male ancestor of theirs would be a common ancestor to everyone today. This wouldn't necessarily be Eve's husband. For all we know, she may have had more than one. But her daughters all certainly had the same maternal grandfather. So, at least for now, the only safe conclusion is that Adam was Eve's father.

JOHN TIERNEY *with* LYNDA WRIGHT *in San Francisco and* KAREN SPRINGEN *in Detroit*

A Novel Notion of Neanderthal

"Human unity is no idle political slogan or tenet of mushy romanticism"

Stephen Jay Gould

Stephen Jay Gould teaches biology, geology, and the history of science at Harvard University.

I am not insensible to the great American myth of wide-open western spaces (nurtured, in my formative experience, primarily by the closed domains of Hollywood backlots used for sets of B movies). Still, as a New Yorker now resident in New England, I tend to side with Frost on the correlation between good fences and good neighbors. Nonetheless, I must admit that, once in a while, the folks next door can actually outdo a resident on his own turf. I prefer T. H. Huxley or Charles Lyell—strictly as literature—to many Victorian novelists. Conversely, I regard one important area of my own profession as better enlightened by novelists than by scientists.

Science is constrained by its canons of evidence. Pure speculation, however reined by plausibility or pregnant with insight, does not lie within the rules of our game. But novelists are free, like Milton's "L'Allegro," the embodiment of good cheer:

Come, and trip it as ye go
On the light fantastic toe;
And, in thy right hand lead with thee
The mountain nymph, sweet Liberty.

(I was as happy as the namesake of this poem when I first read these lines during a dull college course, for they resolved one of those little puzzles that weighs, however lightly, on the intellect. I had never understood how you could "trip the light fantastic on the sidewalks of New York" because, in my streetwise parochialism, I had always pictured a traffic beacon.)

Many crucial events in life's history have provided no direct data for their resolution. Yet the art of plausible reconstruction has value to science because we must have frameworks to discipline our thoughts. Writers of fiction can enlighten us in this treacherous domain. No event so poor in evidence has so strongly captured our imagination as the meeting of Neanderthal and Cro-Magnon people in Europe some 30,000 years ago. The people of Cro-Magnon carved intricate figures of horses and deer and painted their caves with an esthetic power never exceeded in the history of human art. Some Neanderthals buried their dead with ceremony and may have adorned their bodies with ocher, but they had no concept (so far as we can tell) of representational art. We feel that something fundamental about our origin, and our "essence," must lie hidden in the character of this contact between our ancestors and our closest collateral relatives. But we have no data at all beyond the temporal and geographic overlap. We do not know if they murdered each other or met with the equivalent of a Paleolithic handshake, ignored each other or interbred.

This combination of fascination and mystery has spawned a minor industry of novel writing—from William Golding (*The Inheritors*), who explored another aspect of human nature in *Lord of the Flies,* to more recent works of the Finnish paleontologist and novelist Bjorn Jurten (*Dance of the Tiger*) and the saga of Ayla as depicted by Jean Auel (*Clan of the Cave Bear* and sequels).

Let me cite just one example, at my own expense, of the novelist's power to enlighten. In the racist tradition, all too common and often unconscious, Cro-Magnons, as modern conquerors, are usually depicted as light-skinned, Neanderthals as dark. In *Meet Your Ancestors* (1945), for example, Roy Chapman Andrews wrote of the Cro-Magnon people:

They have been called the finest physical types the world has ever produced. Probably their skins were white. In fact, if you saw a Cro-Magnon man on Fifth Avenue dressed in sack suit and a Homburg you wouldn't give him a second glance [well, you probably would these days, for his outdated apparel]. Or perhaps you might, if you were a woman, for artists depict him as a debutante's "dream man."

I had unconsciously adopted this stereotype in my mental picture of these people, but Bjorn Kurten's reconstruction explicitly depicts Neanderthal as white, Cro-Magnon as dark. This conjecture surely makes more sense—for Neanderthals were cold-adapted people living near the ice sheet of glacial Europe, while Cro-Magnons may have had a more tropical origin. Since we possess no direct data, a scientific treatise would have no basis for discussing the skin colors of these people. But a novelist is free, and Kurten's well-informed conjecture taught me something about prejudice and the hold of tradition.

For all their breadth and variation, however, one unchallenged assumption pervades the Neanderthal novels. The modes and reasons differ, but Cro-Magnons are superior, and they quickly prevail in all accounts. This contact of ca. 30,000 years ago is portrayed as the "first meeting" of primitive and advanced—and the Neanderthals rapidly succumb. Neanderthals are dazzled by the technological superiority of Cro-Magnons. Golding's primitives are awe-struck by a Cro-Magnon boat with sails, because they have never thought beyond a floating log when they needed to cross a river. Kurten's watch dumbfoundedly as a Cro-Magnon artist carves the likeness of an animal in wood. The brains of Auel's Neanderthals are so stuffed with memory that they cannot initiate anything new. Of the Cro-Magnon heroine, Ayla, Auel writes, "In nature's way, her kind was destined to supplant the ancient, dying race."

This notion of *temporal succession*—superior supplanting primitive—is common to both major theories about the biological relationship of Cro-Magnon to Neanderthal. In one view, Neanderthals represent an ancestral stage in a progressive sequence of general advance toward modern humans. (The next step to Cro-Magnon then occurs outside Europe. Neanderthals become primitive survivors in a European backwater, and the emigrating Cro-Magnons wipe them out.) In the second view, Neanderthals are a side branch, not an ancestral stock. Yet their early division from an advancing central stock guarantees their backwardness and rapid defeat. Thus, even the novelists, with the maximal range of reasonable conjecture, have never challenged the cardinal premise of conventional wisdom—that modern people arrived in Eurasia far later than primitive Neanderthals, contacted them once, and quickly prevailed.

In this context, a report by H. Valladas and five colleagues generated astonishment in press accounts throughout the world ("Thermoluminescence Dating of Mousterian 'Proto-Cro-Magnon' Remains From Israel and the Origin of Modern Man," *Nature,* February 18, 1988, pp. 614–16). Neanderthals are a Eurasian group dating from about 125,000 to 150,000 years ago, for their first known occurrence, to about 30,000 years ago, for their supposedly singular replacement by modern Cro-Magnons. Anthropologists have puzzled for a long time over a few Eurasian sites that yield anatomically modern human remains but seem to be substantially older than the canonical 30,000-year date for contact and conquest. For example, the Qafzeh caves of Israel contain anatomically modern humans in association with species of rodents usually considered to have been victims of extinction during the early days of Neanderthal in Eurasia. Nonetheless, the presumption of nonoverlap between moderns and Neanderthals (until the crucial and momentary 30,000-year replacement) has been so strong that these sites have remained in limbo, usually rationalized in the literature as "probably" 40,000 years old or less.

Valladas and colleagues have confounded this tradition by reporting a date of 90,000 years for the anatomically modern humans of Qafzeh. You might cling to the old view by arguing that the Levant is not Europe and lies close to the favored African source for modern human origins. Perhaps the Levant was a long staging ground for a western European invasion 60,000 years later. But this resolution will not work, because Israel and the Near East also house abundant and well documented remains of classical Neanderthals clearly younger than the Qafzeh moderns. Thus, the geographic potential for contact between moderns and Neanderthals must have existed for nearly 60,000 years before the novelists' western European apocalypse. Yet moderns did not supplant Neanderthals.

I must admit that I am not fully confident about the 90,000-year date for Qafzeh because the technique of thermoluminescence dating (called TL in the trade), although applied in the most modern and meticulous way by Valladas and colleagues, includes some intrinsic, theoretical uncertainty. (Press accounts, in their lamentable tradition of reporting only claims, and omitting any critical discussion of procedure and methodology, have bypassed this issue entirely—and simply reported the 90,000-year date as though it possessed the factuality of a new fossil bone. I do so wish that this tradition could be broken. Science is a methodology for the testing of claims, not a list of oracular pronouncements about the nature of nature.)

As natural materials are exposed to ionizing radiation, both from the external environment and from the breakdown of isotopes in their own composition, they accumulate energy in the form of electrons trapped at defects in the crystal lattices of their constituent minerals. When the materials are heated, these electrons are driven off, often producing a visible "puff" of light, called thermoluminescence and first reported by Robert Boyle in October 1663 after he took a diamond to bed and warmed it against his naked body. (I shall refrain from the obvious vulgarities, but must report that Boyle considered his diamond as especially sensitive because he viewed his own constitution as "not of the hottest.") TL is not the ordinary red-hot glow of conventional heating, but a distinct emission of light at lower temperature caused by release of these trapped electrons. In any case, the intensity of the TL peak might measure the age of a sample since these electrons accumulate through time.

But how could we use TL to date ancient humans? Clays and flints record their own age, not the moment of human use. Unless, of course, human use has heated the materials and released their TL, thus setting the TL clock back to zero. The subsequent accumulation of new TL will then record the time since human heating. Unsurprisingly, this method was first developed for dating pottery, since clays are fired at temperatures sufficiently high to release TL and reset the clock to zero. The method has been quite successful, but its application is neither straightforward nor unambiguous. In particular, no lawlike, universal rate governs the accumulation of TL; one has to measure the local influx of ionizing radiation from surrounding materials. This requires a firm knowledge of the postburial history of an artifact. In practice, gauges are usually buried for a year at sites where artifacts were found. The excess of an artifact's TL over this yearly dose should, in principle, determine its age.

But Neanderthals and early moderns didn't make pottery. However, they did occasionally drop flint tools and flakes into their fires. Thus, the reported TL dates at Qafzeh and other early sites are based on burned flints—and I am not entirely confident that human campfires invariably burned long enough or hot enough to reset the TL clocks to zero. However, I think that Valladas and colleagues have presented the best possible case, given intrinsic uncertainties of the method. They dated twenty flints from Qafzeh, and all fell in the narrow range of 82,400 to 109,900 years. Moreover, the associated mammalian fauna of Qafzeh, as previously mentioned, has been hinting for years that these anatomically modern humans predated the later Neanderthals of the Levant. (See M. J. Aitken, *Thermoluminescence Dating,* Academic Press, 1985. I also thank Tim White of Berkeley and John Shea of Harvard for their generous help in discussion and supplying references for several topics discussed in the essay.)

For the past thirty years or so, the main excitement in studies of human evolution has centered on discoveries about our early history—from the dawn of the first known australopithecine more than 3 million years ago, to the later transition to our own genus *Homo,* to the evolution and spread of *Homo erectus* from Africa throughout the Old World. The fascination of the opposite end—the much more recent origin of our own species, *Homo sapiens*—has received relatively little attention because no real breakthroughs have been made. This situation has changed dramatically in the last few years because two independent sources of data seem to be converging upon a firm, exciting conclusion that has been intensely surprising (but shouldn't be) to most people—*Homo sapiens* is the product of a relatively recent, discrete event of branching speciation in Africa, not the result of a continuous process of worldwide advance. The redating of Qafzeh provides a confirming link in this story— hence its status as the central item in this essay.

Genetics and paleontology are the partners of this reinterpretation. (For a good review of this important subject, see C. B. Stringer and P. Andrews, "Genetic and Fossil Evidence for the Origin of Modern Humans," *Science,* March 11, 1988, pp. 1263–68.) As discussed in my essay of June 1987, the genealogical tree of modern humans, as reconstructed from the evolution of mitochondrial DNA, contains two major branches: one with only Africans; the other with additional Africans, plus everybody else. This topology implies an African source for the most recent common ancestor. (Although origin in the Levant with multiple migrations back to Africa is not excluded, no data support this more complex reconstruction.) If we are willing to accept a constant rate for the evolution of mitochondrial DNA (unproved, but supported by data now available from other groups), then all non-African racial diversity in *Homo sapiens* is only 90,000 to 180,000 years old, while the common ancestral stock of all modern humans probably lived no more than 250,000 years ago, and perhaps a good deal more recently.

Genetic data cannot tell us what these ancestral people looked like or date their origin with certainty. Perhaps this ca. 200,000-year-old common ancestor was a brutish, small-brained fellow—and the selective blessings of mentality then promoted the evolution of modern characters in both great branches of our family tree. Only the direct evidence of paleontology can resolve this issue.

Happily, fossil data are beginning to suggest an interesting conclusion. The oldest-known anatomically modern humans are probably the South African remains from the Klasies River caves, dated at some 80,000 to 130,000 years old. The redate of Qafzeh indicates about the same age for anatomically modern humans in the Levant. We still do not know the form of the ca. 200,000-year-old common ancestor, but if Klasies and Qafzeh are essentially us, then at least we can say that half the history of our species involves little change of anatomy. Mired in my own biases of punctuated equilibrium, I rather suspect that the 200,000-year-old forebear won't look much different from us either.

Where does this reinterpretation leave Neanderthal, who looks quite a bit different from us—not the Alley Oop caveman primitive of legend, but different nonetheless. Neanderthals have been controversial ever since their first discovery in 1856. (They were found in a valley of the Düssel River named for the minor poet Neander. Valley, in German is *Tal* or, in an older spelling often used in the nineteenth century, *Thal,* hence chronic confusion over the variant spellings Neandertal and Neanderthal. In any case, the word was always pronounced "tal" whatever its spelling, and the common pronunciation with English "th" is just plain wrong—a good example of the common confusion between orthography and content.)

Some leading anthropologists have interpreted Neanderthal as a stage in a general trend to modern humans, hence as our direct ancestor. This view was defended by the Czech-born leader of American paleontology earlier in this century, Ales Hrdlička; also by Franz Weidenrich in the last generation and by C. Loring Brace in our own.

The extreme version of the alternative was presented by the great French anthropologist Marcellin Boule. In a series of detailed monographs on the well-preserved Neanderthal skeleton of La Chapelle-aux-Saints, Boule constructed the apish stereotype later assimilated by pop culture as the brutish, stoop-shouldered caveman—club in one hand, wife's hair in the other.

Boule's Neanderthal, presented to the world just before World War I, slouched because he couldn't straighten his knees, bent forward because his backbone formed a single curve, slung his heavy head forward, and walked on the outer edge of his foot because his semi-prehensile big toe stuck out to the side and couldn't be used for proper support.

Boule's account was surely wrong, unfortunately mired in his own racist desire to compare these primitives with some modern groups that he wished to disparage, and partly based (though not so much as legend proclaims) on the arthritis, not the original anatomy, of his specimen. But in retrospect, bolstered by the redate of Qafzeh, Boule was probably right in his central claim—that Neanderthal is a branch of the human bush completely separated from *Homo sapiens,* and not at all part of our ancestry; and also that Cro-Magnons must have evolved elsewhere and lived contemporaneously with Neanderthals, long before their contact in western Europe some 30,000 years ago. The redating of Qafzeh is a vindication of Boule's primary conclusion:

Now these Cro-Magnons, which seem to replace Neanderthals abruptly in our country, must have lived before then in another place, unless we are willing to propose a mutation so great and so abrupt as to be absurd [from *Les Hommes fossiles,* 1946 edition, p. 267].

Boule's Neanderthal was an apish primitive. Modern anatomical reconstructions reveal a stocky, heavy-set, cold-adapted skeleton with a brain as big as ours—a creature well designed for the climates of glacial Europe. But while Neanderthals have been promoted from primitive to merely different, they have not—and this is the crucial point—become more like us.

During the twenty years that I have studied this field, general consensus has ranked Neanderthal within our own species, as a cold-adapted European race, *Homo sapiens neanderthalensis.* But if the dating of Qafzeh holds, and if the general view that ties all modern humans to a recent African root continues to gain strength, then this consensus must give way. If Neanderthals and modern humans lived in the Levant—and maintained their integrity without interbreeding—for 60,000 years before the great replacement in western Europe, then the two are separate species by the primary criterion of reproductive isolation. We shall have to return to the older view of Neanderthal as a separate species, *H. neanderthalensis.*

A much deeper issue underlies this entire debate. We are astonished to learn that all modern humans are products of a recent branching event in a single place, probably Africa. We are surprised that Neanderthal may be a separate branch of the human bush, not a more primitive ancestor. We are used to conceptualizing evolution as a tale of transformation within a continuous lineage—think of the museum parade of horses, from eohippus (fox-terrier sized, of course!) to Seabiscuit, or the line of human ascent from *Australopithecus,* naked in the African bush, to John Q. Businesssuit. Mired in this prejudice, for example, the *Auckland Sun* (February 19, 1988) reported the Qafzeh redating with this lurid leading paragraph (well, they do walk upside down out there in New Zealand, so maybe we shouldn't be surprised): "Evolutionary theories were turned back to front this week when scientists claimed modern humans existed before Neanderthal Stone Age cavemen."

We shall be truly wiser when we understand that the Qafzeh redate did not turn evolutionary theory upside down. Rather, the separation and prolonged simultaneous existence of Neanderthals and moderns as distinct species fits beautifully with a proper understanding of evolution. The only casualty of Qafzeh is a cultural prejudice of gradual, continuous advance as the canonical style of evolutionary change.

Evolution, at geological scales, is fundamentally about bushes and branching. Modern *Homo sapiens* and the extinct Neanderthals are two distinct branches, two contemporaneous species for most of their existence, if the data and arguments of this essay hold up to future scrutiny. Evolutionary trends usually work this way. The transition from reptiles to mammals, for example, is not the slow movement of a large population in lock-step from cold to warm blood, and from jawbones to earbones. Trends arise within a forest of distinct branches. Most of these branches die; a few are successful and produce more branches like themselves to fuel the transition. Trends are propagated by the differential birth and death of distinct branches, not the wholesale, gradual transformation of a single great entity. Mammals arose because the most mammallike species within a particular group of reptiles tended to live longer or branch off more daughter species. The robust australopithecines died: *Homo habilis* lived. Neanderthals became extinct; *Homo sapiens* survived.

Scientists are subject to the same biases of thinking; the press and general public hold no monopoly upon bloody-mindedness. Professional understanding of human evolution has long been hampered by a preference for viewing trends as the gradual transformation of "whole things," rather than the differential success of some kinds of little branches versus others. Stringer and Andrews, in the article cited previously, distinguished two basic views of human evolution. The "multi-regional model" embodies the older view of trends as gradual transformation. It holds that *Homo sapiens* evolved over a large part of the Old World in a coordinated transition from African and Eurasian *Homo erectus.* Contact and gene flow was sufficient, according to this view, to forge *Homo erectus* from Nairobi to Beijing to Jakarta into a functioning whole, then gradually transformed by natural selection into modern humanity.

The second view, often called Noah's Ark among anthropologists, holds that most ancestral lines died, and that modern humans descend from a local group that eventually spread throughout the world. Everything discussed in this article—from the redating of Qafzeh to the status of Neanderthal to genetic and paleontological evidence for a common, temporally shallow root of all humanity in

Africa—stands as a ringing confirmation of this second theory.

Yet as I advocate this second view with such delight (for its fits well with my own preferences for punctuated equilibrium), I strongly reject its designation as Noah's Ark. I have no objection to flippancy or to biblical metaphor, but only to the inappropriate implications of this name. The Deluge was a disaster outside the ordinary course of nature. If all modern humans stem from the fortunate survivors of a debacle, then our evolution seems unusual among the trends of life's history. But nothing could be more ordinary than the derivation of a successful stock from a single event of branching. Evolution works this way nearly all the time.

Human unity is no idle political slogan or tenet of mushy romanticism (I speak of the biological meaning, not the ethical concept that science cannot touch). All modern humans form an entity united by physical bonds of descent from a recent African root; we are not merely the current state of a tendency, as the multi-regional model suggests. Our unities are genealogical; we are an object of history. This insight is evolution's finest contribution to our greatest quest—the injunction inscribed as one of two cardinal precepts upon the Delphic oracle (according to Plutarch), and later invoked by Linnaeus as the very definition of the name he gave us, *Homo sapiens*: Know thyself.

Life as a

Hunter-gatherer

Richard E. Leakey

For at least two million years our ancestors followed a technologically simple but highly successful way of life. The initial strategy of the opportunistic scavenging of carrion combined with the organized collection of plant foods gradually evolved into a hunting-and-gathering way of life, the transition probably taking place somewhere between one million and half-a-million years ago. Not until relatively recently, between 20,000 and 10,000 years go, did that long-established lifestyle begin to be replaced by systematic food production in the form of pastoralism or agriculture. The change came late in our history, but it developed with astonishing speed and is now virtually total. Only a handful of people, living in isolated parts of the globe, still subsist by the ancient hunter-gatherer way of life.

Hunting-and-gathering was a permanent and stable feature of our biological evolution through *Homo* *erectus* to early *Homo sapiens* and finally to modern man. Given the importance of hunting-and-gathering through the many thousands of generations of our forebears, it may well be that this way of life is an indelible part of what makes us human. Prehistorians like Glynn Isaac try to piece together scraps of evidence from the fossil record to discover what they can about early human behaviour. . . . This kind of work has revealed a great deal, but, inevitably, it is limited in what it can expose of complex social behaviour. We know that until the advent of agriculture, humans made a living by gathering plant foods and hunting or scavenging meat, activities that centered on some form of home base. We can assume from this that there must have been some social organization, but the fossil record remains silent about what it was like to be a member of such a hunter-gatherer group. It indicates nothing of what was impor-

tant to individuals in the group or what moral codes they adhered to, and it only hints at the skills required in order to survive. Of course, one can never know for certain the answers to these questions. But one can obtain some clues through the careful study of contemporary hunter-gatherers.

THE IMAGE OF HUNTER-GATHERER SOCIETIES

Nineteenth-century anthropologists viewed hunter-gatherers as fossilized societies, primitive savages who had somehow slipped unnoticed and unnoticing into the modern world. This is, of course, nonsense. The hunter-gatherers were as modern in biological terms as the explorers who 'discovered' them; they just happened to be sustaining themselves by an ancient method. Misconceptions about non-agricultural people abounded, often inspired by Thomas Hobbes's seventeenth-century notion of life in a state of nature: 'No arts; no letters; no society; and which is worst of all, continual fear and danger of violent death; and the life of man, solitary, poor, nasty, brutish, and short.'

During the past couple of decades, and particularly in the last ten years, the image of hunter-gatherers has undergone a transformation. Writing in his classic book *Stone Age Economics,* anthropologist Marshall Sahlins argued that in studying hunter-gatherers, Western anthropologists must not impose Western, that is, materialistic, ethics on their subjects. This goes farther than just overcoming the revulsion of nineteenth-century explorers at certain food items. (The consumption of large, juicy insect larvae, for example, was often assumed to be the desperate act of starving people, whereas the hunter-gatherers considered them to be great delicacies.) Marshall Sahlins refers to the different goals of the different societies: the pursuit of wealth, property and prestige in the one, and something totally different in the other. He even goes as far as to suggest that the hunting-and-gathering way of life is 'the original affluent society . . . in which all the people's wants are easily satisfied.' As it happens, the hunting-and-gathering economy is not an incessant search for food, as many anthropologists have supposed, but a system that allows a good deal more leisure than is possible in either agricultural or industrial society.

Marshall Sahlins's conclusion rests in part on an important study carried out on the !Kung San (formerly called Bushmen, a derogatory term coined by Dutch colonialists in southern Africa), who live close to the border between Botswana and Namibia, on the northern fringe of the Kalahari Desert. Since 1963 a number of researchers, principally based at Harvard University, have been analysing many aspects of the !Kung's hunter-gather way of life. Since the project began the inevitable march of 'progress' has impinged on the region and only a very small number of people in the area still hunt-and-gather for a living, the rest having been persuaded to settle down as agri-

culturalists. Some of the !Kung have even been recruited by the South African government as anti-terrorist trackers along the Botswana—Namibia border. The transition from a nomadic to a settled existence has in fact been highly instructive about the social components of each way of life. . . .

Richard Lee, one of the principal investigators, recalls his motives for embarking on the study: 'I wanted to get away from the earlier misconceptions about hunter-gatherers. I wanted to find out what were the important elements of their way of life, without romanticizing them either in the Hobbesian "nasty, brutish, and short" manner or by putting them in a Garden of Eden.' Richard Lee is confident that his work is a legitimate way of gaining a glimpse of the past. 'The !Kung are a good model,' he claims, 'because, compared with prehistoric hunters and gatherers, they are living in a very marginal environment. Hunters of the past would have had the pick of rich resources and would undoubtedly have had an easier time of it than do the modern San.' The strength of the conclusions based on the study of the !Kung is that they are largely corroborated by other observations—some anecdotal, some scientific—on hunter-gatherers in many parts of the world. Through such peoples one can gain a valuable impression of the social and technical implications of the hunter-gatherer existence. One does not see exact replicas of our ancestors, but one can understand the principles that governed their lives.

LIFE ON THE EDGE OF THE KALAHARI

To many people, the name Kalahari conjures images of a desert of unrelenting aridity. To the !Kung, however, it is home and has been for at least 10,000 years. It is a place where they make a very reasonable living in a manner that, until recently, had remained unchanged for millennia. Richard Lee describes the area in the following manner: 'The first impression of a traveller to this region is of an im-

mense flatness where the sky dominates the landscape. The Aha Hills rise only a hundred metres above the surrounding plain, and from their top one sees what seem to be endless vistas of brush and savannah stretching to the horizon in every direction. . . . At several points in the landscape the sandy plain is broken by dry river courses. . . . They rarely hold water, perhaps twice in a decade, but when they do the flow can be considerable. . . . At night the stars overhead have an unbearable beauty, with the crystal clear high desert air and the central spine of the Milky Way galaxy arching overhead. It is with good reason that the !Kung name the Milky Way *!ku !ko !kumi,* the backbone of the sky.'

The desert winds have sculpted the sands into long, low red-topped dunes which run from east to west. Groves of mongongo nut trees cover many of the dune ridges, a feature of Kalahari life that is vital to the !Kung both for food and water. Gigantic baobab trees stand here and there, often the largest physical object within view. Everywhere is 'unbroken, unhumanized bush.'

Richard Lee chose an isolated group of !Kung to study, in an area he called the Dobe, which has nine water holes and inhabited by about 450 people. He tackled and overcame the immense challenge of learning the !Kung language: 'The !Kung word can be described as an explosion of sound surrounded by a vowel. The bundle of clicks, fricatives and glottal stops that begins most words makes !Kung a difficult language to record, let alone to speak.' (The use of !,/, and other such marks in written !Kung represents the various clicks and explosive sounds.)

Once settled with his chosen group of !Kung, Richard Lee inevitably was exposed to the predominant feature of hunter-gatherer life: its mobility. During the wet summer season, from October to May, the small foraging bands erect modest temporary camps among the mongongo nut groves, moving on to new camps every few weeks. The band moves, not in a constant and desperate search for food, but because the longer people stay in one place the further they must walk each day in order to collect food. It is a question of convenience, not a flight from starvation.

The foraging bands at this time of year are small, having about six families in them. At least some of the families are likely to be related to each other, either by blood or by marriage. In any case, the !Kung create an extensive network of informal affiliations throughout their neighbouring bands. Giving gifts and receiving them (not trading) are essential elements in weaving together the social fabric of !Kung life, and relationships within and between bands are complex and close.

The numerical composition of a foraging band, roughly thirty people, has been called one of the 'magic numbers' of hunter-gatherer life. Throughout the world hunting-and-gathering people have as the core of their social and economic life a band of about this size. It appears to be the optimum combination of adults and children for exploiting the widespread plant and animal foods that hunter-gatherers live on: fewer than this and the social structure is weakened; more, and the work effort has to be increased in order to collect enough food for everyone. . . . Only when the mode of production changes from the basic hunting-and-gathering system to more settled agriculture do groups larger than thirty become viable over long periods.

When the dry winter months come, the !Kung congregate around permanent water holes in concentrations of a hundred or more people. This 'public' phase of their life is very important. It is the time of intense socializing, large-scale trance-dancing and curing, initiations, story-telling, exchange of gifts and marriage-brokering. If one sees the dispersed summer camps as being connected by an invisible network of kinship, friendship and material obligation, then the winter is the time when the net is pulled together, bonds are strengthened and new alliances made.

This highly valued public phase of !Kung life is not without its drawbacks, however. The unusual concentrations of people inevitably means that people

have to do more work: they have to travel farther to collect plant food and to find animals to hunt. And with the high-density living there often comes personal conflict. As soon as the rains begin, people once again disperse in small bands to the mongongo groves. The bands are, however, not necessarily of the same composition as those of the previous summer: the public phase is an opportunity for people to join with others with whom they would prefer to live and for tensions and conflicts to be resolved by the splitting up of some bands.

Public-phase camps and the fission and fusion of bands are very common among foraging people. For instance, the G/wi San of the much more arid Central Kalahari live in small bands for about 300 days of the year without any standing water. They survive for most of the time on moisture obtained from melons and tubers. During the summer rains, however, they congregate around the few meagre and ephemeral water holes. The ostensible reason for the coming together is to take advantage of the standing water, which is briefly available. But the opportunity for intense socializing is not lost, and one suspects that the prospect of mixing with relatively large numbers of people is anticipated with even more relish than is the chance of drinking from a pool.

Hunter-gatherer peoples frequently give elaborate reasons why they come together in large groups and then break up again, but the real motive seems to be a strong need for formal and informal socializing within a large number of relatives, friends and affiliates. While non-human primates frequently live in social groups of about thirty individuals, they do not usually come together in the larger groups that are such a feature of the human hunter-gatherer way of life.

Hobbes's view that non-agricultural people have 'no society' and are 'solitary' could hardly be more wrong. To be a hunter-gatherer is to experience a life that is intensely social. As for having 'no arts' and 'no letters,' it is true that foraging people possess very little in the form of material culture,

but this is simply a consequence of the need for mobility. When the !Kung move from camp to camp they, like other hunter-gatherers, take all their worldly goods with them: this usually amounts to a total of 12 kilograms (26 pounds) per person, just over half the normal baggage allowance on most airlines. There is an inescapable conflict between mobility and material culture, so the !Kung carry their culture in their heads, not only their backs. Their songs, dances and stories form a culture as rich as that of any people.

In spite of the apparently inhospitable aspect of the northern Kalahari, it does in fact support a large number of wild animals. Richard Lee explains: 'To give some idea of abundance, fresh warthog, steenbok and duiker tracks can be seen every day of the year. Kudu, wildebeest and gemsbok tracks might be seen several times a week. Tracks of giraffe, eland, hartebeest and roan antelope would be seen perhaps once a month or once in two months; buffalo have been sighted only about a dozen times in ten years, zebra perhaps three times and impala only once in the same period.' The natural array of plant foods is impressive too. 'The !Kung are superb botanists and naturalists with an intimate knowledge of their environment,' Richard Lee says. 'Over 200 species of plant are known and named by them, and of these a surprisingly high proportion is considered by the !Kung to be edible.'

THE ROLE OF WOMEN

Referring specifically to the !Kung, Richard Lee gave a paper at a symposium in 1966 entitled *What hunters do for a living*. This revealed that, contrary to popular conception, meat constitutes only thirty to forty percent of the diet. Moreover, in studies of other hunter-gatherers in similar latitudes, the same sort of figure cropped up again and again. The conclusion was inescapable: plant foods are the staple of hunter-gatherer life. Only in the higher latitudes, where the changing seasons make plant foods an unreliable resource, do hunter-gatherers turn to fish or meat for the bulk of their diet.

In virtually all foraging people, as with the !Kung, it is the women who do most of the gathering of plant foods while the men do most of the hunting. There are exceptions, of course, such as the Agta people of the Philippines where the women share the hunting with the men. But in the vast majority of cases, there is a sexual division of labour. The most obvious reason for this arrangement is the incompatibility between the demands of the hunt—the long distances travelled while tracking prey and the quiet and stealth that is critical during the final stalk—and the problems involved in carrying weighty and noisy infants.

!Kung women give birth once every three to four years. Once again, the birth interval of roughly four years is a worldwide phenomenon among hunter-gatherer peoples, and it appears to be a biological response to the physical demands of mobility. Very young children must be carried while gathering and on migrations from an old camp to a new location. Transporting two children *and* gathering food would be extremely arduous. Richard Lee has calculated the amount of work which would be involved in carrying infant- and food-loads if the birth intervals were one year, two years, three years and so on. At the shorter intervals the work load is enormous and decreases rapidly when the birth interval is about four years, but does not drop significantly as the birth interval gets longer than four years. The world's hunter-gatherers therefore appear to have hit upon the optimum spacing entirely independently of each other. Only with a sedentary existence, such as in an agricultural economy, can women have babies more frequently without imposing on themselves an enormous carrying burden.

Why some kind of crèche system is not more common among foraging people is a mystery, but it may be because the mother's presence is necessary for suckling, which, with !Kung mothers, goes on for three or four years, often long after milk has ceased to flow. This extended suckling may be a physiological mechanism for preventing ovulation and therefore reducing the chances of another pregnancy. On the other hand, a crèche would make long birth spacing less necessary and eliminate the need for prolonged suckling.

The consequence of the sexual division of labour and the long birth interval is that food gathering is a highly social activity involving several mothers and their young, whereas hunting is a much more solitary affair, usually undertaken by a pair of men, possibly with an 'apprentice' adolescent. The economic differences between hunting and gathering are also profound. A woman can gather in one day enough food for her family for three days, and she seldom fails. A man may bring down a large animal that will feed the band for several weeks, or he may come home with only a small spring hare. Often he returns empty-handed.

According to Lee's calculations, !Kung men work just over twenty-one hours a week in contributing meat to the camp whereas women spend slightly more than twelve hours a week supplying plant foods which constitute about seventy percent of the diet. When all other forms of work—including making tools and housework, but excluding child care—are added together, a man's week is over forty-four hours and a woman's forty hours. But as women do most of the child care, their total work load is greater than the men's. Richard Lee considers that the women do not feel themselves exploited: they have economic prestige and political power, a situation denied to many women in the 'civilized' world.

THE ETHICS OF HUNTER-GATHERERS

Anyone going into a !Kung camp and expecting to find a cache of food is in for a surprise. Hunter-gatherers simply do not lay up stocks against future shortages. Such an 'extraordinary' attitude provoked nineteenth-century anthropologists into commenting that hunter-gatherers behaved 'as if the game were locked up in a stable,' and that they had 'not the slightest thought of, or care for, what the morrow may bring forth.' Rodney Needham, writing in 1954, said that foraging people have 'a confidence in the capacity of the environment to support them, and in their own ability to extract their livelihood from it.'

Food storage would run counter to the !Kung's habit of sharing food, particularly meat. Perhaps because it is a relatively rare commodity, meat is highly prized by the !Kung, as it is among most hunter-gatherers. When an animal is killed, the hunter (or rather the person whose arrow struck the prey—and that is not always the same person as he who shot the arrow) initiates an elaborate process of sharing the raw meat. The sharing runs along the lines of kinship, alliances and obligations. Lorna Marshall, a pioneer in !Kung studies, once witnessed the butchering of an eland, the largest of the African antelopes, and she counted sixty acts of meat distribution within a short time of the initial sharing. The network of sharing and obligation is very important among the !Kung. Richard Lee emphasizes the point strongly: 'Sharing deeply pervades the behaviour and values of !Kung foragers, within the family and between families, and it is extended to the boundaries of the social universe. Just as the principle of profit and rationality is central to the capitalist ethic, so is sharing central to the conduct of social life in foraging societies.'

This ethic is not confined to the !Kung: it is a feature of hunter-gatherers in general. Such behaviour, however, is not automatic; like most of human behavior, it has to be taught from childhood. 'Every human infant is born with the capacity to share and the capacity to be selfish,' Richard Lee says. That which is nurtured and developed is that which each individual society regards as most valuable.

In the same vein as the sharing ethic comes a surprising degree of egalitarianism. The !Kung have no chiefs and no leaders. Problems in their society are mostly solved long before they mature into anything that threatens social harmony. Although the !Kung are very thinly distributed overall—occupying on average about 4 square kilometres (1.5 square miles) per person—their camps, by contrast, are an intense compression of humanity. People's conversations are common property, and disputes are readily defused through communal bantering. No one gives orders or takes them. Richard Lee once asked /Twi!gum whether the !Kung have headmen. 'Of course we have headmen,' he replied, much to Richard Lee's surprise. 'In fact, we are all headmen; each one of us is a headman over himself!' /Twi!gum considered the question and his witty answer to be a great joke.

The stress on equality demands that certain rituals are observed when a successful hunter returns to camp. The object of these rituals is to play down the event so as to discourage arrogance and conceit. 'The correct demeanour for the successful hunter,' explains Richard Lee, 'is modesty and understatement.' A !Kung man, /Gaugo, described it this way: 'Say that a man has been hunting. He must not come home and announce like a braggart, "I have killed a big one in the bush!" He must first sit down in silence until I or someone else comes up to his fire and asks, "What did you see today?" He replies quietly, "Ah, I'm no good for hunting. I saw nothing at all . . . maybe just a tiny one." Then I smile to myself because I now know he has killed something big.' The bigger the kill, the more it is played down.

'The theme of modesty is continued when the butchering and carrying party goes to fetch the kill the following day,' Richard Lee explains. The helpers joke, complaining that surely the hunter did not need so many people to carry such a puny kill. And the hunter will agree, suggesting that they just cut out the liver and go and look for something more worthwhile. The jesting and understatement is strictly followed, again not just by the !Kung but by many foraging people, and the result is that although some men are undoubtedly more proficient hunters than others, no one accrues unusual prestige or status because of his talents.

When one examines the technology of the hunter, and that of the other aspects of !Kung life, one is very impressed not by its complexity or sophistication but rather by its simplicity. A club and bows-and-arrows, the arrows tipped with insect-larvae poison, are the hunter's prime equipment, though they also use hooks for retrieving spring hares from their burrows, snares for entrapping small animals, and net-bags made from animal sinews for carrying various items. For plant-food gathering, the technical array is even more modest: a digging stick and some kind of container. The !Kung women use a kaross, which is made from antelope hide, in which they can transport the nuts, fruits, roots and berries, together with their infant. Back at camp, crude stones are sufficient for the initial cracking open of the plentiful and valued mongongo nut. A wooden mortar and pestle are all that is required for pounding the inner nut meat, so as to render it digestible to the young and the old, or to mix it with other foods. And as water, or rather lack of it, dominates !Kung life, containers, such as ostrich eggshells or bags made from animal stomachs, are also important.

By contrast with the simple equipment used in hunting-and-gathering, the *skill* demanded is prodigious. Hunters must be able to identify an animal from its tracks, know how old it is, how long ago it passed by, whether it was running or idling, and whether it is injured or healthy. Once within striking distance of the prey, considerable cunning is needed to approach close enough for a telling shot with the diminutive arrows. Only the smallest antelope is knocked down by such a shot and most prey has to be tracked for several hours, sometimes days, before the poison kills it.

The !Kung are finely tuned to their environment, reading it closely and more thoroughly than people from a non-foraging society could ever comprehend. Two ethologists, Nicholas Blurton-Jones and Melvin Konner, once talked with the !Kung hunters to see how much of the animal world they

understood. They were astonished at the !Kung knowledge: 'Some !Kung observations which we refused to believe were later proved correct when checked with ethologists who have worked in Africa,' they admitted.

Gathering also requires a great deal of skill. Patricia Draper, who has made a special study of women in !Kung society, puts it this way: 'The !Kung economy looks simple in comparison with other more diversified economies with greater division of labour, but from the point of view of the individual actor, subsistence is quite complex. For example, although it is simple enough to pick up nuts or melons once one is standing where they are found, it requires enough strength to walk 16 kilometres [10 miles] or more per day carrying a full day's harvest and perhaps a child. A woman needs to know where various foodstuffs are to be found, in what season they are edible, and how to keep oriented in the bush. !Kung women, like their men, pay close attention to animal tracks as they pass through the bush; and they tell the men about recent game movements when they return home in the evening.'

It is clear when looking at a wide range of hunter-gatherers that there are significant similarities in the way they run their lives. These similarities seem to be imposed by their way of life, and they are therefore important in forming an impression of the general character of our ancestors' lives. We can make the following general statements about hunter-gatherers:

The main social and economic focus of the hunter-gatherer existence is the home base, probably occupied by about six families. The main social consequence of the dual pursuit of meat and plant foods is a sexual division of labour, with the males doing most of the hunting and the females most of the gathering. The quest for meat is surprisingly unrewarding, and unless plant foods are too seasonal to act as a staple they will provide the largest proportion of the diet. The practice of bringing plant and animal foods back to a home base where they are shared with all members of the band demands a highly developed sense of co-operation and equality. The system also allows for an unusually large amount of spare time which people divide between visiting relatives and friends in nearby bands and entertaining visitors at their own camp. Indeed, the degree of socialization is intense and reaches a pitch when, for a short while, bands coalesce into larger groups. Above all, foraging people deploy tremendous skill and only minimal technology in exploiting their environment.

As Richard Lee says, 'We mustn't imagine that this is the exact way in which our ancestors lived. But I believe that what we see in the !Kung and other foraging people are patterns of behaviour that were crucial to early human development.' Of the several types of hominid that were living two to three million years ago, one of them—the line that eventually led to us—broadened its economic base by sharing food and including more meat in its diet. The development of a hunting-and-gathering economy was a potent force in what made us human.

Is It Our Culture, Not Our Genes, That Makes Us Killers?

**Richard E. Leakey
and Roger Lewin**

Richard Leakey, like his famous mother and father, continues to push back the date at which true humans emerged from the evolutionary process. Roger Lewin is the science editor of New Scientist.

"The blood-bespattered, slaughter-gutted archives of human history from the earliest Egyptian and Sumerian records to the most recent atrocities of the Second World War accord with early universal cannibalism, with animal and human sacrificial practices or their substitutes in formalized religions, and with the worldwide scalping, head-hunting, body-mutilating and necrophilic practices of mankind in proclaiming this common bloodlust differentiator, this predaceous habit, this mark of Cain that separates man dietetically from his anthropodial relatives and allies him rather with the deadliest of Carnivora." The message of these stirring words, written by Paleoanthropologist Raymond Dart, is clear: humans are unswervingly brutal, possessed of an innate drive to kill each other.

On the same subject, the Nobel Prize winner Konrad Lorenz, one of the founders of modern ethology, wrote with even more eloquence: "There is evidence that the first inventors of pebble tools—the African australopithe-cines—promptly used their weapons to kill not only game, but fellow members of their species as well. Peking Man, the Prometheus who learned to preserve fire, used it to roast his brothers: beside the first traces of the regular use of fire lie the . . . roasted bones of *Sinanthropus pekinensis* himself."

Lorenz sounded these dramatic phrases 14 years ago in his celebrated book *On Aggression,* the main burden of which is that the human species carries with it an inescapable legacy of territoriality and aggression, instincts which must be ventilated lest they spill over in ugly fashion. All these—archaeological evidence of cannibalism, the notion of territorial and aggressive instincts, of an evolutionary career as killer apes—were woven together to form one of the most dangerously persuasive myths of our time: mankind is incorrigibly belligerent; war and violence are in our genes.

This essentially pessimistic view of human nature was assimilated with unseemly haste into a popular conventional wisdom, an assimilation that was further enhanced by Desmond Morris (with *The Naked Ape*) and Robert Ardrey (with *African Genesis, The Territorial Imperative, Social Contract,* and more recently *The Hunting Hypothesis*). We emphatically reject this conventional wisdom for three reasons: first, on the very general premise that no theory of human nature can be so firmly proved as its proponents imply; second, that much of the evidence used to erect this aggression theory is simply not relevant to human behavior; and last, that clues that do impinge on the basic elements of human nature argue much more persuasively that we are a cooperative rather than an aggressive animal.

The rules for human behavior are simple, we believe, precisely because they offer such a wide scope for expression. By contrast, the proponents of innate aggression try to tie us down to narrow, well-defined paths of behavior: humans are aggressive, they propose, because there is a universal territorial instinct in biology; territories are established and maintained by displays of aggression; our ancestors acquired weapons, turning ritual displays into bloody combat, a development that was exacerbated through a lust for killing. And according to the Lorenzian school, aggression is such a crucial part of the territorial animals' survival kit that it is backed up by a steady rise in pressure for its expression. Aggression may be released by an appropriate cue, such as a threat by another animal, but in the protracted absence of such cues the pressure eventually reaches a critical point at which the behavior bursts out spontaneously. The difference between a piece of behavior that is elicited by a particular type of stimulus, and one that will be expressed whether or not cues occur is enormous, and that difference is central to understanding aggression in the human context.

There is no doubt that aggression and territoriality are part of modern life: vandalism is a distressingly familiar part of the urban scene, and there is war, an apparent display of territoriality and aggression on a grand scale. Are these unsavory aspects of modern living simply part of an inescapable legacy of our animal origins? Or are they phenomena which have entirely different causes?

To begin with, it is worth taking a broad view of territoriality and aggression in the animal world. Why are some animals territorial? Simply to protect resources, such as food, a nest or a similar reproductive area. Many birds defend one piece of real estate in which a male may attract and court a female, and then move off to another one, also to be defended, in which they build a nest and rear young. Intruders are soon met with territorial displays, the intention of which is quite clear. The clarity of the defender's response, and also of the intruder's prowess, is the secret of nature's success with these so-called aggressive encounters.

Such confrontations are strictly ritualized, so that on all but the rarest occasions the biologically fitter of the two wins without the infliction of physical damage on either one. This "aggression" is in fact an exercise in competitive display rather than physical violence. The biological common sense implicit in this simple behavioral device is reiterated again and again throughout the animal kingdom. For a species to transgress, there must be extremely unusual circumstances. We cannot deny that with the invention of tools, an impulse to employ them occasionally as weapons might have caused serious injury, there being no stereotyped behavior patterns to deflect their risk. And it is possible that our increasingly intelligent prehuman ancestors may have understood the implications of power over others through the delivery of one swift blow with a sharpened pebble tool. But is it likely?

The answer must be no. An animal that develops a proclivity for killing its fellows thrusts itself into an evolutionarily disadvantageous position. Because our ancestors almost always lived in small bands, in which individuals were closely related to one another, and had as neighbors similar bands which also contained blood relations, in most acts of murder the victim would more than likely have been kin to the murderer. As the evolutionary success is in the production and well-being of as many descendants as possible, an undifferentiated innate drive for killing individuals of one's own species would soon have wiped that species out. Humans, as we know, did not blunder up an evolutionary blind alley, a fate that innate, unrestrained aggressiveness would undoubtedly have produced.

To argue, as we do, that humans are innately non-aggressive toward one another is not to imply that we are of necessity innately good-natured toward our fellows. In the lower echelons of the animal kingdom the management of conflict is largely through genetically-seated mock battles. But farther along the evolutionary path, carrying out the appropriate avoidance behavior comes to depend more and more on learning, and in social animals, the channel of learning is social education. The capacity for that behavior is rooted in the animal's genes, it is true, but its elaboration depends also on learning.

For instance, among the Micronesian Ifaluk of the western Pacific, real violence is now so thoroughly condemned that "ritual" management of conflict is taught in childhood. The children play boisterously, as any normal children do; however a child who feels that he or she is being treated unfairly will set off in pursuit of the offender—but at a pace that will not permit catching up. As other children stand around, showing looks of disapproval, the chase may end with the plaintiff throwing pieces of coconut at the accused—once again with sufficient care so as to miss the target! This is ritual conflict, culturally based, not genetic.

Animal conflict occurs both between animals of different species and between individuals of the same species, and under differing environmental conditions. Anyone who argues for inbuilt aggression in Homo sapiens must see aggression as a universal instinct in the animal kingdom. It is no such thing. Much of the research on territoriality and aggression concerns birds. Because they usually must build nests, in which they will then spend a good deal of time incubating eggs, and still longer rearing their young, it is a biological necessity for them to protect their territory. It is therefore not surprising that most birds possess a strong territorial drive. But simply because greylag geese and mockingbirds, for instance, enthusiastically defend their territory, we should not infer that all animals do so. And it is not surprising that hummingbirds show considerably more territorial aggression than lions, even though the king of beasts is a lethal hunter. Our closest animal relatives, the chimpanzees and gorillas, are notably nonterritorial. Both of these species are relatively mobile and so they can forage for food over a wide area.

The animal kingdom therefore offers a broad spectrum of territoriality, whose basic determining factor is the mode of reproduction and style of daily life. Indeed, an animal may find it necessary to assert ownership of land in one situation and not in another.

That territoriality is flexible should not be surprising. If food resources and space are scarce, then there may well be conspicuous territorial behavior. Some individuals will fail to secure sufficient food or a place in which to rear a brood. These individuals are, of course, the weakest, and this is what survival of the fittest through natural selection really means.

Territorial behavior is therefore triggered when it is required and remains dormant when it is not. The Lorenzians, however, take a different view; aggression, they say, builds up inexorably, to be released either by appropriate cues or spontaneously in the absence of appropriate cues. A safety valve suggested by Lorenzians for human societies is competitive sport. But such a suggestion neglects the high correlation between highly competitive encounters and associated vandalism and physical violence—as players, referees and crowds know to their cost through Europe and the Americas. More significantly, research now shows a close match between warlike behavior in countries and a devotion to sport. Far from defusing aggression, highly organized, emotionally charged sporting events generate even more aggression and reflect the degree to which humans' deep propensity to group identity and cohesion can be manipulated.

We can say therefore that territoriality and aggression are not universal instincts as such. Rather they are pieces of behavior that are tuned to particular life-styles and to changes in the availability of important resources in the environment.

When the practice of hunting and gathering was becoming firmly rooted in the fertile soil of prehuman society, our ancestors would of course not have operated sophisticated kinship networks. But we do know that chimpanzees know who are their brothers and sisters and who are not. And we know too that chimpanzees and baboons do migrate between their various troops. The biological benefits of reducing tension and conflict between groups through exogamy almost certainly would have been achieved early in hominid evolution. The notion of hostile neighboring hordes is an image born of the mistaken belief in a belligerence written ineradicably into the human genetic blueprint.

Food shortage, either on the hoof or rooted in the ground, must nevertheless have been a cause of potential conflict between bands. Indeed, severe famine may well have forced hominids into belligerent confrontation with one another in open competition for the scarce food. And the band that lost out may even have ended as the victors' supper. But there is neither evidence nor any reason to suggest that hominid flesh, either roasted or raw, appeared on our ancestors' diet, specifically as a source of food, in any but the most extreme circumstances. A much more likely consequence of conflict over food resources, so far as can be judged from what we know of both animals and present-day hunter-gatherers, would have been the dispersal of bands and

even the temporary scattering of individuals, a practice that ensures the best use of the limited food that is available.

Along with lions, humans are one of the few mammals who on occasion deliberately eat each other. When a male lion wins control of a pride, he will often consume the young cubs and set about producing offspring of his own. Ruthless and wasteful though it may appear, the biological reason for the dominant male's behavior is evident: the offspring produced by the pride will have been sired by a very powerful animal, providing a brutal but efficient method of natural selection. Cannibalism in humans, however, takes place for different reasons.

TWO KINDS OF HUMAN CANNIBALISM

Broadly, there are two sorts of cannibalism and the distinction between them is crucial. First, there is the eating of members of one tribe of individuals by another—usually as the end result of raids; such is the conventional version of the practice, and it is known as exocannibalism. In the second form, known as endocannibalism, people eat members of their own tribe.

Human cannibalism takes place primarily as part of some kind of ritual. Even among the infamous tribes in the highlands of New Guinea, the context is one of extensive tribal ritual. Months of preparation—weaving symbolic adornments and the carving of elaborate wooden images—precede a raid, and it is abundantly clear that the entire exercise has a powerful unifying effect on the tribe. The habits of the New Guinea tribes are, in any event, extremely rare, and as against cannibalism manifested in this extreme form we may set the other extreme, in which people swallow a small morsel of a dead relative as a mark of love and respect.

Altogether, then, the notion that humans are inherently aggressive is simply not tenable. We cannot deny that 20th-century humans display a good deal of aggression, but we cannot point to our evolutionary past either to ex-

plain its origins or to excuse it. There are many reasons why a youth may "spontaneously" smash a window or attack an old lady, but an inborn drive inherited from our animal origins is probably not one of them. Human behavior is extraordinarily sensitive to the nature of the environment, and so it should not be particularly surprising that a person reared in unpleasant surroundings, perhaps subjected to material insecurity and emotional deprivation, should later behave in a way that people blessed with a more fortunate life might regard as unpleasant. Urban problems will not be solved by pointing to supposed defects in our genes while ignoring real effects in social justice.

The fallacy of thus adducing our animal origins should be evident for wars as well. Wars are planned and organized by leaders intent on increasing their power. In war men are more like sheep than wolves: they may be led to manufacture munitions at home, to release bombs from 10,000 feet up, or to fire long-range guns and rockets—all as part of one great cooperative effort. It is not insignificant that those soldiers who engage in hand-to-hand fighting are subjected to an intense process of desensitization before they can do it.

With the growth of agriculture and of materially based societies, warfare has increased steadily in ferocity, culminating in our current capability to destroy even the planet. We should not look to our genes for the seeds of war; those seeds were planted when, 10,000 years ago, our ancestors for the first time planted crops and began to be farmers. The transition from the nomadic hunting way of life to the sedentary one of farmers and industrialists made war possible and potentially profitable.

Possible, but not inevitable. For what has transformed the possible into reality is the same factor that has made human beings special in the biological kingdom: culture. Because of our seemingly limitless inventiveness and our vast capacity for learning, there is an endless potential for difference among human cultures, as indeed may be witnessed throughout the world. An important element of culture, however, consists in those central values that make up an ideology. It is social and political ideologies, and the tolerance or lack of it between them, that brings human nations to bloody conflict. Those who argue that war is in our genes not only are wrong, but in addition they commit the crime of diverting attention from the real cause of war.

Our supreme biological irony underlies the entire issue of organized war in modern societies—the cooperative nature of human beings. Throughout our recent evolutionary history, particularly since the rise of a hunting way of life, there must have been extreme selective pressures in favor of our ability to cooperate as a group: organized food-gathering and hunts are successful only if each member of the band knows his task and joins in with the activity of his fellows. The degree of selective pressure toward cooperation, group awareness and identification was so strong, and the period over which it operated was so extended, that it can hardly have failed to have become embedded to some degree in our genetic makeup.

We are not suggesting that the human animal is a cooperative, group-oriented automaton. That would negate what is the prime evolutionary heritage of humans: their ability to acquire culture through education and learning. We are essentially cultural animals with the capacity to formulate many kinds of social structures; but a deep-seated urge toward cooperation, toward working as a group, provides a basic framework for those structures.

Unfortunately, it is our deeply rooted urge for group cooperation that makes large-scale wars not only possible, but unique in their destructiveness. Animals that are essentially self-centered and untutored in coordinated activity could neither hunt large prey nor make war. Equally, however, massive warfare would not be possible without the inventive intelligence that has produced the increasingly sophisticated hardware of human conflict. It is therefore as unhelpful to blame the scourge of war on our cooperativeness as it would be to blame it on our intelligence. To do either is to evade the real issue—those ideological values and behavioral habits on which nations are based, through which governments manipulate their people.

If we wish to, we can change our social structures without any fear of some primal urge welling to the surface and sucking us back into some atavistic pattern. We are, after all, the ultimate expression of a cultural animal; we have not totally broken free of our biological roots, but neither are we ruled by them.

Credits/ Acknowledgments

Cover design by Charles Vitelli

1. Natural Selection
Facing overview—New York Public Library.

2. Primates
Facing overview—United Nations photo by George Love.

3. Fossil Evidence
Facing overview—Courtesy of the American Museum of Natural History.

4. Late Hominid Evolution
Facing overview—Australian Information Service. 119-122—Photos by Erik Trinkaus.

ANNUAL EDITIONS ARTICLE REVIEW FORM

■ NAME: _____ DATE: _____

■ TITLE AND NUMBER OF ARTICLE: _____

■ BRIEFLY STATE THE MAIN IDEA OF THIS ARTICLE: _____

_____

_____

_____

_____

■ LIST THREE IMPORTANT FACTS THAT THE AUTHOR USES TO SUPPORT THE MAIN IDEA:

_____

_____

_____

_____

_____

_____

_____

■ WHAT INFORMATION OR IDEAS DISCUSSED IN THIS ARTICLE ARE ALSO DISCUSSED IN YOUR
TEXTBOOK OR OTHER READING YOU HAVE DONE? LIST THE TEXTBOOK CHAPTERS AND PAGE
NUMBERS:

_____

_____

_____

_____

_____

_____

_____

■ LIST ANY EXAMPLES OF BIAS OR FAULTY REASONING THAT YOU FOUND IN THE ARTICLE:

_____

_____

_____

_____

■ LIST ANY NEW TERMS/CONCEPTS THAT WERE DISCUSSED IN THE ARTICLE AND WRITE A
SHORT DEFINITION:

_____

_____

_____

_____

_____

*Your instructor may require you to use this Annual Editions Article Review Form in any number of ways:
for articles that are assigned, for extra credit, as a tool to assist in developing assigned papers, or simply
for your own reference. Even if it is not required, we encourage you to photocopy and use this page;
you'll find that reflecting on the articles will greatly enhance the information from your text.

ANNUAL EDITIONS:
PHYSICAL ANTHROPOLOGY 92/93
Article Rating Form

Here is an opportunity for you to have direct input into the next revision of this volume. We would like you to rate each of the 26 articles listed below, using the following scale:

1. **Excellent: should definitely be retained**
2. **Above average: should probably be retained**
3. **Below average: should probably be deleted**
4. **Poor: should definitely be deleted**

Your ratings will play a vital part in the next revision. So please mail this prepaid form to us just as soon as you complete it.
Thanks for your help!

Annual Editions revisions depend on two major opinion sources: one is our Advisory Board, listed in the front of this volume, which works with us in scanning the thousands of articles published in the public press each year; the other is you—the person actually using the book. Please help us and the users of the next edition by completing the prepaid article rating form on this page and returning it to us. Thank you.

Rating	Article	Rating	Article
	1. The Growth of Evolutionary Science		15. The Scars of Human Evolution
	2. A Pox Upon Our Genes		16. Dawson's Dawn Man: The Hoax at Piltdown
	3. The Ticking of a Time Bomb		17. New Fossil Is Forcing Family Tree Revisions
	4. Curse and Blessing of the Ghetto		
	5. Emerging Viruses		18. Sizing Up Human Intelligence
	6. Germ Wars		19. Scavenger Hunt
	7. Racial Odyssey		20. What Was the Acheulean Hand Ax?
	8. Everything *Else* You Always Wanted to Know About Sex . . . But That We Were Afraid You'd Never Ask		21. Bamboo and Human Evolution
			22. Hard Times Among the Neanderthals
	9. Machiavellian Monkeys		23. The Search for Adam and Eve
	10. These Are Real Swinging Primates		24. A Novel Notion of Neanderthal
	11. What Are Friends For?		25. Life as a Hunter-Gatherer
	12. Suburban Chimp		26. Is It Our Culture, Not Our Genes, That Makes Us Killers?
	13. Lucy's Uncommon Forebear		
	14. Bone Wars		

(Continued on next page)

ABOUT YOU

Name_____ Date_____

Are you a teacher? ☐ Or student? ☐

Your School Name _____

Department _____

Address _____

City _____ State _____ Zip _____

School Telephone # _____

YOUR COMMENTS ARE IMPORTANT TO US!

Please fill in the following information:

For which course did you use this book? _____

Did you use a text with this Annual Edition? ☐ yes ☐ no

The title of the text? _____

What are your general reactions to the Annual Editions concept?

Have you read any particular articles recently that you think should be included in the next edition?

Are there any articles you feel should be replaced in the next edition? Why?

Are there other areas that you feel would utilize an Annual Edition?

May we contact you for editorial input?

May we quote you from above?

ANNUAL EDITIONS: PHYSICAL ANTHROPOLOGY 92/93

BUSINESS REPLY MAIL

First Class   Permit No. 84   Guilford, CT

Postage will be paid by addressee

The Dushkin Publishing Group, Inc.
Sluice Dock
DPG **Guilford, Connecticut 06437**

No Postage
Necessary
if Mailed
in the
United States